Oracle 10g/11g Data and Database Management Utilities

Master twelve must-use utilities to optimize the efficiency, management, and performance of your daily database tasks

Hector R. Madrid

BIRMINGHAM - MUMBAI

Oracle 10g/11g Data and Database Management Utilities

First published: June 2009

Production Reference: 1220609

Published by Packt Publishing Ltd.
32 Lincoln Road
Olton
Birmingham, B27 6PA, UK.

ISBN 978-1-847196-28-6

www.packtpub.com

Cover Image by Vinayak Chittar (vinayak.chittar@gmail.com)

Credits

Author
Hector R. Madrid

Reviewers
Hans Forbrich

Peter McLarty

Ulises Lazarini

Acquisition Editor
James Lumsden

Development Editor
Dhiraj Chandiramani

Technical Editor
John Antony

Indexer
Rekha Nair

Editorial Team Leader
Gagandeep Singh

Project Team Leader
Priya Mukherji

Project Coordinator
Leena Purkait

Proofreader
Lesley Harrison

Production Coordinator
Dolly Dasilva

Cover Work
Dolly Dasilva

About the Author

Hector R. Madrid is a highly respected Oracle professional with 20 years of experience as a full time DBA. He has been working with Oracle databases from version 5.0 up to the latest 11g release. He was the first Oracle Certified Master in Latin America and he holds the Oracle Certified Professional certificate for all Oracle versions starting with 7.3 up to 11g.

He obtained a bachelor's degree in Electronic Engineering from the Metropolitan Autonomous University in 1992, with a major in Digital Systems and Computers. He obtained a Master's degree in Computer Science from the same University. He has collaborated with Oracle Corp. as an instructor teaching the database track since 1996.

Hector works as a database consultant for several major firms, dealing with a wide range of DBA requirements, ranging from daily DBA tasks to defining and maintaining mission critical and high availability systems.

He has presented different technical papers at several Oracle conferences. He is the author of the Blog 'Oracle by Madrid' a Blog specializing in Oracle database topics.

To my parents Higinio Rivera and Teresa Madrid who taught me the basis of who I am now.

My wife Claudia and my daughter Alexandra for their extraordinary patience and support during the development of this book

Hans Forbrich, a respected Oracle ACE Director, who has forged each letter of this title with knowledge and experience, for his valuable technical feedback and all his comments both in this book and in general in the Oracle community.

About the Reviewer

Hans Forbrich has been around computers for 40 years. Indeed, while studying for his BSc EE in the 1970s he worked as a contract programmer to help pay for school. Hans has been working with Oracle products since 1984. In the field service group at Nortel he was introduced to Oracle Database version 4. He joined Oracle Canada to work in the Communications vertical from 1996 to 2002. In 2003 Hans started Forbrich Computer Consulting Ltd., which has become a successful international Oracle consultancy and Oracle training partner based in St. Albert, near Edmonton, Alberta, Canada.

As an Oracle ACE Director and OCP, Hans frequently responds in various Oracle Forums, teaches for Oracle University, consults with Oracle customers on maximizing value from Oracle licenses, and speaks at Oracle User Group conferences around the world. He holds a strong belief that Oracle products provide significant value and the key to extracting that value—and reducing the effective cost of the product—is in understanding the product and using the right tool for the job.

I thank my wife of 27 years for her patience, especially while I experiment in the lab. And also, I thank my two sons for their patience, their assistance at computer setups, and help with those same experiments. (I am proud to note that Son #1, aka Employee #2, aka Chief Network & Systems Administrator, has achieved his MSc EE this past year!) Finally I thank Edmonton Opera and my colleagues there for allowing me to break away from computers and unwind on stage with the Edmonton Opera Chorus.

Peter McLarty has worked with technology for over 25 years. He has been working with Unix and databases for over 10 years with 8 years experience as an Oracle DBA. Peter has worked with Oracle 7.3 through to Oracle 11. Peter has a number of years experience supporting Oracle Application Server. He has experience with RAC and Oracle Maximum Availability Architecture. Peter maintains his own web site with articles about many topics of interest to him and not always about databases or Oracle. Peter has a diverse background in IT supporting his DBA skills and is now involved in Architecture and System Assurance. Peter works for Pacific DBMS, whose office is in Margate, Queensland. Peter is married with 2 children, and several pets to support. When he is not doing things with computers he likes to follow his football team or study things about Asia and learn Thai.

I would like to thank my family for giving me peace to review this book.

Ulises Lazarini is the president of Consultoria Informatica Lazarini, and a partner of Oracle with more than 10 years experience of working with Oracle databases. He has also been an OCP member since Oracle 7.3.4, 8, 8i, 9i, 10g, and so on.

He has been an Oracle instructor in the kernel field for more than 12 years. Ulises has been a speaker at Oracle Open World (September 2008, "Migration from Siebel 7.8 running on SQL Server to Oracle 10g RAC") and a DBA Consultant on two successful Oracle database cases. He has been very active in installing and monitoring RAC environments for OLTP and data warehouse databases.

He has been responsible for high availability on global databases.

Table of Contents

Preface

Does your database seem complicated? Are you finding it difficult to work with it efficiently? Database administration is part of a daily routine for all database professionals. Using Oracle Utilities, administrators can benefit from improved maintenance windows, optimized backups, faster data transfers, and more reliable security, and can in general do more with the same time and resources.

You don't have to reinvent the wheel, just learn how to use Oracle Utilities properly to achieve your goals. That is what this book is about; it covers topics which are oriented towards data management, session management, batch processing, massive deployment, troubleshooting, and how to make the most out of frequently used DBA tools to improve your daily work.

Data management is one of the most frequently required tasks; doing a backup is a must-do task for any company. Data management includes several tasks such as data transfers, data uploading and downloading, reorganizing data, and data cloning, among many others. If people learn to use a tool and things appear to go well, few will question if their approach is optimal. Often it is only when maintenance windows start shrinking; due to the ever increasing amount of data and need for business availability, that problems with any particular approach get identified. People tend to get used to using the old export/import utilities to perform data management and if it works, they probably will consider the problem solved and continue to use an obsolete tool. This book explores further possibilities and new tools. It makes the user question if his/her current environment is optimized and teaches the reader how to adopt more optimized data management techniques focusing on the tools and requirements most frequently seen in modern production environments.

What this book covers

Chapter 1 deals with Data Pump. Data Pump is a versatile data management tool. It is much more than just an exp/imp upgrade; it allows remapping, dump file size estimation, restartable tasks, network transfers, advanced filtering operations, recovering data after a commit has been issued, and transferring data files among different oracle versions. It includes a PL/SQL API so it can be used as a base to develop data pump-based systems.

Chapter 2 involves a description of the SQL*Loader. It describes how SQL* Loader is the tool to upload plain text format files to the database. If SQL* Loader properly configured, you can greatly increase the speed with which uploads are completed. Loading data to take care of the character set will avoid unnecessary headaches, and you can optimize your loading window. There are several tips and tricks to load different character sets to the database and load binary data to BLOB fields. This tool can be used to load data on the fly and you will learn how to proactively configure it to get a smooth load.

Chapter 3 is all about External Tables. The external table is a concept Oracle introduced in 9i to ease the ETL (Extraction Transformation and Loading) DWH process. An external table can be created to map an external file to the database so you can seamlessly read it as if it was a regular table. You can extend the use of the external tables concept to analyze log files such as the alert.log or the network log files inside the database. The external table concept can be implemented with the Data Pump drivers; this way you can easily and selectively perform data transfers among databases spanning different Oracle versions.

Chapter 4 specializes in advanced techniques involved in optimizing the Recovery Manager. Recovery Manager can be optimized to minimize the impact in production environments; or it can run faster using parallel techniques. It can be used to clone a database on the same OS or transport it over different platforms, or even change the storage method between ASM and conventional file system storage and vice versa.

Chapter 5 talks about the Recovery Manager. Recovery manager first appeared back in 8.0, but it was not until 9i that it began to gain popularity among DBAs as the default backup/recover tool. It is simple and elegant and the most frequently used commands are pretty simple and intuitive. This chapter presents several practical database recovery scenarios.

Chapter 6 is about Session Management. The users are the main reason why the DBA exists. If it were not for the users, there would be no database activity and there would be no problems to be solved. How can you easily spot a row lock contention problem? What should be done to diagnose and solve this problem? What does it mean to kill a user session? Managing sessions means you can regulate them by means of Oracle profiles; this may sooner or later lead to snipped sessions; what are those snipped sessions? How do you get rid of them? This chapter discusses several user session management issues.

Chapter 7 talks about the Oracle Scheduler. The Oracle Scheduler is a powerful tool used to schedule tasks in Oracle. This tool can perform simple schedules as well as complex schedules; you need to understand time expressions and the Oracle scheduler architecture to take advantage of this utility.

Chapter 8 will teach you about Oracle Wallet Manager. Oracle Wallet Manager is the cornerstone and entry point for advanced security management. You can use it to manage certificates and certificate requests. You can store identity certificates and retrieve them from a central location, or you can use the registry in a Windows environment. You can hide passwords without using OS Authentication mechanisms by storing the user password inside the wallet.

Chapter 9 deals with security of the system. Most people worry about having a valid backup that can be used to effectively recover data, but not all of them are concerned about the backup security; if a backup can be used to recover data, this doesn't actually mean the data will be recovered at the same site where it was taken from. OWM is a tool which can be used to have the backup encrypted, so sensitive data can be secured not only from the availability point of view, but also from the confidentiality point of view. Security has to do also with identifying who the real user is; this can be achieved with the enterprise user. This chapter explains step by step how to set up an environment with enterprise identity management using the Enterprise Security Manager.

Chapter 10 talks about Database Configuration Assistant. Creating a database is one of the first tasks the user performs when installing Oracle, but this tool goes far beyond the simple task of creating the database; it can be used to manage templates, create a database in silent mode, and configure services in an RAC environment. Configuring database options and enabling the Enterprise Manager DB Control can be done here. DBCA is also the easy way to start up and configure an Automatic Storage Management (ASM) environment.

Chapter 11 provides details about the Oracle Universal Installer. Installing Oracle is more than just a next → next button pressing activity; OUI is a tool to manage software. Most people care about database backups, as well as configuration file backups, but what about the Oracle installer repository? This set of files is most often underestimated unless a hardware failure makes the DBA understand what Oracle software maintenance is. OUI can perform silent and batch installations; it can also perform installations from a central software depot accessible through the Web.

Chapter 12 is about the Enterprise Manager Configuration Assistant. Most DBAs use EM as the basic DBA administration tool; it is a very intuitive database management console. Most people depend on it to easily perform most of the administration and operation tasks that otherwise would be time consuming to complete through character console mode. But what happens when it is not available, either because of a change in the network topology or a firewall that restricts access to the managing port? Then the user needs to have the console reconfigured to bring it back into operation. EMCA is the character mode tool used to perform this task.

Chapter 13 talks about OPatch. Patching the RDBMS is required to keep the software up to date. When a patchset is to be applied OUI is used, but when a single patch or a CPU is to be applied OPatch must be used. You will learn how to perform a basic patch application task, list the patch inventory, find out if a patch has already been applied, maintain the software and the software inventory, and learn how and when to perform a patch application while the database is up and running.

What you need for this book

This book requires the reader to know the basics of SQL, and have some experience with Oracle 10g and 11g databases.

This book covers an Oracle database installation on Linux, although the techniques detailed are equally applicable to other operating systems.

Who this book is for

This book is aimed at all Oracle professionals who wish to employ must-use data and database utilities, and optimize their database interactions.

Entry-level users can acquaint themselves with the best practices needed to get jobs done in a timely and efficient manner. Advanced users will find useful tips and How-Tos that will help them focus on getting the most out of the database, utilities, and fine-tune batch process.

Conventions

In this book, you will find a number of styles of text that distinguish between different kinds of information. Here are some examples of these styles, and an explanation of their meaning.

Code words in text are shown as follows: "We can include other contexts through the use of the `include` directive."

A block of code will be set as follows:

```
BEGIN
    dbms_resource_manager_privs.grant_switch_consumer_group(
        grantee_name    => 'SCOTT',
        consumer_group  => 'OLTP',
        grant_option    => FALSE
    );
END;
```

When we wish to draw your attention to a particular part of a code block, the relevant lines or items will be shown in bold:

```
ALPHA =
  (DESCRIPTION =
    (ADDRESS = (PROTOCOL = TCP)(HOST = alpha)(PORT = 1522))
    (ADDRESS = (PROTOCOL = TCP)(HOST = alpha)(PORT = 1521))
    (CONNECT_DATA =
      (SERVER = DEDICATED)
      (SERVICE_NAME = alpha)
    )
  )
```

Any command-line input or output is written as follows:

```
orapki wallet create -wallet <Path to Wallet>
```

New terms and **important words** are shown in bold. Words that you see on the screen, in menus or dialog boxes for example, appear in our text like this: "From the main menu choose the **Operations** menu and then select the **Add Certificate Request** submenu, a form as shown in the following screenshot will be displayed where you can capture specific information.".

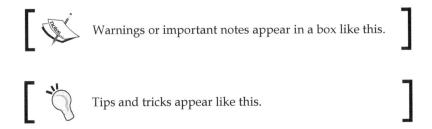

Warnings or important notes appear in a box like this.

Tips and tricks appear like this.

Reader feedback

Feedback from our readers is always welcome. Let us know what you think about this book—what you liked or may have disliked. Reader feedback is important for us to develop titles that you really get the most out of.

To send us general feedback, simply drop an email to feedback@packtpub.com, and mention the book title in the subject of your message.

If there is a book that you need and would like to see us publish, please send us a note in the **SUGGEST A TITLE** form on www.packtpub.com or email suggest@packtpub.com.

If there is a topic that you have expertise in and you are interested in either writing or contributing to a book, see our author guide on www.packtpub.com/authors.

Customer support

Now that you are the proud owner of a Packt book, we have a number of things to help you to get the most from your purchase.

Downloading the example code for the book

Visit http://www.packtpub.com/files/code/6286_Code.zip to directly download the example code.

The downloadable files contain instructions on how to use them.

Errata

Although we have taken every care to ensure the accuracy of our contents, mistakes do happen. If you find a mistake in one of our books—maybe a mistake in text or code—we would be grateful if you would report this to us. By doing so, you can save other readers from frustration, and help us to improve subsequent versions of this book. If you find any errata, please report them by visiting http://www.packtpub.com/support, selecting your book, clicking on the **let us know** link, and entering the details of your errata. Once your errata are verified, your submission will be accepted and the errata added to any list of existing errata. Any existing errata can be viewed by selecting your title from http://www.packtpub.com/support.

Piracy

Piracy of copyright material on the Internet is an ongoing problem across all media. At Packt, we take the protection of our copyright and licenses very seriously. If you come across any illegal copies of our works in any form on the Internet, please provide us with the location address or website name immediately so that we can pursue a remedy.

Please contact us at copyright@packtpub.com with a link to the suspected pirated material.

We appreciate your help in protecting our authors, and our ability to bring you valuable content.

Questions

You can contact us at questions@packtpub.com if you are having a problem with any aspect of the book, and we will do our best to address it.

1
Data Pump

Storage technology is improving day by day, and the more storage that becomes available at a low cost, the more data appears to fill it up. Managing high volumes of data becomes impractical if we take the traditional export/import approach, as this tool is very limited. Let's remember that export/import has been available in Oracle for a very long time, it dates back to Oracle Release 5, and it has been adapted to incorporate some meaningful new features. When 10g first appeared, a complete re-engineering took place and a new product was conceived to meet today's data management requirements. It was the **Data Pump**.

Data Pump allows better manageability, and performance; it can be parameterized to meet particular data management requirements, such as direct export/import operations between different databases (or even different versions, starting with 10g Release 1). It can remap data object definitions, and access them by means of either a **Command Line Interface (CLI)** batch or interactive interface. In turn, the data pump **Application Programming Interface (API)** allows a programmer to embed data pump code inside a regular PL/SQL application so that it manages its own data without requiring a direct **Database Administrator (DBA)** or **Database Owner (DBO)** intervention.

Data Pump features

Data Pump provides these features:

- Better performance and more manageability than the old export/import
- It is a server side tool
- Resume / suspend control
- Network Mode
- Restartable
- Fine grained object Selection
- Provides a Metadata API

Oracle Data Pump is a facility available since Oracle 10g Release 1. It first appeared back in 2003. It enables high speed data and metadata transfers. It is an efficient, manageable, adaptive tool that can be used in more than one mode; namely, the regular command line interface, the suspended mode, the network mode, and the PL/SQL API mode. Besides the CLI interface, it is used by Enterprise Manager, SQL*Loader (by means of the external data pump table driver), the PL/SQL API, and other clients.

Data Pump is a productive tool designed to make the DBA's life easier. It can be easily set to a suspended mode and brought back to work wherever it was stopped. A session does not need an interactive connection to perform data management, so it can leave an unattended job and it can be resumed any time. This tool doesn't need to generate a file to transfer data in a database-to-database mode; it is the so called network mode, which is very useful when a single load is performed. When this data transfer mode is used, data does not have to be erased afterwards as there is no intermediate file created to move the data. The network mode is similar to the conventional named pipes which are used to perform data transfers on the fly; however, this traditional approach is not available on all **Operating Systems (OSes)** (Windows does not support named pipes). If a task is launched, even if a degree of parallelism hasn't been specified, it can be modified at run time, so resource consumption can be increased or decreased at will.

Data Pump allows high speed data movement from one database to another. The expdp command exports data and metadata to a set of OS files known as a dump file set. Compared with the traditional export/import tool set, Data Pump allows a DBA to easily clone accounts, move objects between tablespaces and change other object features at load time without being required to generate an SQL script to have the object modified, rebuilt and loaded. This kind of on-the-fly object redefinition is known as the remap feature. Data Pump performance is significantly better than that of the old export/import tools.

Data Pump architecture

Data Pump is a server side tool; even if it is remotely invoked, all the command actions and file generation will take place on the host where the database resides, and all directory objects refer to paths in the server. **Oracle Data Pump** requires a Master Table which is created in the user's schema when a Data Pump session is open. This table records the Data Pump's session status and if the job has to be stopped (either on purpose or due to an unexpected failure), the Data Pump knows where it was when it is brought back to work. This table is automatically purged once the job is finished. The master table will match the job name given, by means of the command line parameter job_name, or Oracle can choose to generate a name for it, in case this parameter hasn't been defined.

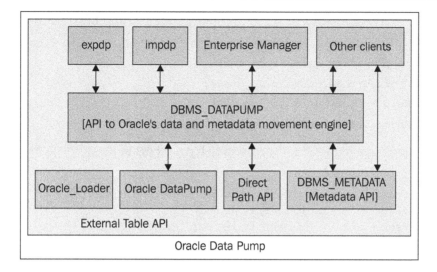

Oracle Data Pump

Oracle Data Pump has a master process that is responsible for orchestrating the data pump work. This master process is automatically created when either an **impdp** or **expdp** is started. Among other things, this process is responsible for populating the master table and spawning several worker processes (in case Data Pump has been directed to work in parallel mode).

Setting up the practical scenarios

Data Pump is a server side tool. In order for it to work with the remote file system it requires an access to the file by means of Oracle directory objects. On the database you must create directory objects and make sure the physical paths at the OS level are readable and writable by the oracle user. The examples provided assume a default database was created with the default oracle demo schemas; we'll be using the SCOTT, HR, SH, and OE demo schemas; when the database is created make sure the default demo accounts are selected.

Let's connect with the SYS administrative account by means of a regular SQL command line interface session, in this example the SYS user is used only for demonstration purposes, and the goal of SYS is to create the directory objects and grant privileges on these directories to the demo users. You can use any user who has been granted privileges to read and write on a directory object.

```
$ sqlplus / as sysdba
```

Let's create two directories, one for the default dump files and the other for the default log dest:

```
SQL> create directory default_dp_dest
  2  as '/home/oracle/default_dp_dest';
SQL> create directory default_log_dest
  2  as '/home/oracle/default_log_dest';
```

Some privileges are required for the users to have access to these oracle directories:

```
grant read, write on directory default_dp_dest to scott;
grant read, write on directory default_dp_dest to hr;
grant read, write on directory default_dp_dest to sh;
grant read, write on directory default_dp_dest to oe;

grant read, write on directory default_log_dest to scott;
grant read, write on directory default_log_dest to hr;
grant read, write on directory default_log_dest to sh;
grant read, write on directory default_log_dest to oe;

grant create database link to scott;
grant create database link to hr, oe, sh;

grant exp_full_database to scott, hr, sh, oe;
```

In this example, the `exp_full_database` privilege is granted to the demo accounts. This is done to allow the users to work on the database, but you can restrict them to only manage the data that belongs to their schemas.

Data Pump export

Data Pump export (`expdp`) is the database utility used to export data, it generates a file in a proprietary format. The generated file format is not compatible with the one generated by the old export (`exp`) utility.

Data Pump export modes

Data Pump export modes define the different operations that are performed with Data Pump. The mode is specified on the command line using the appropriate parameters. Data Pump has the following modes:

- **Full export mode:** This mode exports the whole database; this requires the user to have the `exp_full_database` role granted.

- **Schema mode**: This mode selects only specific schemas, all objects belonging to the listed schemas are exported. When using this mode you should be careful, if you direct a table to be exported and there are objects such as triggers which were defined using a different schema, and this schema is not explicitly selected then the objects belonging to this schema are not exported.

- **Table mode**: The tables listed here are exported, the list of tables, partitions, and dependent objects are exported. You may export tables belonging to different schemas, but if this is the case then you must have the `exp_full_database` role explicitly granted to be able to export tables belonging to different schemas.

- **Tablespace mode**: This mode allows you to export all tables belonging to the defined tablespace set. The tables along with the dependent objects are dumped. You must have the `exp_full_database` role granted to be able to use this mode.

- **Transportable tablespace mode**: This mode is used to transport a tablespace to another database, this mode exports only the metadata of the objects belonging to the target set of listed tablespaces. Unlike tablespace mode, transportable tablespace mode requires that the specified tables be completely self-contained.

Data Pump Export provides different working interfaces such as:

- **Command line interface**: The command line interface is the default and the most commonly used interface. Here the user must provide all required parameters from the OS command line.

- **Parameter file interface**: In this mode the parameters are written in a plain text file. The user must specify the parameter file to be used for the session.

- **Interactive command** line **interface**. This is not the same interactive command line most users know from the regular exp command. This interactive command line is used to manage and configure the running jobs.

A simple Data Pump export session

Now let's start with our first simple Data Pump export session. This will show us some initial and important features of this tool.

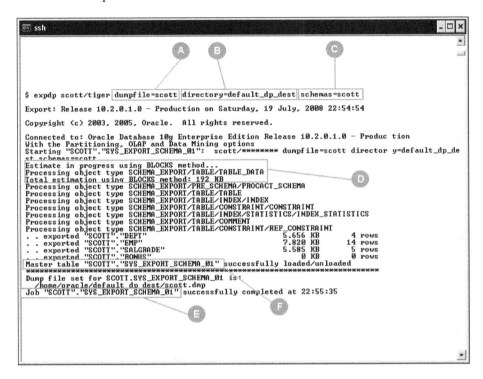

Here we will start with a basic Data Pump session to perform a simple logical backup. The command `expdp` has the following arguments:

Initially we define a **Dumpfile (A)**. As it will be managed by means of a **database directory object (B)** it is not necessary to define the path where the dump file will be stored. Remember, the directory objects were previously defined at the database level. This session will export a user's **Schema (C)**. No other parameters are defined at the command prompt and the session begins.

It can be seen from the command output that an **estimation (D)** takes place; this estimates the size of the file at the file system, and as no other option for the estimation was defined at the command line it is assumed the **BLOCKS** method will be used. The estimation by means of the BLOCKS method isn't always accurate, as it depends on the blocks sampled. Block density is a meaningful error factor for this estimation, it is better to use STATISTICS as the estimation method.

At the output log, the **Master table** (F) where the job running information is temporarily stored can be seen. The job name takes a **default name** (E). It is a good practice to define the job name and not let Oracle define it at execution time, if a DBA names the Job, it will be easier to reference it at a later time.

Data Pump export filtering operations

At the command line, filtering options can be specified. In this example, it is used to define the tables to export, but we can also specify whether the dump file will (or will not) include all other dependent objects.

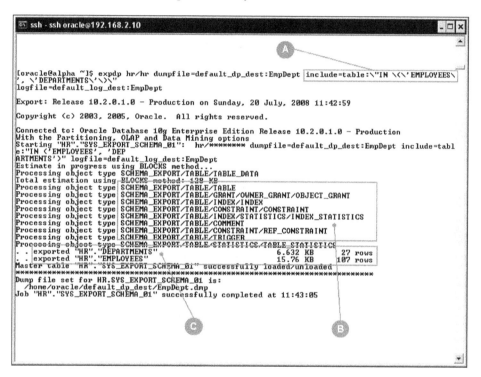

The **include** (A) and `exclude` options are mutually exclusive, and in this case as `include` was declared at the command line and it requires special characters, those must be *escaped* so the OS doesn't try to interpret them. When a longer `include` or `exclude` option is required, it is better to use a parameter file, where the escape characters are not required.

All the **filtered objects** (**C**) to be exported were saved in the dump file along with their **dependent objects** (**B**). If you change the command line with the following, it will prevent all the indexes being exported:

```
$ expdp hr/hr dumpfile=default_dp_dest:EmpDeptNoIndexes
tables=EMPLOYEES,DEPARTMENTS exclude=INDEX:\"LIKE \'\%\'\"
logfile=default_log_dest:EmpDeptNoIndexes
```

As can be seen, the `exclude` or `include` clause is actually a `where` predicate.

Use of parameter file

Using a parameter file simplifies an otherwise **complex to write** command line, it also allows the user to define a library of repeatable operations, even for simple exports. As previously seen, if a filtering (object or row) clause is used — some extra operating system escape characters are required. By writing the filtering clauses inside a parameter file, the command line can be greatly simplified.

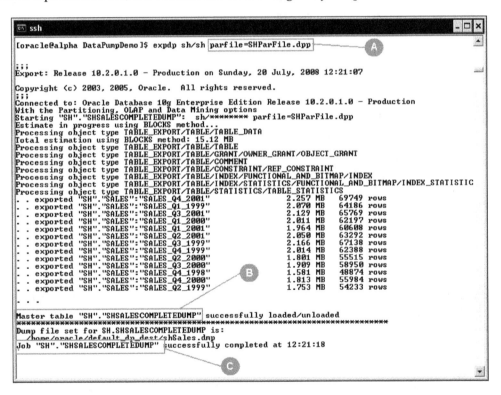

Comparing this command line (**A**) against the previously exposed command lines, it can be seen that it is more readable and manageable. The **SHParFile.dpp** file from the example contains these command options:

```
USERID=sh/sh
DUMPFILE=shSales
DIRECTORY=default_dp_dest
JOB_NAME=shSalesCompleteDump
TABLES=SALES
LOGFILE=default_log_dest:shSales
```

The parameter file is a plain text format file. You may use your own naming conventions. Oracle regularly uses .par for the parameter files, in this case it used .dpp to denote a Data Pump parameter file. The file name can be dynamically defined using environment variables, but this file name formatting is beyond the scope of Oracle and it exclusively depends on the OS variable management.

JOBNAME (C) is the option to specify a non-default job name, otherwise oracle will use a name for it. It is good practice to have the job name explicitly defined so the user can **ATTACH** to it at a later time, and related objects such as the **Master table** (**B**) can be more easily identified.

Retrieve original data

In some circumstances, it may be useful to export the image of a table the way it existed before a change was committed. If the database is properly configured, the database flashback query facility — also integrated with dpexp — may be used. It is useful for obtaining a consistent exported table image.

In this example a copy of the original HR.EMPLOYEES table is made (HR.BAK_EMPLOYEES), and all the tasks will update the BAK_EMPLOYEES table contents. A **Restore Point** is created so that you can easily find out the exact time stamp when this change took place:

```
SQL> CREATE RESTORE POINT ORIGINAL_EMPLOYEES;

Restore point created.

SQL> SELECT SCN, NAME FROM V$RESTORE_POINT;

       SCN NAME
---------- ----------------------------------
    621254 ORIGINAL_EMPLOYEES
SQL> SELECT SUM(SALARY) FROM EMPLOYEES;

SUM(SALARY)
-----------
    691400
```

This is the way data was, at the referred SCN. This number will be used later, to perform the expdp operation and retrieve data as it was, at this point in time.

Next a non-reversible update on the data takes place.

```
SQL> UPDATE BAK_EMPLOYEES SET SALARY=SALARY*1.1;
107 rows updated.
SQL> COMMIT;
Commit complete.
SQL> SELECT SUM(SALARY) FROM BAK_EMPLOYEES
SUM(SALARY)
-----------
    760540
```

Here we have a time reference and the goal is to restore data as it was.

Below are the contents of the data pump parameter file used to retrieve data.

```
USERID=hr/hr
DIRECTORY=default_dp_dest
DUMPFILE=hrExpAtRestorePoint
JOB_NAME=hrExpAtRestorePoint
TABLES=BAK_EMPLOYEES
LOGFILE=default_log_dest:hrExpAtRestorePoint
FLASHBACK_SCN=621254
```

The parameter FLASHBACK_SCN states the point in time from when the table is to be retrieved.

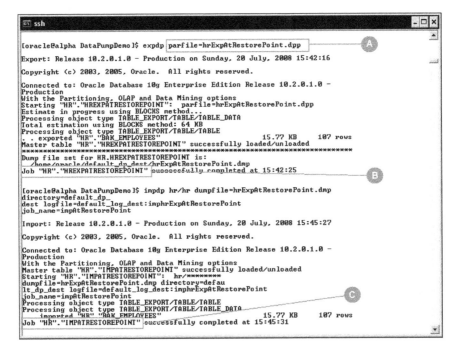

Once the backup is taken, the current table is dropped. When the import takes place it rebuilds the table with the data, as it was before. The import parameter file has been temporarily modified so it defines the log file name, and it includes only the minimum required parameters for the `impdp` task (**C**).

```
USERID=hr/hr
DIRECTORY=default_dp_dest
DUMPFILE=hrExpAtRestorePoint
JOB_NAME=ImpAtRestorePoint
TABLES=BAK_EMPLOYEES
LOGFILE=default_log_dest:hrImpAtRestorePoint
```

Once the import job is finished, a query to the current table shows the data 'as it was', prior to the update command.

```
SQL> select sum(salary) from bak_employees;

SUM(SALARY)
-----------
     691400
```

Data Pump export space estimation

Proactively estimating the amount of space required by an export file prevents physical disk space shortages. Data Pump has two methods to estimate the space requirements: Estimation by block sampling (BLOCKS) or estimation by object statistics (STATISTICS).

```
ESTIMATE={BLOCKS | STATISTICS}
```

- **BLOCKS** – The estimate is calculated by multiplying the number of database blocks used by the target objects times the appropriate block sizes.

- **STATISTICS** – The estimate is calculated using statistics for each table. For this method to be as accurate as possible, all tables should have been analyzed recently.

The second method leads to more accurate results and can be performed in a more efficient way than the BLOCKS method; this method requires reliable table statistics.

It can be seen from an export execution, that space estimation is always carried out, and the default estimation method is BLOCKS. The BLOCKS method is used by default as data blocks will always be present at the table, while the presence of reliable statistics cannot be taken for granted. From performance and accuracy perspectives it is not the best choice. It takes longer to read through the whole table, scanning the data block to estimate the space required by the dump file. This method may not be accurate as it depends on the block data distribution. This means that it assumes all block data is evenly distributed throughout all the blocks, which may not be true in every case, leading to inaccurate results. If the STATISTICS keyword is used, it is faster; it only has to estimate the file size from the information already gathered by the statistics analysis processes.

Taking the export of the SH schema with the ESTIMATE_ONLY option and the option BLOCKS, the estimation may not be as accurate as the STATISTICS method. As these test results shows:

ESTIMATE_ONLY	Reported Estimated Dump File Size
BLOCKS	15.12 MB
STATISTICS	25.52 MB
ACTUAL FILE SIZE	29.98 MB

From the above results, it can be seen how important it is to have reliable statistics at the database tables, so any estimation performed by data pump can be as accurate as possible.

Dump file multiplexing

Data Pump export is an exporting method that is faster than the old exp utility. Export speed can between 15 and 45 times faster than the conventional export utility. This is because the original export utility uses only conventional mode inserts, whereas Data Pump export uses the direct path method of loading, but in order for it to reach the maximum possible speed it is important to perform the parallel operations on spindles other than those where the database is located. There should be enough I/O bandwidth for the export operation to take advantage of the dump file multiplexing feature.

The options used to generate an export dump in parallel with multiplexed dump files are:

```
USERID=sh/sh
DUMPFILE=shParallelExp01%u,shParallelExp02%u
DIRECTORY=default_dp_dest
JOB_NAME=shParallelExp
TABLES=SALES
LOGFILE=default_log_dest:shParallelExp
ESTIMATE=statistics
PARALLEL=4
```

Notice the `%u` flag, which will append a two digit suffix to the Data Pump file. These options will direct export data pump to generate four dump files which will be accessed in a round robin fashion, so they get uniformly filled.

The resulting export dump files are:

```
shParallelExp0101.dmp
shParallelExp0102.dmp
shParallelExp0201.dmp
shParallelExp0202.dmp
```

Transporting data among different versions

Data Pump allows data transfers among different Oracle versions that support the feature. (Note the feature was introduced in Oracle Database 10g Release. 1). The database must be configured for compatibility of 9.2.0 or higher. This feature simplifies data transfer tasks. In order for this to work it is important to consider the source version versus the destination version. It works in an ascending compatible mode, so a Data Pump export taken from a lower release can always be read by the higher release, but an export taken from a higher release must be taken with the VERSION parameter declaring the compatibility mode. This parameter can either take the value of COMPATIBLE (default) which equals the compatible instance parameter value, LATEST, which equals the metadata version or any valid database version greater than 9.2.0. This last statement doesn't mean Data Pump can be imported on a 9.2.0 database. Rather, it stands for the recently migrated 10g databases which still hold the compatible instance parameter value set to 9.2.0.

If the COMPATIBLE parameter is not declared an export taken from a higher release won't be read by a lower release and a run time error will be displayed.

When performing data transfers among different database versions, you should be aware of the Data Pump compatibility matrix:

Data Pump client and server compatibility:

expdp and impdp client version	10.1.0.X	10.2.0.X	11.1.0.X
10.1.0.X	Supported	Supported	Supported
10.2.0.X	NO	Supported	Supported
11.1.0.X	NO	NO	Supported

Each Oracle version produces a different Data Pump file version, when performing expdp/impdp operations using different Data Pump file versions you should be aware of the file version compatibility.

Version Data Pump Dumpfile Set	Written by database with compatibility	Can be imported into Target		
		10.1.0.X	10.2.0.X	11.1.0.X
0.1	10.1.X	Supported	Supported	Supported
1.1	10.2.X	No	Supported	Supported
2.1	11.1.X	No	No	Supported

Data Pump export interactive mode

Data Pump is meant to work as a batch utility, but it also has a prompt mode, which is known as the interactive mode. It should be emphasized that the data pump interactive mode is conceptually different from the old interactive export/import mode. In this release, the interactive mode doesn't interfere with the currently running job, it is used to control some parameter of the running job, such as the degree of parallelism, kill the running job, or resume job execution in case of a temporary stop due to lack of disk space.

In order for the user to ATTACH to a running job in interactive mode, the user must issue the *Ctrl-C* keystroke sequence from an attached client. If the user is running on a terminal different from the one where the job is running, it is still possible to attach to the running job by means of the explicit ATTACH parameter. It is because of this feature that it is useful to not let Oracle define the job name.

Once attached there are several commands that can be issued from the open Data Pump prompt:

Command	Description (Default)
CONTINUE_CLIENT	Return to logging mode. Job will be re-started if idle
EXIT_CLIENT	Quit client session and leave the job running
HELP	Summarize interactive commands
KILL_JOB	Detach and delete job
PARALLEL	Change the number of active workers for current job PARALLEL=
START_JOB	Start/resume current job. START_JOB=SKIP_CURRENT will start the job after skipping any action which was in progress when job was stopped
STATUS	Frequency (seconds) job status is to be monitored where the default (0) will show new status when available STATUS=[interval]
STOP_JOB	Orderly shutdown of job execution and exits the client. STOP_JOB=IMMEDIATE performs an immediate shutdown of the Data Pump job

In this scenario the expdp **Command Line Interface** (CLI) is accessed to manage a running job. First a simple session is started using the command:

```
expdp system/oracle dumpfile=alphaFull directory=default_dp_dest full=y
job_name=alphaFull
```

The JOB_NAME parameter provides a means to quickly identify the running job.

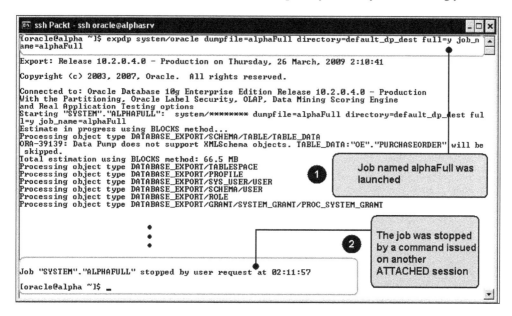

Once the job is running on a second OS session a new `expdp` command instance is started, this time using the ATTACH command. This will open a prompt that will allow the user to manage the running job.

```
expdp system/oracle attach=alphaFull
```

After showing the job status it enters the prompt mode where the user can issue the previously listed commands.

In this case a STOP_JOB command has been issued. This notifies the running session that the command execution has been stopped, the job output is stopped and the OS prompt is displayed. After a while the user reattaches to the running job, this time the START_JOB command is issued, this resumes the job activity, but as the `expdp` session was exited no more command output is displayed. The only way the user can realize the job is running is by querying the DBA_DATAPUMP_JOBS view or by browsing the log file contents.

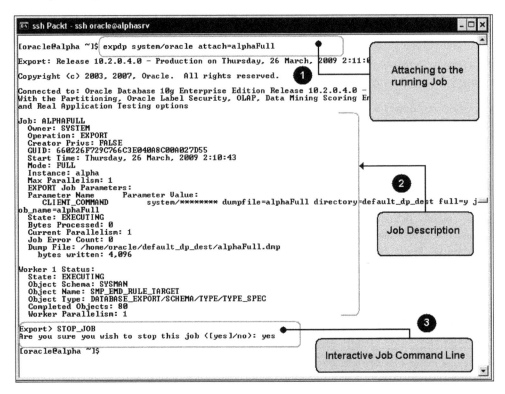

 The ATTACH command does not require the job name if there is only a single JOB running. If there is more than one concurrent job running then the user must specify the job name.

Data Pump restart capability

In case of failure or any other circumstances that prevent the Data Pump job from successfully ending its work, an implicit recommencing feature is activated. The job enters a suspended mode that allows the DBA to attach this feature to the job. It is important to emphasize that the master job table must positively identify the interrupted job, otherwise it won't be possible to restart the job once the circumstance behind the failure has been properly corrected.

In order for the user to attach to the job, it must be connected with the ATTACH command line option properly set. At this point, it becomes evident why it is a good practice to have a name for the data pump job, other than the default system generated name.

Getting information about the export job

When a Data Pump task takes place, it can be monitored to find out if everything is running fine with it. A view named DBA_DATAPUMP_JOBS can be queried to check the task status.

```
SQL> select * from dba_datapump_jobs;
```

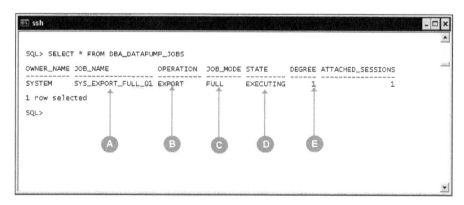

In this query it can be seen that a **FULL (C) EXPORT (B)** data pump job named **SYS_EXPORT_FULL_01 (A)** is in **Executing State (D)**. It is executing with a default parallel **degree** of **1 (E)**. In case of trouble, the status changes and it would be time to work with the CLI mode to **ATTACH** to the job and take corrective action.

Data Pump import

Data Pump import (`impdp`) is the tool used to perform the data import operation, it reads the data from a file created by Data Pump export. This tool can work in different modes such as:

- **Full import mode**: This is the default operation mode. This mode imports the entire contents of the source dump file, and you must have the `IMP_FULL_DATABASE` role granted if the export operation required the `EXP_FULL_DATABASE` role.

- **Schema mode**: A schema import is specified using the `SCHEMAS` parameter. In a schema import, only objects owned by the current user are loaded. You must have the `IMP_FULL_DATABASE` role in case you are planning to import schemas you don't own.

- **Table mode**: This mode specifies the tables, table partitions and the dependent objects to be imported. If the `expdp` command required the `EXP_FULL_DATABASE` privilege to generate the dump file, then you will require the `IMP_FULL_DATABASE` to perform the import operation.

- **Tablespace mode**: In this mode all objects contained within the specified set of tablespaces are loaded.

- **Transportable tablespace mode**: The transportable tablespace mode imports the previously exported metadata to the target database; this allows you to plug in a set of data files to the destination database.

- **Network mode**: This mode allows the user to perform an import operation on the fly with no intermediate dump file generated; this operation mode is useful for the one time load operations.

The Data Pump import tool provides three different interfaces:

- **Command Line Interface**: This is the default operation mode. In this mode the user provides no further parameters once the job is started. The only way to manage or modify running parameters afterwards is by entering interactive mode from another Data Pump session.

- **Interactive Command Interface**: This prompt is similar to the interactive `expdp` prompt, this allows you to manage and modify the parameters of a running job.

- **Parameter File Interface**: This enables you to specify command-line parameters in a parameter file. The `PARFILE` parameter must be specified in the command line.

Remap function

One of the most interesting import data pump features is the `REMAP` function. This function allows the user to easily redefine how an object will be stored in the database. It allows us, amongst many other things, to specify if the tables to be loaded will be remapped against another schema (`REMAP_SCHEMA`). It also changes the tablespace where the segment will be stored (`REMAP_TABLESPACE`). In case of a full data pump import, the function can also remap where the database files will be created by means of the `REMAP_DATAFILE` keyword.

Let's show the `REMAP_SCHEMA` facility. It is common practice to have a user's schema cloned for testing or development environments. So let's assume the HR schema is to be used by a recently created HRDEV user, and it requires all the HR schema objects mapped in its schema.

Create the HRDEV user. In this case the user HRDEV is created with the RESOURCE role granted. This is only for demonstration purposes, you should only grant the minimum required privileges for your production users.

```
SQL> create user HRDEV ident
  2    identified by ORACLE
  3    default tablespace USERS;
User created.
SQL> grant CONNECT, RESOURCE to HRDEV;
Grant succeeded.
```

Export the HR Schema objects using the following command:

```
$ expdp system/oracle schemas=HR dumpfile=DEFAULT_DP_DEST:hrSchema
logfile=DEFAULT_LOG_DEST:hrSchema
```

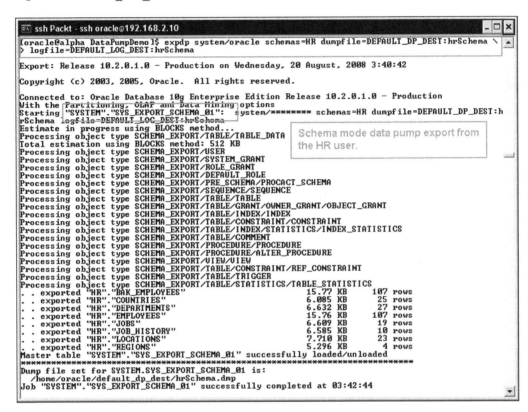

Import the HR Schema objects and remap them to the HRDEV user's schema. Using the following command:

```
$ impdp system/oracle \

dumpfile=DEFAULT_DP_DEST:hrSchema \

logfile=DEFAULT_LOG_DEST:hrSchema \ REMAP_SCHEMA=HR:HRDEV
```

The import session runs as follows:

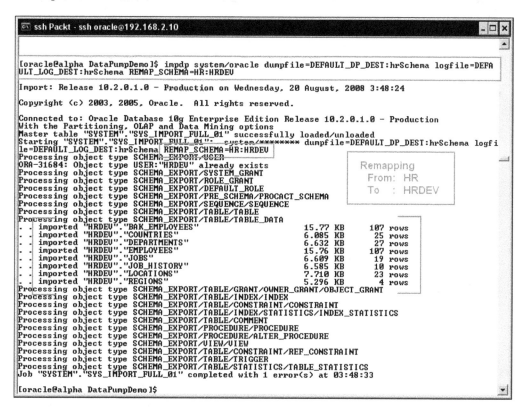

The HRDEV schema automatically inherits, by means of a cloning process (REMAP_SCHEMA), 35 objects from the HR schema, which includes tables, views, sequences, triggers, procedures, and indexes.

Data Pump import network mode

One of the most interesting data pump features is the network mode, which allows a database to receive the data directly from the source without generating an intermediate dump file. This is convenient as it saves space and allows a networked pipeline communication between the source and the destination database.

The network import mode is started when the parameter NETWORK_LINK is added to the impdp command, this parameter references a valid database link that points to the source database. This link is used to perform the connection with a valid user against the source database. A simple CREATE DATABASE LINK command is required to setup the source database link at the target database.

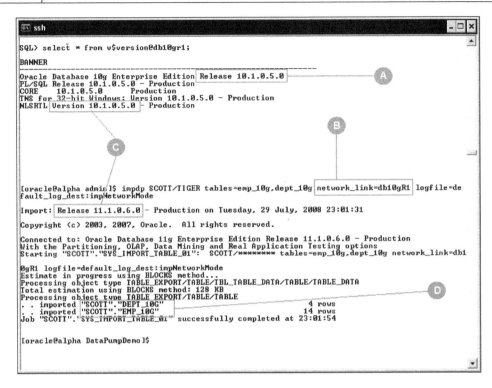

```
SQL> select * from v$version@db10gr1;

BANNER
--------------------------------------------------------
Oracle Database 10g Enterprise Edition Release 10.1.0.5.0
PL/SQL Release 10.1.0.5.0 - Production
CORE    10.1.0.5.0    Production
TNS for 32-bit Windows: Version 10.1.0.5.0 - Production
NLSRTL Version 10.1.0.5.0 - Production




[oracle@alpha admin]$ impdp SCOTT/TIGER tables=emp_10g,dept_10g network_link=db10gR1 logfile=de
fault_log_dest:impNetworkMode

Import: Release 11.1.0.6.0 - Production on Tuesday, 29 July, 2008 23:01:31

Copyright (c) 2003, 2007, Oracle.  All rights reserved.

Connected to: Oracle Database 11g Enterprise Edition Release 11.1.0.6.0 - Production
With the Partitioning, OLAP, Data Mining and Real Application Testing options
Starting "SCOTT"."SYS_IMPORT_TABLE_01":  SCOTT/******** tables=emp_10g,dept_10g network_link=db1
0gR1 logfile=default_log_dest:impNetworkMode
Estimate in progress using BLOCKS method...
Processing object type TABLE_EXPORT/TABLE/TBL_TABLE_DATA/TABLE/TABLE_DATA
Total estimation using BLOCKS method: 128 KB
Processing object type TABLE_EXPORT/TABLE/TABLE
. . imported "SCOTT"."DEPT_10G"                           4 rows
. . imported "SCOTT"."EMP_10G"                           14 rows
Job "SCOTT"."SYS_IMPORT_TABLE_01" successfully completed at 23:01:54

[oracle@alpha DataPumpDemo]$
```

.It can be seen that the import operation takes place at the 11g database; meanwhile the export is taken from a 10g Release 1 database by network mode using a database link created on the 11g side. This example is a classical data migration from a lower to a higher version using a one-time export operation.

The source database is **10.1.0.5.0 (A)**, and the destination database version is **11.1.0.6.0 (C)**. There is a database link named **db10gR1 (B)** on the 11g database. In order for this export to work it is important to consider version compatibility. In network mode the source database must be an equal or lower version than the destination database, and the database link can be either public, fixed user, or connected user, but *not* current user. Another restriction of the data pump network mode is the filtering option; only full tables can be transferred, not partial table contents.

At the target site a new database link is created:

```
CREATE DATABASE LINK DB10GR1
CONNECT TO <username> IDENTIFIED BY <password> using <TNSAlias>;
```

This alias is used at import time:

```
impdp <username>/<password> network_link=<DBLink> tables=<List of Tables
to Import> logfile=<Directory Object>:file_name
```

The network import mode provides a practical approach for one-time data transfers. It is convenient and reduces the intermediate file management that is usually required.

Improving performance with Data Pump

There are some considerations the user should pay attention, in order to take full advantage of this tool. When performing a data pump export operation it can perform faster if using parallelism, but if this is not used properly, the process may end up serializing, which is very likely to happen if the dump files are written to the same disk location.

When performing a data pump import operation, we should consider the same parallelism issue. If using an enterprise edition, the degree of parallelism can be set and can be tuned so that there will be several parallel processes carrying out the import process. It is advisable to ensure the number of processes does not exceed twice the number of available CPU's.

Also, the tablespace features are important. The tablespace should be *locally managed* with **Automatic Segment Space Management (ASSM)**; this will allow the insert process to perform faster.

Other features that should be considered are related to database block checking. Both `db_block_ckecking` and `db_block_checksum` impose a performance penalty. It has been reported by some users that this penalty is meaningful when batch loading takes place. It is advisable to either disable these parameters or reduce the emphasis. Those instance parameters are dynamic, so they can be modified during the operation.

Other instance parameters to consider are those related to parallelism, the `parallel_max_servers`, and `parallel_execution_message_size`. When using parallelism, the `large_pool_size` region should be properly configured.

Working with the Data Pump API

The Data Pump API allows the PL/SQL programmer to gain access to the data pump facility from inside PL/SQL code. All the features are available, so an export/import operation can be coded inside a stored procedure, thus allowing applications to perform their own programmed logical exports.

The stored program unit that leverages the data pump power is DBMS_DATAPUMP.

This code shows a simple export data pump job programmed with the DBMS_DATAPUMP API.

This sample code required the DBMS_DATAPUMP program units to perform the following tasks:

- FUNCTION OPEN
- PROCEDURE ADD_FILE
- PROCEDURE METADATA_FILTER
- PROCEDURE START_JOB
- PROCEDURE DETACH
- PROCEDURE STOP_JOB

The account used in the next example is used merely for demonstration purposes. In a practical scenario you can use any user that has the execute privilege granted on the DBMS_DATAPUMP package and the appropriate privileges on the working directories and target objects.

```
conn / as sysdba
set serveroutput on
DECLARE
 dp_id        NUMBER;          -- job id
BEGIN
  -- Defining an export DP job name and scope
  dp_id := dbms_datapump.open('EXPORT','SCHEMA',NULL,'DP_API_EXP_
DEMO','COMPATIBLE');
  -- Adding the dump file
  dbms_datapump.add_file(dp_id, 'shSchemaAPIDemo.dmp', 'DEFAULT_DP_
DEST',
  filetype => DBMS_DATAPUMP.KU$_FILE_TYPE_DUMP_FILE);
  -- Adding the log file
  dbms_datapump.add_file(dp_id, 'shSchemaAPIDemo.log', 'DEFAULT_LOG_
DEST',
  filetype => DBMS_DATAPUMP.KU$_FILE_TYPE_LOG_FILE);
  -- Specifying schema to export
  dbms_datapump.metadata_filter(dp_id, 'SCHEMA_EXPR', 'IN (''SH'')');
  -- Once defined, the job starts
  dbms_datapump.start_job(dp_id);
  -- Once the jobs has been started, the session is dettached.
Progress can be monitored from dbms_datapump.get_status.
  -- in case it is required, the job can be attached by means of the
dbms_datapump.attach() function.
  -- Detaching the Job, it will continue to work in background.
  dbms_output.put_line('Detaching Job, it will run in background');
  dbms_datapump.detach(dp_id);
```

```
     -- In case an error is raise, the exception
     -- is captured and processed.
EXCEPTION
   WHEN OTHERS THEN
     dbms_datapump.stop_job(dp_id);
END;
/
```

Data Pump 11g new features

'The features described so far are valid in both 10g and 11g, but there are specific features available only in 11g such as:

- Compression
- Encrypted dump file sets
- Enhancements for Data Pump external table management
- Support for XML data types

Compression

The compression feature in 10g is related to the metadata, not the actual data part of the dump files. With 11g, this feature was improved to allow either the metadata, the row data or the complete dump file set to be compressed. This shrinks the dump file set by 10 to 15 percent.

Encrypted dump file sets

In 11g it is possible to use the encrypted dump file sets feature to have the dump set encrypted. Data Pump in 11g includes other keywords to manage encryption, such as ENCRYPTION_ALGORITHM, and ENCRYPTION_MODE which requires the **Transparent Data Encryption** (TDE) feature to perform the encryption process. This feature will be addressed in more depth in the security chapter

Enhancements for Data Pump External Tables

In 10g, when a row in an external table was corrupted, it led to the entire process being aborted. Data Pump 11g is more tolerant under these circumstances, allowing the process to continue with the rest of the data.

Single partition transportable for Oracle Data Pump

With this feature, it is possible to move just one partition or sub partition between databases without having the need to move the whole table. A partition can be added as part of an existing table or as an independent table.

Overwrite dump files

In 10g dump files had to be removed by the DBA prior to any attempt to overwrite them. In 11g a new keyword was added, REUSE_DUMPFILES, which defaults to 11g, and when activated simply overwrites the existing dump files (if they already exist).

XML Datatypes

In previous Data Pump releases, the XML data type was not supported, all Oracle XML data types are supported with Oracle Data Pump. You can use all other datatypes, however you should be aware that the Data Pump driver for external tables restricts the use of certain data types.

Summary

Data Pump is one of the least known and under-exploited data management tools in Oracle, in part due to the widely used regular export/import utility. Most user's are used to the old tool and as the data pump export dump file is not compatible with the old utilities, there is a point of no return when starting to use the Data Pump utility. However, when the user gets acquainted with the Data Pump features and feels more comfortable using this alternative for regular data management processes, they will notice how productivity and manageability improve.

Data Pump allows more flexible data management scenarios than its predecessor, the regular export/import utilities. Once the power of Data Pump is deployed by the user on the DBA's day-to-day tasks, Data Pump will automatically be positioned as the de-facto data management tool. It is available in all Oracle editions starting from 10g Release 1. Getting to know this tool allows the DBA to plan much more flexible scenarios.

In the next chapter another useful data management tool will be addressed, SQL*Loader, a tool that is used to perform plain file loads to the database.

2
SQL*Loader

Transferring data in plain text file format is common when performing tasks such as loading a database for the first time, data warehouse maintenance, ASCII backups, or spatial data management. Knowing how to efficiently use and tailor this tool allows the user to optimize the time invested in performing one of the most labor intensive and time consuming maintenance tasks.

During the upload process it is important to foresee any space allocation issues that may prevent the load process from successfully finishing. It is important to either gauge the tablespace requirements, or proactively launch automatic space management tasks.

It is important to know how to perform the data load with different character sets, so that users don't risk losing data, and to ensure that even if the data load completes successfully it doesn't end up showing those boring 'question marks' because of character set incompatibilities.

There are several ways to perform the load of large objects, such as long texts or multimedia files. By knowing the issues, and the caveats that should be considered, the user will be able to perform a data load more efficiently.

SQL*Loader basics

Sometimes, an external source provides data in an unwanted format. As database users, we can only deal with whatever way the data has been formatted, and do our best to load it. Sometimes an interface has to be built specifically to perform a complex format load. The purpose of SQL*Loader is not only to provide a plain format data loader tool, but also a means to allow a complex data set to be loaded. The user can leverage the power of SQL*Loader by:

- Loading several data files on the same session
- Specifying a particular character sets to be loaded
- Conditionally loading data
- Performing pre-loading phases
- Loading data from a variety of sources, including named pipes
- Loading either logical or physical records
- Loading regular data as well as Large Objects and object/relational data
- Taking advantage of parallelism and direct path loads to accelerate the load process

SQL*Loader's architecture is both simple and elegant. It requires at least one or two input files to start processing data, one of them is the datafile and the other the control file; it may produce two or three output files, one for the log file, another for the bad file and another file known as discard file.

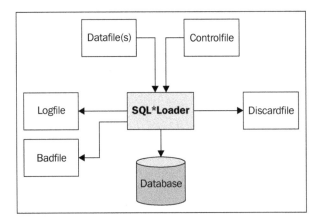

Looking at the above diagram, SQL*Loader files are defined as follows:

Datafile: This is the actual plain-data file. This datafile must have a consistent format (along with its contents) according to the predefined format described by the control file. This is the source file and under certain circumstances, such as a one-time load, this file may also have the control file contents embedded. There may be more than one datafile for a single data load, the number of datafiles is specified in the control file.

Controlfile: This file describes the way data is structured; it specifies whether the record will have a commonly used record delimited by a carriage return, or a record that spans several lines. This control file specifies if the record is a fixed size column record or if the columns are delimited by an exclusive character in a variable size record format. It can specify: the data types, lengths, precision, character set, use of secondary data files, different data files, record structure, and many other data description parameters.

The control file uses format free syntax, which means control file contents can span multiple lines and can contain multiple space characters to separate keywords. Control file commands are case insensitive, but it should be pointed out that quoted strings are literally read.

In summary, the control file describes the input (what and how to read), the output (where and when to load), and the mapping between the two.

Logfile: Once a data loading session is over, all meaningful activity is recorded in the log file. This is a plain format file where session activity is recorded. The logfile describes the control file specifications, the amount of data loaded, the elapsed time to complete the load, information about defective rows, and the parameters used during a selective data load. The script to create an external table can also be found here if the proper command line option is specified.

Discardfile: All records that didn't match any condition specified during a conditional load are, if specified, sent to the discard file. The user can specify the maximum number of discarded records to be sent to the discard file before aborting the load process. The discard file is optional and the user must explicitly request its creation.

Badfile: If a malformed record is found, or if a record doesn't meet a particular constraint condition, it is sent to the bad file. There it may have a second chance to be loaded once the defect has been corrected. There are a maximum number of records allowed during a load to be considered defective, and by default this number is 50. Once the maximum number of bad records is reached, the load process is automatically aborted and proper log information is recorded at the log file.

Preparing the demo environment

We will require a demo user to perform the loads, a regular tablespace, and some
basic privileges for the SQL*Loader demo user. The paths and other particular
references are included as mere examples, and to meet the syntax requirements.
Actual implementations may differ. During the development of
these demonstrations, data from either the HR or SCOTT schemas was used.
The next examples use the SYS user to perform administrative tasks, it is only for
demonstration purposes, any user with privileges to create a tablespace is enough
to setup the environment, and any user who has permission to insert data into a
given table is enough to perform the data loading procedure. The paths used and
the Oracle SID referred here are just based on a specific demo database used.

```
connect / as sysdba
create tablespace sqlldrdemo
datafile '/u01/oracle/oradata/beta/sqlldr01.dbf' size 32m
autoextend on next 16m;

create user sqlldrdemo
identified by oracle
default tablespace sqlldrdemo
quota unlimited on sqlldrdemo;

grant connect, resource to sqlldrdemo;

connect  sqlldrdemo/oracle

create table emp
        (empno number(4) not null,
         ename char(10),
         job char(9),
         mgr number(4),
         hiredate date,
         sal number(7,2),
         comm number(7,2),
         deptno number(2))
tablespace sqlldrdemo;

create table dept
        (deptno number(2),
         dname char(14) ,
         loc char(13) )
tablespace sqlldrdemo;
```

Our first simple load

Let' start working with the basics. In this scenario we will perform a simple load where the main points will be presented. A simple source datafile will be loaded and exposed to the main points a simple load has to consider.

In order for you to perform the first basic load, a simple text file has to be created; this file will be the control file. The control file defines how the load will be executed, it specifies the target table(s), the data file format, what to do in case of error, and which other special features will be either used or not.

This first control file was taken from the demonstrations available from the Oracle Home once the companion disk (demo section) has been installed. This is the ulcase1.ctl control file. The comments are specified by using two hyphens at the beginning of the line. All text following the hyphens up to the end of the line is considered a comment and it is not interpreted.

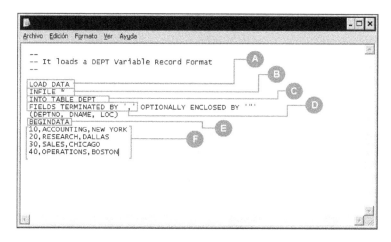

LOAD DATA: The beginning of the file starts with the keyword LOAD DATA (**A**). It assumes the target table is empty. In case there is data already loaded, and depending on what exactly is being planned we can either APPEND or REPLACE. If no modifier is specified, then it means the table must be empty before attempting to insert data, otherwise a runtime error will show up. The user must have at least the SELECT privilege on the table. If the option APPEND is used, it means that we can just proceed to insert data; the user must be careful with the unique and primary key constraints. For the REPLACE option, all data in the table will be removed prior to starting the load; the user must have the SELECT and DELETE privileges to be able to perform the operation with this option. It should be pointed out that deleting a complete table may lead to severe performance problems, so it is better to use the TRUNCATE option, it will be faster and as it applies over all the data rows, it performs significantly faster than the REPLACE option.

INFILE (B): This option can be used to specify where the source data file is. It can be a simple one time relative small load, as shown in the example. In this case, there is no need to have a separate source data file, so it can be embedded in the same file as that of the control file. As shown on the image, this option is specified at the start (*) (**B**), indicating that the data section will start as the first row right after the **BEGINDATA (E)** keyword is found, and it will stop at the end of file (**F**). In this case there can be no more control file commands from this point on. Any additional control file commands will be treated as malformed rows and will be sent to the bad file. In case another datafile needs to be specified, it could be defined from the file with the same INFILE keyword. It can also be defined with the command line argument DATA.

There are three ways to specify how data is organized; in fixed or variable field length (**D**) or in stream format.

Once the control file has been created, a typical SQL*Loader command line would read like this:

```
sqlldr username/password control=controlFileName.ctl
```

In this case, the username and password appear as the first parameter, so we do not need to specify the user-id keyword. Next the control file is declared, as the INFILE * keyword was specified inside the file, no datafile specification is required. Log file and Bad File names are automatically generated, and those files will hold the same name as that of the control file with the default file extensions *.ctl and *.bad.

As an example, the command line issued to start the first load is:

```
sqlldr sqlldrdemo/oracle ulcase1
```

You should notice that it is assumed that both the demo user and the demonstration tables were properly created. The script ulcase1.sql creates the tables EMP and DEPT.s.

The SQL*Loader log file

This file describes the execution details, and shows exactly what happened. In case of any failure this is the first place to go for troubleshooting. Let's take a look at the details of a log file generated after the execution of the previous load example.

Header: A generic header is shown where the RDBMS version is shown along with the time this tool was invoked, plus some copyright information.

File names (A): At least three file names are specified, the first stands for the **control file** name used to perform the load, the second one for the **data file**, in this case, as the INFILE * keyword was specified, the data file holds the same name as that of the control file. In case any defective rows were to be found, those would have been sent to the **bad file**, and as no name was specified for this file, it holds by default the same name used for the control file plus the .bad as its file extension. And finally the **discard file**; in this case this was not a conditional load, so there was no need to have this file specified.

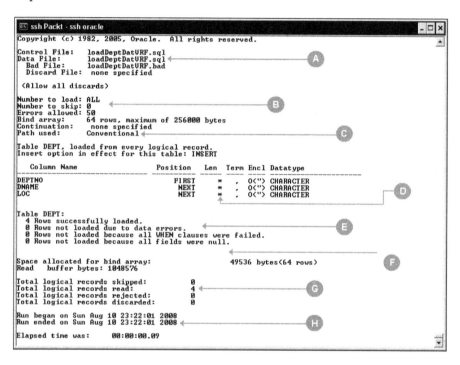

```
ssh Packt - ssh oracle                                                  _ □ ×
Copyright (c) 1982, 2005, Oracle.  All rights reserved.

Control File:     loadDeptDatURF.sql
Data File:        loadDeptDatURF.sql ◄─────────────────────    Ⓐ
  Bad File:       loadDeptDatURF.bad
  Discard File:  none specified

(Allow all discards)

Number to load: ALL
Number to skip: 0                                             Ⓑ
Errors allowed: 50
Bind array:      64 rows, maximum of 256000 bytes
Continuation:     none specified
Path used:        Conventional ◄──────────────────────       Ⓒ

Table DEPT, loaded from every logical record.
Insert option in effect for this table: INSERT

    Column Name              Position   Len  Term Encl Datatype
   ------------------------- --------- ----- ---- ---- --------
DEPTNO                        FIRST      *    ,  O(") CHARACTER
DNAME                         NEXT       *    ,  O(") CHARACTER      Ⓓ
LOC                           NEXT       *    ,  O(") CHARACTER

Table DEPT:
   4 Rows successfully loaded.
   0 Rows not loaded due to data errors.
   0 Rows not loaded because all WHEN clauses were failed.       Ⓔ
   0 Rows not loaded because all fields were null.

Space allocated for bind array:              49536 bytes(64 rows)
Read   buffer bytes: 1048576                                    Ⓕ

Total logical records skipped:    0
Total logical records read:       4 ◄──────────────────         Ⓖ
Total logical records rejected:   0
Total logical records discarded:  0

Run began on Sun Aug 10 23:22:01 2008
Run ended on Sun Aug 10 23:22:01 2008 ◄──────────────           Ⓗ

Elapsed time was:     00:00:00.09
```

The number of rows to load was **ALL (B)**, which is the default. If a load failed for some reason, then it is possible to restart the load at a specified row, skipping the other N previous rows; this fact is reported here. As mentioned, (by default) the maximum number of allowed defective rows is fifty, if the fiftieth error shows up, the load is automatically aborted and this information is reported. The number of permissible defective rows can be changed. In cases where no errors are allowed, zero must be specified.

Path used (C): This could say Direct or Conventional, depending on which kind of data load was used.

Data file format (D): In this particular case, a variable record size was specified. This can be seen just by the order of the columns plus a star sign as the value of the length column.

Execution details (**E**): This provides the number of successfully loaded rows, the number of defective rows, and the number of discarded and the number of null records found.

The space allocated for the bind array (**F**) is reported here. In this case, as a variable record size was requested, the bind array is prepared with an additional amount of memory, and compared with a fixed file size format. The bind array is meaningfully bigger, and this fact is considered for performance issues during data load.

Finally, the **timing** (**H**) is reported plus a **summary** (**G**) of all the records that were either skipped, read, rejected or discarded, plus the total elapsed time, which counts from the time the command is started (from the command line) up to the moment when the SQL*Loader utility finishes and closes its session.

Fixed record size format load

This format has records fixed in length. Padded spaces are used at the end of each field, if required, to have the column fixed in size. This kind of format has better load performance than the variable sized format. It is easier to define at the control file specification, and its length is always interpreted in character length semantics.

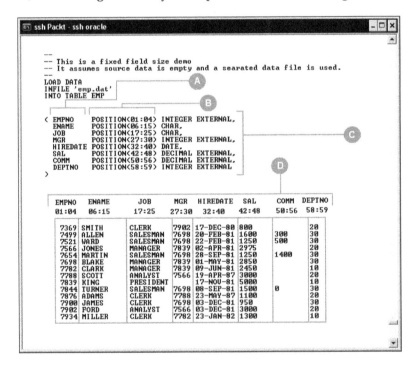

In a fixed record format, the control file specifies the **column name** (**A**), the physical position of the column in the file, starting to count with the column 1 and specified by the keyword **POSITION** (**B**), and the specific **data type** (**C**).

It is important to point out that the date format specified at the control file assumes the data file matches the default date format, according to the configured locale. If this condition is not met, then a malformed date format error will be shown and the load is very likely to be aborted due to the maximum defective row limit. If a different format is specified at the data file, then a date mask must be specified next to the DATE type declaration.

```
HIREDATE POSITION(32:40) DATE "DD-MON-RR"
```

Once this initial fixed field size is executed, the log file will read as follows:

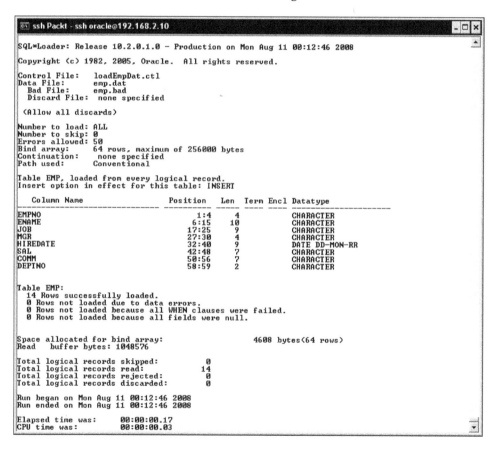

Variable record size format load

This allows more flexibility than the fixed record format, but it requires a field separator character, different from any character used by the data. The variable record format is always read in byte length semantics. This is the most common way of loading exported spreadsheets (.csv files). For repeated loads of CSVs, it is suggested to use External Tables (explained in the next chapter).

Compared with the fixed size, the variable record size data file will use less physical space when stored in the OS, but the size of the bind array used to perform the load will be significantly bigger, so this should be considered when choosing which format to use to perform the data load.

Taking a look at this code snippet, it can be seen that in order for the user to define a variable length record size—a delimiter is required. This character must be unique and not form part of the actual data to be loaded.

```
LOAD DATA
INFILE *S
INTO TABLE ABC
FIELDS TERMINATED BY ':'
(ID, ABC)
BEGINDATA
27:ABCDEFGHIJKLMNOPQRSTUVWXYZ
28:ABCDEFGHIJKLMNOPQRSTUVWXYZ
29:ABCDEFGHIJKLMNOPQRSTUVWXYZ
30:ABCDEFGHIJKLMNOPQRSTUVWXYZ
31:ABCDEFGHIJKLMNOPQRSTUVWXYZ
32:ABCDEFGHIJKLMNOPQRSTUVWXYZ
33:ABCDEFGHIJKLMNOPQRSTUVWXYZ
34:ABCDEFGHIJKLMNOPQRSTUVWXYZ
35:ABCDEFGHIJKLMNOPQRSTUVWXYZ
36:ABCDEFGHIJKLMNOPQRSTUVWXYZ
```

Stream record format load

This is a flexible way to specify data input. The 'end of record' character is determined as data is read. If a record delimiter is not specified at the control file, then either the carriage return or the carriage return and line feed are used to delimit the record, depending on the particular operating system used. A file is in stream record format when the records are not specified by size; instead SQL*Loader forms records by scanning for the record terminator. This is a flexible way to define the data input format, but it should be noted that a performance penalty applies for this format.

We will assume data is produced in this format, and the control file used to perform the data load has been configured accordingly:

```
--
-- It loads a DEPT Variable Record Format with Stream record
organization
--
LOAD DATA
INFILE 'loadDeptDatStream.dat' "str '|'"
TRUNCATE
INTO TABLE DEPT
FIELDS TERMINATED BY ',' OPTIONALLY ENCLOSED BY '"'
(DEPTNO, DNAME, LOC)
```

Here we can see the new `str` keyword, which declares which string sequence is used to define the end of the record. By the way, the option used to perform the load is TRUNCATE, which instructs SQL*Loader to perform the workload once current data has been truncated. It is faster than the REPLACE option.

The data format used during this test was:

```
10,ADMINISTRATION,SEATTLE,|20,MARKETING,TORONTO,|30,PURCHASING,SEATTLE,
|40,HUMAN RESOURCES,LONDON,|50,SHIPPING,SOUTH SAN FRANCISCO,
|60,IT,SOUTHLAKE,|70,PUBLIC RELATIONS,MUNICH,|80,SALES,OXFORD,
|90,EXECUTIVE,SEATTLE,|100,FINANCE,SEATTLE,|110,ACCOUNTING,SEATTLE,
|120,TREASURY,SEATTLE,|130,CORPORATE TAX,SEATTLE,
|140,CONTROL AND CREDIT,SEATTLE,|150,SHAREHOLDER SERVICES,SEATTLE,
|160,BENEFITS,SEATTLE,|170,MANUFACTURING,SEATTLE,
|180,CONSTRUCTION,SEATTLE,|190,CONTRACTING,SEATTLE,
|200,OPERATIONS,SEATTLE,|210,IT SUPPORT,SEATTLE,|220,NOC,SEATTLE,
|230,IT HELPDESK,SEATTLE,|240,GOVERNMENT SALES,SEATTLE,
|250,RETAIL SALES,SEATTLE,|260,RECRUITING,SEATTLE,
|270,PAYROLL,SEATTLE,|
```

In this data sample, just ignore the carriage return character. The data is a continuous stream whose records are delimited by the pipe character.

When defining the delimiter string these additional escape sequences can be used:

- \n indicates a line feed
- \t indicates a horizontal tab
- \f indicates a form feed
- \v indicates a vertical tab
- \r indicates a carriage return

Specifying a particular character set

A commonly seen requirement is loading data in a character set different from the WE8ISO family. When performing a load with a particular character set it should be specified with the NLS_LANG environment variable. In case it is not specified this way, it must be declared at the control file with the CHARACTERSET parameter. The character set will automatically be converted to the specified character set as long as the target database supports the conversion, otherwise a question mark will be loaded instead, indicating that the target database either didn't understand the conversion or the character set at the target database is not a superset of the source character set data.

In this example a load takes place using different character sets on this table, the purpose of the table is to store a multilingual error catalog:

```
CREATE TABLE ERRORCATALOG
  (
    LANGUAGE VARCHAR2(3),
    ERROR_NUMBER NUMBER(6),
    ERROR_STRING NVARCHAR2(1000)
  );
```

The first datafile to store is in Japanese, the second demo is Chinese and several other control files are prepared to load different languages for this multilingual demonstration table.

The Japanese datafile is:

The prepared control file for this session declares the character set as `JA16SJIS`, to perform this load:

```
load
characterset JA16SJIS
append
into table ERRORCATALOG
fields terminated by '|'  optionally enclosed by '"'
( LANGUAGE ,ERROR_NUMBER ,ERROR_STRING )
```

In this example a Chinese data file is loaded, as shown:

The control file used to perform this load declares the character set as `ZHS16GBK`

```
load
characterset ZHS16GBK
append
into table ERRORCATALOG
fields terminated by '|'  optionally enclosed by '"' ( LANGUAGE
,ERROR_NUMBER ,ERROR_STRING )
```

Once the different control files have been prepared, all the datafiles are loaded. By querying the table from iSQL*Plus, we get the resulting catalog:

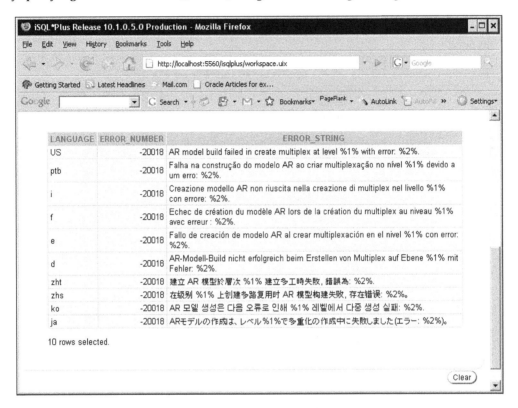

Load on the fly

SQL*Loader has a powerful interface that allows loads from different sources; it can read data from disk, tape or a named pipe. This feature allows loads on the fly without the creation of an intermediate data file, which is a very convenient strategy for loads that will only take place once and whose data source is dynamic. Let's have a named pipe created, so there is no datafile in-between, and data is directly consumed by the database through SQL*Loader.

On the OS prompt, let's create a named pipe. A process will then send data to the named pipe and SQL*Loader will read it from there.

This data load procedure is not available for Windows as this platform does not allow the use of the named pipes required to perform the data load on the fly.

At a Unix prompt, let's create a regular named pipe:

```
mkfifo abcpipe.dat
```

Send data to the named pipe and leave the process in the background:

```
cat abc.dat > abcpipe.dat &
```

Load data from the named pipe:

```
sqlldr sqlldrdemo/oracle direct=true control=abc data=abcpipe.dat
```

It can be seen that SQL*Loader performs the load seamlessly. The data source was obtained from the named pipe and then read and loaded by SQL*Loader.

You can remove the named pipe, just like any other regular file:

```
rm abcpipe.dat
```

The advantage of this approach is that there is no intermediate file created, saving space and performing a clean one time load from a dynamic data source.

Direct path versus Conventional path load

If SQL*Loader is properly configured the load can be sped up in a meaningful way by means of the direct path load. Direct path was a new feature introduced in Oracle 7.3, and it hasn't changed too much since then. Direct path is an Oracle feature that allows an insertion process to go directly to the database files without using the database transactional mechanism. It allows the data load process to be performed in the fastest possible way. It must be noted that there is a price to pay in the transaction and recoverability models for the increased processing speed.

When a conventional path load takes place, SQL*Loader fills a bind array buffer and passes it to the Oracle database so it is processed by means of regular SQL INSERT commands — SQL*Loader performs a batch insert assembling 64 rows (by default). Afterwards a commit command is issued. This approach makes the database buffer to allocate resources to perform the insert, and generates a transaction that is logged by the redo log buffer, and sent to the redo log files. After the checkpoint process is fired, the dirty database block buffers are sent from the database buffer cache to its final destination (the database files) by means of the **Database Writer (DBWR)** process.

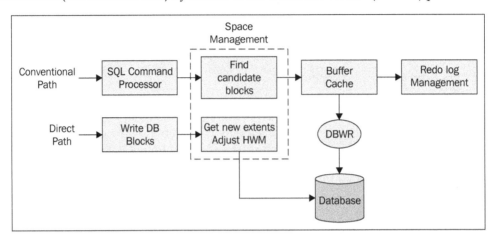

On the other hand, the direct path engine uses the column array structure to format Oracle data blocks and build index keys. It assembles the database blocks externally. Once they are ready, SQL*Loader simply finds out where the segment high water mark is placed, then adjusts and inserts the database blocks directly to the database files. During direct path insert mode, redo information may or may not be generated depending on the logging mode, or if the 'force logging' database mode has been enabled, so there could be some serious recoverability issues.

In order for SQL*Loader to work in direct path mode it is enough to declare the DIRECT=Y command line parameter. Some considerations must be present in order for you to take advantage of this feature, as explained here:

- Use **Locally Managed Tablespace (LMT)**
- Use ASSM
- Allocate space before, don't let dynamic space allocation be triggered during the load
- Make sure you have enough space, not only for the data to be loaded, but also for the index segments

There is a price to pay for the additional performance boost that you should be aware of.

Direct path load pros

- The primary benefit of direct path load is that it is faster than the conventional path load
- It performs data saves, skipping the database buffer cache
- It doesn't have to wait for the DBWR background process to write to the database files
- It can be parallelized

Direct path load cons

- It may require more space as direct path load looks for never used blocks beyond the high water mark. If the user is not aware of this, several bubbles of partially used blocks may remain below the **High Water Mark (HWM)**.
- It allows no concurrent transactions to take place at the target table at while the load is in progress.
- It doesn't fire triggers.
- It doesn't validate check constraints.
- The character set must be consistent with that of the database; otherwise character conversion may take place.

In this demo a simple table has been created. This table holds two columns, one is the id and the other is a varchar2 column. 8 million rows were inserted, and then those rows were extracted to a text datafile. On the first exercise the load takes place by means of the conventional path. On the second test, the load is performed by means of direct path loads. The results are:

	Case 1	**Case 2**	**Case 3**	**Case 4**
Path	Conventional	Direct	Conventional	Direct
Primary Key	No	No	No	No
Extent pre-allocation	No	No	Yes	Yes
Time	914s	14.6s	883.2s	13.9s

From the tests, meaningful time differences between a conventional and a direct path load can be shown. So it is worth considering the possibility of loading data in direct path mode.

	Case 5	Case 6
Path	Conventional	Direct
Primary Key	Yes	Yes
Extent pre-allocation	No	No
Time	944s	50s

During this test, a primary key constraint was added. The primary key related index took 1 minute 16.4 seconds. Considering this, if the table already has indexes, in the case of direct path load, it takes less time to leave the index and perform the load than inserting the whole data and rebuilding the index afterwards. In the case of conventional path loading, if the table already has indexes, it takes about the same time to complete the load with or without indexes. It should be pointed out that the more indexes there are, the more effort is required to maintain them. On direct loads, the indexes are maintained by data saves; it uses temporary extents and then merges this data to the maintained indexes. On the other hand a conventional path maintains the indexes with regular transactional procedures. Depending on the number of indexes it may be better to set them to an **unusable** state and have them rebuilt after the load has finished.

Loading Large Objects (LOBs)

There are several ways to load multimedia files. This kind of data is provided in a raw format, so the most suitable data type to store this information in is: the **Binary Large Object (BLOB)**. Both the LONG and LONG RAW are not considered in this discussion as it is not good practice to preserve these kinds of columns.

The long data type is considered deprecated for the new features; it has been a constant throughout all the new releases, starting with 8.0. Most of the new features are supported for LOB data types, but not for LONG data types.

A LOB is a data type that stores a Large Object, and it can be of BLOB, **Character Large Object (CLOB)**, **National Character Large Object (NCLOB)** or BFILE specific data type. It is useful to employ large objects to store multimedia files (binary LOBs), large amounts of text such as descriptions, commentaries, or the particular case of XMLType columns. Text can also be specified in national character sets. There are two kinds of LOBs:

- **Internal LOBs**: They are stored inside the database and are protected by the transactional mechanism of the database and the regular backup policies.
- **External LOBs**: They live outside the database and are at the sole responsibility of the user for protection and maintenance. The BFILE keeps only the information of the path to the external file, inside the database.

Loading a LOB can be done from either a primary datafile, which happens to be in line in the same datafile, or from a secondary lob file, which is a more natural way to address multimedia files, and reduces the overhead of handling records to delimit the lob data.

LOB data can be present in predetermined size fields. In the next control file code you can see the amount of data reserved for the LOB. As the LOB is not guaranteed to always have the same size, the lob data can be padded with blank spaces. The way to load this data is by means of either CHAR or RAW data types.

Let's first prepare the CLOB load demonstration table:

```
CREATE TABLE CLOBDEMO (
    NAME         VARCHAR2(16),
    DESCRIPTION CLOB
);
```

A control file that loads CLOB data into the previously create table is then prepared:

```
LOAD DATA
INFILE 'demo.dat' "STR '|'"
APPEND
INTO TABLE CLOBDEMO(
    NAME          POSITION(01:16)     CHAR,
    DESCRIPTION   POSITION(18:256)    CHAR DEFAULTIF DESCRIPTION=BLANKS
)
```

The data comes in a record delimited format with fixed field size.

 Note: we saw the record delimiter parameter before in the stream section.

```
first            This is the first demo record for the lob
Second line of the first record|second        This is the second
demo record for the lob
Second line of the second record|third        This is the third
demo record for the lob
Second line of the third record|
```

Loading multimedia files

This is another case of LOB loading, in this case the BLOB data type is used to store binary data. When loading records from the same data file, there is an overhead involved to find out the record length. Loading from a secondary data file is more suitable for loading LOB data. When loading LOB data this way there is no requirement that the LOB field fits in memory, the load takes place by reading from the LOB file in 64K chunks.

When loading data from a LOB file, there are two ways to specify the LOB file; it can be specified either statically or dynamically. In the first case, the file is specified in the same control file. In the case of a dynamically defined LOB file, the file is specified within the data file and it is read into a FILLER field (from the datafile) which is then used as a parameter in the control file to specify where the LOB file is.

A FILLER field acts as a place holder; it is not read as actual data, its position is just considered in the data file to find other field positions or, in this case, to read its information as source of data for a dynamic 'variable' inside the same control file.

Let's first prepare the table for this demonstration:

```
CREATE TABLE image_table (
      image_id    NUMBER(5),
      file_name   VARCHAR2(30),
      image_data BLOB
);
```

In the example, the load is performed by means of a dynamically specified LOB file name.

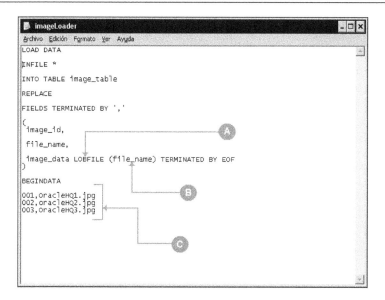

In the control file, the LOBFILE keyword was specified; it declares that the next field to load is a CLOB field (**A**) which takes **file_name** (**B**) as a parameter. The first column of the data file is just a regular numeric column; the second column stands for the LOB file name. This format is suitable for loading image and multimedia files, which by nature are found as standalone files.

Once the files have been loaded it is possible to use any BLOB viewer to retrieve them from the database. By means of a BLOB viewer, a GIF or JPEG can be retrieved and displayed on a regular browser, just like any other image.

Resumable load

When a lengthy load takes place, the last thing a user wants to see is an ORA- error or any other error displayed on the console. This is an emerging issue which usually has to do with a lack of resources to finish the job. There should be enough free space not only for the data to be loaded, but also for the related indexes as well. As SQL*Loader has a default number of rows to commit in a batch load, there is no risk of exhausting the undo regions during a conventional data load.

While performing a lengthy load with a constrained time frame it is better (for peace of mind) to reduce the possibility of any unforeseen circumstances arising that may prevent the successful completion of the task. That is why storage levels must be evaluated to ensure there is enough free space to hold the massive load, otherwise it will have to be restarted by means of a recalculation of the SKIP value to jump to the point of failure, and continue the load from that point on.

Another more practical approach is to use the **RESUMABLE** feature. This feature was first introduced in Oracle 9i Release 1. If an error occurs there are two options. Create a PL/SQL script intelligent enough to diagnose and automatically correct the error, this PL/SQL stored unit would be triggered by the **AFTER SUSPEND** system trigger. If there is no PL/SQL script, a **SUSPEND** feature may be used in favor of the user, allowing the user to take a time-out before the process finally crashes, this time will allow the user to avoid a scenario similar to this one:

```
$ sqlldr sqlldrdemo/oracle direct=y control=abc.ctl
SQL*Loader: Release 10.2.0.1.0 - Production on Mon Aug 11 20:45:17 2008
Copyright (c) 1982, 2005, Oracle.  All rights reserved.
SQL*Loader-2026: the load was aborted because SQL Loader cannot continue.
Load completed - logical record count 2917806.
$
```

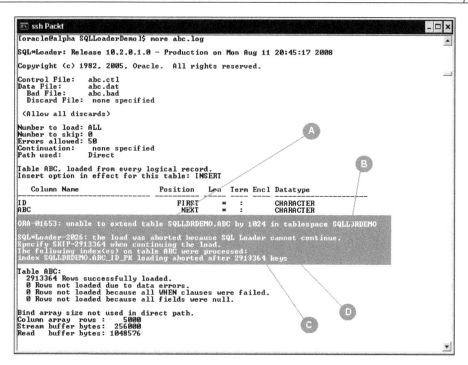

```
ssh Packt                                                              _ □ ×
[oracle@alpha SQLLoaderDemo]$ more abc.log

SQL*Loader: Release 10.2.0.1.0 - Production on Mon Aug 11 20:45:17 2008

Copyright (c) 1982, 2005, Oracle.  All rights reserved.

Control File:   abc.ctl
Data File:      abc.dat
  Bad File:     abc.bad
  Discard File: none specified

 (Allow all discards)

Number to load: ALL
Number to skip: 0
Errors allowed: 50
Continuation:   none specified
Path used:      Direct

Table ABC, loaded from every logical record.
Insert option in effect for this table: INSERT

    Column Name          Position   Len  Term Encl Datatype
---------------------------------------------------------------------------
ID                          FIRST     *   :         CHARACTER
ABC                          NEXT     *   :         CHARACTER
ORA-01653: unable to extend table SQLLDRDEMO.ABC by 1024 in tablespace SQLLDRDEMO

SQL*Loader-2026: the load was aborted because SQL Loader cannot continue.
Specify SKIP=2913364 when continuing the load.
The following index(es) on table ABC were processed:
index SQLLDRDEMO.ABC_ID_PK loading aborted after 2913364 keys

Table ABC:
  2913364 Rows successfully loaded.
  0 Rows not loaded due to data errors.
  0 Rows not loaded because all WHEN clauses were failed.
  0 Rows not loaded because all fields were null.

Bind array size not used in direct path.
Column array  rows :     5000
Stream buffer bytes: 256000
Read   buffer bytes: 1048576
```

In the above slide it can be seen that the load was aborted because SQL*Loader cannot continue. It had reached 2,917,806 rows out of 8,000,000 rows, so it is far from being finished. The log shows an **ORA-01653** error (**A**), which means that the tablespace has reached its maximum capacity and can no longer grow. As it is not possible to keep on loading data, it immediately shows the abort message, and on the SQL*Loader side there is nothing else to do but to suggest the DBA continue the load at a later time once the problem has been solved using the SKIP=2913364 command line clause, specified at (**C**). There it can be seen in the log file that the related index was processed up to the last saved key (**D**).

There is another more efficient and proactive way to deal with these kinds of loads. The resumable feature will take care of the load process, and will diagnose and troubleshoot things according to what the DBA has programmed. It is assumed the DBA is proactive enough to foresee all possible events so that the load runs unattended, or at least the DBA must program a process to send an alert to the operator in charge, so the operator can react accordingly.

In this second example, the operator will launch SQL*Loader, this time with the RESUMABLE feature enabled. In order for the user to use the resumable feature, it must have the RESUMABLE privilege granted.

```
$ sqlplus / as sysdba
SQL> grant RESUMABLE to SQLLDRDEMO;
Grant succeeded.
```

Let the load begin, and this time use the keywords:

- resumable: This keyword enables the RESUMABLE feature; by default its value is FALSE.

- resumable_name: This declares what the name of the resumable identifier will be; displayed at the DBA_RESUMABLE view.

- resumable_timeout: This is the time to wait in case an outstanding issue arises. The operator must detect, diagnose, and correct the problem before this time expires. By default it waits 7,200 seconds.

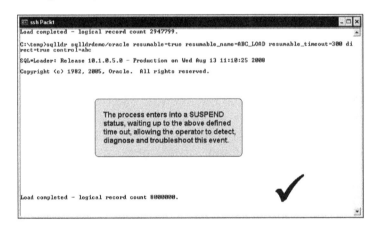

In this example the command line used was:

```
$ sqlldr sqlldrdemo/oracle resumable=true resumable_name=ABC_LOAD
resumable_timeout=300 direct=true control=abc
```

Here, the **resumable** keyword was defined as true, a name is used to identify the resumable event and a 5 minute time out was declared. In this scenario an operator has to identify the problem by querying the DBA_RESUMABLE view; once identified, fix the problem and let the resumable feature exit on its own from the suspend mode to successfully finish the load.

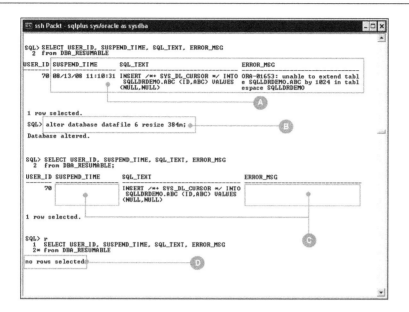

By querying the **DBA_RESUMABLE** view (**A**), it can be seen that a problem with an
INSERT statement arose, this problem produced an ORA-01653 error, the same as the
one reported in the previous log file.

The operator reacts and manually increases the size of the delinquent datafile (**B**),
providing enough space for the process to continue.

Once the problem has been fixed the process continues. As long as there are no
more problems, both the SUSPEND_TIME and ERROR_MSG columns will display null
values (**C**). As soon as the process finishes the entry, the **DBA_RESUMABLE** view is
cleared (**D**).

This approach happens to be more manageable, but it still requires manual
intervention. During a batch load scheduled during a constrained time frame at
(let's say) three o'clock in the morning, it is better to be peacefully resting in bed,
rather than waiting for your mobile to display an alert because the process has
aborted and the load has to be launched again. In this case a special system trigger is
coded, the AFTER SUSPEND trigger.

The resumable feature triggers when an outstanding associated event is about to
abort the process, issuing a SUSPEND event to the database. An AFTER SUSPEND trigger
fires and it executes the routine the DBA has programmed.

In this scenario an `AFTER SUSPEND` trigger is created:

```
$ sqlplus / as sysdba
create trigger SQLLDR_RESUMABLE_HANDLER
after suspend on database
begin
  execute immediate 'alter database datafile 6 resize 384m';
end;
/
```

This trigger will fire and will increase the size of the datafile where the load takes place. The PL/SQL code is only for demonstration purposes, the handler procedure should be intelligent so it is able to diagnose what the source of the problem is, and react accordingly.

Once the trigger has been programmed, the load will take place once again, and this time it requires no operator intervention. As soon as the process enters into the `SUSPEND` mode, the database will fire the system event trigger `AFTER SUSPEND`, and automatically increase the size of the faulty tablespace. Once the root problem has been automatically fixed the load will simply continue just as if nothing had happened.

As the resumable feature is a database feature, it is useful not only for SQL*Loader, but also for any other database batch related process that requires self-healing routines to keep the process up and running. There is an API named `DBMS_RESUMABLE` that can be used inside PL/SQL code.

Parallel load

A parallel load can be used to perform the data load more efficiently. It is a suitable data load strategy for partitioned tables. When performing the load the data file is partitioned so that each single session grabs its piece of data and all the sessions can execute the job simultaneously on the same table.

In order for the user to enable parallel loading, once the data has been split into several files, the clause `PARALLEL=TRUE` must be specified for each session. If the user is working on a Unix like operating system, then the workload can be left running as a background process.

```
sqlldr sqlldrdemo/oracle control=pload01.ctl DIRECT=TRUE PARALLEL=TRUE
&
sqlldr sqlldrdemo/oracle control=pload02.ctl DIRECT=TRUE PARALLEL=TRUE
&
sqlldr sqlldrdemo/oracle control=pload03.ctl DIRECT=TRUE PARALLEL=TRUE
&
sqlldr sqlldrdemo/oracle control=pload04.ctl DIRECT=TRUE PARALLEL=TRUE
&
```

In this example, four processes execute the data load in parallel. The degree of parallelism must be tuned, so that the process doesn't end up serializing due to data file access problems.

When performing a parallel load some issues should be considered:

- Indexes are not maintained and will be marked as UNUSABLE, so the user must schedule an index maintenance task afterwards.

- The user should look for the constraint status after the load. Both constraints and triggers must be manually enabled after the load.

General performance booster tips

In order to take advantage of maintenance windows to perform the data load, here is some advice for improving load performance and better using the time frame.

- When performing a load, do not use logical records, map in one-to-one physical records to logical records.

- Use LMT with ASSM, this combination is available from Oracle 9i Rel. 2 onwards.

- Use a fixed size field data file format over the variable sized with delimiter characters.

- Try to avoid character set conversions, try to use the same character set on the client side and at the server side.

- If possible use direct load; this is the fastest way to load data.

- When loading data try to have the data preordered at the data file by the most important index, this way when the index is created the clause NOSORT can be used. The index will be created faster.

- If possible, use parallel loads, and parallel index maintenance.

- When loading LOBS, use **Secondary Data Files (SDF)** instead of embedding them in the same datafile.

- When performing direct path loads, it is advisable to mark indexes as unusable. This way the overhead will be avoided in the temporary tablespace due to the space consumption for the index maintenance task that takes place when data is loaded. Once data load is over, a regular index rebuild operation can be scheduled.

Summary

Loading ASCII data from an external source is a frequent task in data warehouse environments when migrating data from other non-compatible databases. The kind of information and the way it may be formatted are important to consider it is the time to define the control file to execute the load.

When the load takes place it is sensible to take advantage of the time frame, avoiding unexpected issues that may prevent the process from finishing on time, particularly those loads that must be executed on a just-in-time basis. Proactively defining a resumable load will help the user to avoid problems and automatically correct unforeseen issues.

A situation may arise where you would need to load different character sets on the same database, and the user should be aware of the implications and best practices in this situation.

Several kinds of loads can be performed, from just plain and simple fixed record rows to complex formats. Loading a variety of data types, from plain text files to binaries, and large objects is possible. There are several resources the user may consider to use time (efficiently) during maintenance windows.

There are many more data load examples, but analyzing them here goes beyond the scope of this book, you may want to refer to the documentation found at the RDBMS demonstration section in your Oracle Home.

When data loads require some transformation to meet particular requirements it becomes necessary to load data into a stage area where data is taken from to execute data transformation routines. This stage area can be skipped and optimized with the use of external tables; this topic, and others related to external tables, will be covered on the next chapter.

3
External Tables

When working in data warehouse environments, the **Extraction – Transformation – Loading** (ETL) cycle frequently requires the user to load information from external sources in plain file format, or perform data transfers among Oracle database in a proprietary format. This requires the user to create control files to perform the load. As the format of the source data regularly doesn't fit the one required by the Data Warehouse, a common practice is to create stage tables that load data into the database and create several queries that perform the transformation from this point on, to take the data to its final destination.

A better approach, would be to perform this transformation 'on the fly' at load time. That is what External Tables are for. They are basically external files, managed either by means of the SQL*Loader or the data pump driver, which from the database perspective can be seen as if they were regular read only tables.

This format allows the user to think about the data source as if the data was already loaded into its stage table. This lets the user concentrate on the queries to perform the transformation, thus saving precious time during the load phase.

External Tables can serve not only as improvements to the ETL process, but also as a means to manage database environments, and a means of reducing the complexity level of data management from the user's point of view.

The External Table basics

An External Table is basically a file that resides on the server side, as a regular flat file or as a data pump formatted file. The External Table is not a table itself; it is an external file with an Oracle format and its physical location. This feature first appeared back in Oracle 9i Release 1 and it was intended as a way of enhancing the ETL process by reading an external flat file as if it was a regular Oracle table. On its initial release it was only possible to create read-only External Tables, but, starting with 10g — it is possible to unload data to External Tables too.

In previous 10g Releases there was only the SQL*Loader driver could be used to read the External Table, but from 10g onwards it is now possible to load the table by means of the data pump driver. The kind of driver that will be used to read the External Table is defined at creation time. In the case of ORACLE_LOADER it is the same driver used by SQL*Loader. The flat files are loaded in the same way that a flat file is loaded to the database by means of the SQL*Loader utility, and the creation script can be created based on a SQL*Loader control file. In fact, most of the keywords that are valid for data loading are also valid to read an external flat file table.

The main differences between SQL*Loader and External Tables are:

- When there are several input datafiles SQL*Loader will generate a bad file and a discard file for each datafile.

- The CONTINUEIF and CONCATENATE keywords are not supported by External Tables.

- The GRAPHIC, GRAPHIC EXTERNAL, and VARGRAPHIC are not supported for External Tables.

- LONG, nested tables, VARRAY, REF, primary key REF, and SID are not supported.

- For fields in External Tables the character set, decimal separator, date mask and other locale settings are determined by the database **NLS** settings.

- The use of the backslash character is allowed for SQL*Loader, but for External Tables this would raise an error. External Tables must use quotation marks instead.
  For example:

  SQL*Loader

  FIELDS TERMINATED BY ' , ' OPTIONALLY ENCLOSED BY " \ "

  External Tables

  TERMINATED BY ' , ' ENCLOSED BY " ' "

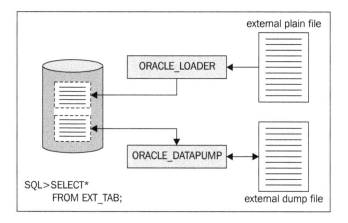

A second driver is available, the ORACLE_DATAPUMP access driver, which uses the Data Pump technology to read the table and unload data to an External Table. This driver allows the user to perform a logical backup that can later be read back to the database without actually loading the data. The ORACLE_DATAPUMP access driver utilizes a proprietary binary format for the external file, so it is not possible to view it as a flat file.

Let's setup the environment

Let's create the demonstration user, and prepare its environment to create an **External Table**. The example that will be developed first refers to the External Table using the ORACLE_LOADER driver.

```
create user EXTTABDEMO
    identified by ORACLE
    default tablespace USERS;

alter user exttabdemo
    quota unlimited on users;

grant     CREATE SESSION,
          CREATE TABLE,
          CREATE PROCEDURE,
          CREATE MATERIALIZED VIEW,
          ALTER SESSION,
          CREATE VIEW,
          CREATE ANY DIRECTORY
to EXTTABDEMO;
```

A simple formatted spool from this query will generate the required external table demonstration data. The original source table is the demonstration `HR.EMPLOYEES` table.

```
select
    EMPLOYEE_ID ||','||
    DEPARTMENT_ID ||','||
    FIRST_NAME ||','||
    LAST_NAME ||','||
    PHONE_NUMBER ||','||
    HIRE_DATE ||','||
    JOB_ID ||','||
    SALARY ||','||
    COMMISSION_PCT ||','||
    MANAGER_ID ||','||
    EMAIL
from        HR.EMPLOYEES
order by EMPLOYEE_ID
```

The above query will produce the following sample data:

The External Table directory is defined inside the database by means of a `DIRECTORY` object. This object is not validated at creation time, so the user must make sure the physical directory exists and the oracle OS user has read/write privileges on it.

```
$ mkdir $HOME/external_table_dest
SQL> CREATE DIRECTORY EXTTABDIR AS '/home/oracle/external_table_dest';
```

The above example was developed in a Linux environment, on Windows platforms the paths will need to be changed to correctly reflect how Oracle has been set up.

Now, the first External Table can be created.

A basic External Table

Here is the source code of the External Table creation.

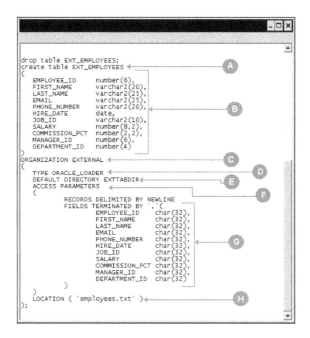

The create table command syntax is just like any other regular table creation (**A**), (**B**), up to the point where the **ORGANIZATION EXTERNAL** (**C**) keyword appears, this is the point where the actual External Table definition starts. In this case the External Table is accessed by the **ORACLE_LOADER** driver (**D**). Next, the external flat file is defined, and here it is declared the Oracle **DIRECTORY** (**E**) where the flat file resides. The **ACCESS PARAMETERS** (**F**) section specifies how to access the flat file and it declares whether the file is a fixed or variable size record, and which other SQL*Loader loading options are declared. The **LOCATION** (**H**) keyword defines the name of the external data file. It must be pointed out that as this is an External Table managed by the **SQL_LOADER** driver the **ACCESS_PARAMETERS** section must be defined, in the case of External Tables based on the **DATAPUMP_DRIVER** this section is not required.

The columns are defined only by name (**G**), not by type. This is permitted from the SQL*Loader perspective, and allows for dynamic column definition. This column schema definition is more flexible, but it has a drawback—data formats such as those in DATE columns must match the database date format, otherwise the row will be rejected. There are ways to define the date format working around this requirement. Assuming the date column changes from its original default format mask "DD-MON-RR" to "DD-MM-RR", then the column definition must change from a simple CHAR column to a DATE with format mask column definition.

Original format:

```
"HIRE_DATE" CHAR(255)
```

Changed format:

```
"HIRE_DATE" DATE "DD-MM-RR"
```

When working with an External Table, the access parameter is not validated at creation time, so if there are malformed rows, or if there are improperly defined access parameters, an error is shown, similar to the one below.

```
ERROR at line 1:
ORA-29913: error in executing ODCIEXTTABLEFETCH callout
ORA-30653: reject limit reached
ORA-06512: at "SYS.ORACLE_LOADER", line 52
```

Once the data is created and all required OS privileges have been properly validated, the data can be seen from inside the database, just as if it were a regular Oracle table.

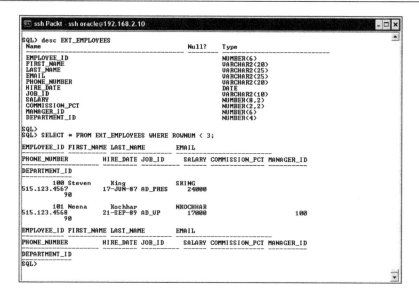

This table is read only, so if the user attempts to perform any DML operation against it, it will result in this error:

```
SQL> delete ext_employees;
delete ext_employees
       *
ERROR at line 1:
ORA-30657: operation not supported on external organized table
```

As the error message clearly states, this kind of table is only useful for read only operations.

This kind of table doesn't support most of the operations available for regular tables, such as index creation, and statistics gathering, and these types of operations will cause an ORA-30657 error too. The only access method available for External Tables is Full Table Scan, so there is no way to perform a selective data retrieval operation.

The External Tables cannot be recovered, they are just metadata definitions stored in the dictionary tables. The actual data resides in external files, and there is no way to protect them with the regular backup database routines, so it is the user's sole responsibility to provide proper backup and data management procedures. At the database level the only kind of protection the External Table receives is at the metadata level, as it is an object stored as a definition at the database dictionary level. As the data resides in the external data file, if by any means it were to be corrupted, altered, or somehow modified, there would be no way to get back the original data. If the external data file is lost, then this may go unnoticed, until the next SELECT operation takes place.

This metadata for an External Table is recorded at the {USER | ALL | DBA}_TABLES view, and as this table doesn't actually require physical database storage, all storage related columns appear as null, as well as the columns that relate to the statistical information. This table is described with the {USER | ALL | DBA}_EXTERNAL_TABLES view, where information such as the kind of driver access, the reject_limit, and the access_parameters, amongst others, are described.

```
SQL> DESC USER_EXTERNAL_TABLES
  Name                            Null?       Type
  ------------------------------  --------    --------------
  TABLE_NAME                      NOT NULL    VARCHAR2(30)
  TYPE_OWNER                                  CHAR(3)
  TYPE_NAME                       NOT NULL    VARCHAR2(30)
  DEFAULT_DIRECTORY_OWNER                     CHAR(3)
  DEFAULT_DIRECTORY_NAME          NOT NULL    VARCHAR2(30)
  REJECT_LIMIT                                VARCHAR2(40)
  ACCESS_TYPE                                 VARCHAR2(7)
  ACCESS_PARAMETERS                           VARCHAR2(4000)
  PROPERTY                                    VARCHAR2(10)
```

This is the first basic External Table, and as previously shown, its creation is pretty simple. It allows external data to be easily accessed from inside the database, allowing the user to see the external data just as if it was already loaded inside a regular stage table.

Creating External Table metadata, the easy way

To further illustrate the tight relationship between SQL*Loader and External Tables, the SQL*Loader tool may be used to generate a script that creates an External Table according to a pre-existing control file.

SQL*Loader has a command line option named EXTERNAL_TABLE, this can hold one of three different parameters {NOT_USED | GENERATE_ONLY | EXECUTE}. If nothing is set, it defaults to the NOT_USED option.

This keyword is used to generate the script to create an External Table, and the options mean:

- NOT_USED: This is the default option, and it means that no External Tables are to be used in this load.

- GENERATE_ONLY: If this option is specified, then SQL*Loader will only read the definitions from the control file and generate the required commands, so the user can record them for later execution, or tailor them to fit his/her particular needs.

- EXECUTE: This not only generates the External Table scripts, but also executes them. If the user requires a sequence, then the EXECUTE option will not only create the table, but it will also create the required sequence, deleting it once the data load is finished. This option performs the data load process against the specified target regular by means of an External Table, it creates both the directory and the External Table, and inserts the data using a SELECT AS INSERT with the APPEND hint.

Let's use the GENERATE_ONLY option to generate the External Table creation scripts:

```
$ sqlldr exttabdemo/oracle employees external_table=GENERATE_ONLY
```

By default the log file is located in a file whose extension is .log and its name equals that of the control file. By opening it we see, among the whole log processing information, this set of DDL commands:

```
CREATE TABLE "SYS_SQLLDR_X_EXT_EMPLOYEES"
(
  "EMPLOYEE_ID" NUMBER(6),
  "FIRST_NAME" VARCHAR2(20),
  "LAST_NAME" VARCHAR2(25),
  "EMAIL" VARCHAR2(25),
  "PHONE_NUMBER" VARCHAR2(20),
  "HIRE_DATE" DATE,
  "JOB_ID" VARCHAR2(10),
  "SALARY" NUMBER(8,2),
  "COMMISSION_PCT" NUMBER(2,2),
  "MANAGER_ID" NUMBER(6),
  "DEPARTMENT_ID" NUMBER(4)
)
ORGANIZATION external
(
  TYPE oracle_loader
  DEFAULT DIRECTORY EXTTABDIR
  ACCESS PARAMETERS
  (
    RECORDS DELIMITED BY NEWLINE CHARACTERSET US7ASCII
    BADFILE 'EXTTABDIR':'employees.bad'
    LOGFILE 'employees.log_xt'
    READSIZE 1048576
    FIELDS TERMINATED BY "," OPTIONALLY ENCLOSED BY '"' LDRTRIM
```

```
REJECT ROWS WITH ALL NULL FIELDS
(
  "EMPLOYEE_ID" CHAR(255)
    TERMINATED BY "," OPTIONALLY ENCLOSED BY '"',
  "FIRST_NAME" CHAR(255)
    TERMINATED BY "," OPTIONALLY ENCLOSED BY '"',
  "LAST_NAME" CHAR(255)
    TERMINATED BY "," OPTIONALLY ENCLOSED BY '"',
  "EMAIL" CHAR(255)
    TERMINATED BY "," OPTIONALLY ENCLOSED BY '"',
  "PHONE_NUMBER" CHAR(255)
    TERMINATED BY "," OPTIONALLY ENCLOSED BY '"',
  "HIRE_DATE" CHAR(255)
    TERMINATED BY "," OPTIONALLY ENCLOSED BY '"',
  "JOB_ID" CHAR(255)
    TERMINATED BY "," OPTIONALLY ENCLOSED BY '"',
  "SALARY" CHAR(255)
    TERMINATED BY "," OPTIONALLY ENCLOSED BY '"',
  "COMMISSION_PCT" CHAR(255)
    TERMINATED BY "," OPTIONALLY ENCLOSED BY '"',
  "MANAGER_ID" CHAR(255)
    TERMINATED BY "," OPTIONALLY ENCLOSED BY '"',
  "DEPARTMENT_ID" CHAR(255)
    TERMINATED BY "," OPTIONALLY ENCLOSED BY '"'
)
)
location
(
  'employees.txt'
)
)
```

The more complete version is shown, some differences with the basic script are:

- All the column definitions are set to CHAR(255) with the delimiter character defined for each column
- If the current working directory is already registered as a regular DIRECTORY at the database level, SQL*Loader utilizes it, otherwise, it creates a new directory definition
- The script specifies where the bad files and log file are located
- It specifies that an all-null column record is rejected

In the case of the EXECUTE keyword, the log file shows that not only are the scripts used to create the External Table, but also to execute the INSERT statement with the /*+ append */ hint. The load is performed in direct path mode.

All External Tables, when accessed, generate a log file. In the case of the ORACLE_LOADER driver, this file is similar to the file generated by SQL*Loader. It has a different format in the case of ORACLE_DATAPUMP driver. The log file is generated in the same location where the external file resides, and its format is as follows:

```
<EXTERNAL_TABLE_NAME>_<OraclePID>.log
```

When an ORACLE_LOADER managed External Table has errors, it dumps the 'bad' rows to the *.bad file, just the same as if this was loaded by SQL*Loader.

The ORACLE_DATAPUMP External Table generates a simpler log file, it only contains the time stamp when the External Table was accessed, and it creates a log file for each oracle process accessing the External Table.

Unloading data to External Tables

The driver used to unload data to an External Table is the ORACLE_DATAPUMP access driver. It dumps the contents of a table in a binary proprietary format file. This way you can exchange data with other 10g and higher databases in a preformatted way to meet the other database's requirements. Unloading data to an External Table doesn't make it updateable, the tables are still limited to being read only.

Let's unload the EMPLOYEES table to an External Table:

```
create table dp_employees
    organization external(
          type oracle_datapump
          default directory EXTTABDIR
          location ('dp_employees.dmp')
    )
as
    select * from employees;
```

This creates a table named DP_EMPLOYEES, located at the specified EXTTABDIR directory and with a defined OS file name.

In the next example, at a different database a new DP_EMPLOYEES table is created, this table uses the already unloaded data by the first database. This DP_EMPLOYEES External Table is created on the 11g database side.

```
create table dp_employees(
EMPLOYEE_ID          NUMBER(6),
FIRST_NAME VARCHAR2(20),
LAST_NAME   VARCHAR2(25),
EMAIL                VARCHAR2(25),
PHONE_NUMBER         VARCHAR2(20),
HIRE_DATE   DATE,
JOB_ID               VARCHAR2(10),
SALARY               NUMBER(8,2),
COMMISSION_PCT       NUMBER(2,2),
MANAGER_ID NUMBER(6),
DEPARTMENT_ID        NUMBER(4)
)
organization external
(
   type oracle_datapump
   default directory EXTTABDIR
   location ('dp_employees.dmp')
);
```

This table can already read in the unloaded data from the first database. The second database is a regular 11g database. So this shows the inter-version upward compatibility between a 10g and an 11g database.

```
SQL> select count(*) from dp_employees;

  COUNT(*)
----------
      107
```

Inter-version compatibility

In, the previous example a 10g data pump generated an External Table that was transparently read by the 11g release.

Let's create an 11g data pump External Table named DP_DEPARTMENTS:

```
create table dp_departments
   organization external(
           type oracle_datapump
           default directory EXTTABDIR
```

```
            access parameters
            (
                    version '10.2.0'
            )
            location ('dp_departments.dmp')
    )
as
    select * from departments
Table created.
SQL> select count(*) from dp_departments;

  COUNT(*)
----------
        27
```

In the previous example it is important to point out that the VERSION keyword defines the compatibility format.

```
access parameters
(
    version '10.2.0'
)
```

If this clause is not specified then an incompatibility error will be displayed.

```
SQL> select count(*) from dp_departments;
select count(*) from dp_departments
*
ERROR at line 1:
ORA-29913: error in executing ODCIEXTTABLEOPEN callout
ORA-39142: incompatible version number 2.1 in dump file
"/home/oracle/external_table_dest/dp_departments.dmp"
ORA-06512: at "SYS.ORACLE_DATAPUMP", line 19
```

Now let's use the 10g version to read from it.

```
SQL> select count(*) from dp_departments;

  COUNT(*)
----------
        27
```

The VERSION clause is interpreted the same way as the VERSION clause for the data pump export, it has three different values:

- **COMPATIBLE**: This states that the version of the metadata corresponds to the database compatibility level.

- **LATEST**: This corresponds to the database version.

- **VERSION NUMBER**: This refers to a specific oracle version that the file is compatible with. This value cannot be lower than 9.2.0.

Data transformation with External Tables

One of the main uses of the External Tables is their support of the ETL process, allowing the user to perform a data load that is transformed to the target format without an intermediate stage table.

Let's read an External Table whose contents are:

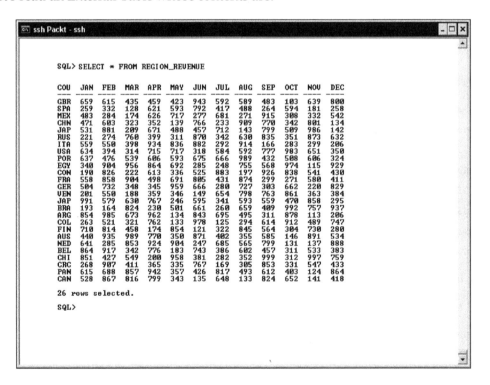

This data can be loaded in a single command to multiple tables. Let's create several tables with the same structure:

```
SQL> desc amount_jan
 Name                   Null?    Type
 ----------------  --------  ------------
 REGION                          VARCHAR2(16)
 AMOUNT                          NUMBER(3)
```

Now we can issue a command to send the data from the External Table to the different tables.

```
INSERT ALL
    INTO AMOUNT_JAN (REGION, AMOUNT) VALUES(COUNTRY, JAN)
    INTO AMOUNT_FEB (REGION, AMOUNT) VALUES(COUNTRY, FEB)
    INTO AMOUNT_MAR (REGION, AMOUNT) VALUES(COUNTRY, JAN)
    INTO AMOUNT_APR (REGION, AMOUNT) VALUES(COUNTRY, JAN)
    INTO AMOUNT_MAY (REGION, AMOUNT) VALUES(COUNTRY, JAN)
    INTO AMOUNT_JUN (REGION, AMOUNT) VALUES(COUNTRY, JAN)
    INTO AMOUNT_JUL (REGION, AMOUNT) VALUES(COUNTRY, JAN)
    INTO AMOUNT_AUG (REGION, AMOUNT) VALUES(COUNTRY, JAN)
    INTO AMOUNT_SEP (REGION, AMOUNT) VALUES(COUNTRY, JAN)
    INTO AMOUNT_OCT (REGION, AMOUNT) VALUES(COUNTRY, JAN)
    INTO AMOUNT_NOV (REGION, AMOUNT) VALUES(COUNTRY, JAN)
    INTO AMOUNT_DEC (REGION, AMOUNT) VALUES(COUNTRY, JAN)
SELECT      COUNTRY,
    JAN,
    FEB,
    MAR,
    APR,
    MAY,
    JUN,
    JUL,
    AUG,
    SEP,
    OCT,
    NOV,
    DEC
FROM        REGION_REVENUE;
```

In this example, we will perform a conditional insert to different tables depending on the value of the amount column. We will first create three tables, one for low, another for average, and a third for high amounts:

```
SQL> create table low_amount(
  2  region       varchar2(16),
  3  month        number(2),
  4  amount       number(3));
Table created.
SQL> create table high_amount as select * from low_amount;
Table created.
```

Now we can read the External Table and have the data inserted conditionally to one of three mutually exclusive targets.

```
INSERT ALL
        WHEN ( JAN <= 500 ) THEN
                INTO LOW_AMOUNT( REGION, MONTH, AMOUNT)
                VALUES ( COUNTRY, '01', JAN )
        WHEN ( FEB <= 500 ) THEN
                INTO LOW_AMOUNT( REGION, MONTH, AMOUNT)
                VALUES ( COUNTRY, '02', FEB )
        WHEN ( MAR <= 500 ) THEN
                INTO LOW_AMOUNT( REGION, MONTH, AMOUNT)
                VALUES ( COUNTRY, '03', MAR )
        WHEN ( APR <= 500 ) THEN
                INTO LOW_AMOUNT( REGION, MONTH, AMOUNT)
                VALUES ( COUNTRY, '04', APR )
        WHEN ( MAY <= 500 ) THEN
                INTO LOW_AMOUNT( REGION, MONTH, AMOUNT)
                VALUES ( COUNTRY, '05', MAY )
        WHEN ( JUN <= 500 ) THEN
                INTO LOW_AMOUNT( REGION, MONTH, AMOUNT)
                VALUES ( COUNTRY, '06', JUN )
        WHEN ( JUL <= 500 ) THEN
                INTO LOW_AMOUNT( REGION, MONTH, AMOUNT)
                VALUES ( COUNTRY, '07', JUL )
        WHEN ( AUG <= 500 ) THEN
                INTO LOW_AMOUNT( REGION, MONTH, AMOUNT)
                VALUES ( COUNTRY, '08', AUG )
        WHEN ( SEP <= 500 ) THEN
                INTO LOW_AMOUNT( REGION, MONTH, AMOUNT)
                VALUES ( COUNTRY, '09', SEP )
        WHEN ( OCT <= 500 ) THEN
                INTO LOW_AMOUNT( REGION, MONTH, AMOUNT)
                VALUES ( COUNTRY, '10', OCT )
        WHEN ( NOV <= 500 ) THEN
                INTO LOW_AMOUNT( REGION, MONTH, AMOUNT)
                VALUES ( COUNTRY, '11', NOV )
        WHEN ( DEC <= 500 ) THEN
                INTO LOW_AMOUNT( REGION, MONTH, AMOUNT)
                VALUES ( COUNTRY, '12', DEC )
        WHEN ( JAN > 500 ) THEN
                INTO HIGH_AMOUNT( REGION, MONTH, AMOUNT)
                VALUES ( COUNTRY, '01', JAN )
        WHEN ( FEB > 500 ) THEN
                INTO HIGH_AMOUNT( REGION, MONTH, AMOUNT)
                VALUES ( COUNTRY, '02', FEB )
        WHEN ( MAR > 500 ) THEN
```

```
                        INTO HIGH_AMOUNT( REGION, MONTH, AMOUNT)
                        VALUES ( COUNTRY, '03', MAR )
              WHEN ( APR > 500 ) THEN
                        INTO HIGH_AMOUNT( REGION, MONTH, AMOUNT)
                        VALUES ( COUNTRY, '04', APR )
              WHEN ( MAY > 500 ) THEN
                        INTO HIGH_AMOUNT( REGION, MONTH, AMOUNT)
                        VALUES ( COUNTRY, '05', MAY )
              WHEN ( JUN > 500 ) THEN
                        INTO HIGH_AMOUNT( REGION, MONTH, AMOUNT)
                        VALUES ( COUNTRY, '06', JUN )
              WHEN ( JUL > 500 ) THEN
                        INTO HIGH_AMOUNT( REGION, MONTH, AMOUNT)
                        VALUES ( COUNTRY, '07', JUL )
              WHEN ( AUG > 500 ) THEN
                        INTO HIGH_AMOUNT( REGION, MONTH, AMOUNT)
                        VALUES ( COUNTRY, '08', AUG )
              WHEN ( SEP > 500 ) THEN
                        INTO HIGH_AMOUNT( REGION, MONTH, AMOUNT)
                        VALUES ( COUNTRY, '09', SEP )
              WHEN ( OCT > 500 ) THEN
                        INTO HIGH_AMOUNT( REGION, MONTH, AMOUNT)
                        VALUES ( COUNTRY, '10', OCT )
              WHEN ( NOV > 500 ) THEN
                        INTO HIGH_AMOUNT( REGION, MONTH, AMOUNT)
                        VALUES ( COUNTRY, '11', NOV )
              WHEN ( DEC > 500 ) THEN
                        INTO HIGH_AMOUNT( REGION, MONTH, AMOUNT)
                        VALUES ( COUNTRY, '12', DEC )
    SELECT  COUNTRY,
            JAN,
            FEB,
            MAR,
            APR,
            MAY,
            JUN,
            JUL,
            AUG,
            SEP,
            OCT,
            NOV,
            DEC
    FROM    REGION_REVENUE;
```

Extending the alert.log analysis with External Tables

Reading the `alert.log` from the database is a useful feature which can help you to find any outstanding error messages reported in this file.

```
create table ALERT_LOG(
    text_line        varchar2(512)
)
 organization external (
    type ORACLE_LOADER
    default directory BACKGROUND_DUMP_DEST
    access parameters(
            records delimited by newline
            nobadfile
            nodiscardfile
            nologfile
    )
    location( 'alert_beta.log')
);
```

Once the External Table has been created, the `alert.log` file can be queried just like any other regular table.

```
SQL> select text_line from alert_log
  2  where text_line like 'ORA-%';

TEXT_LINE
------------------------------------------------------------------------
-------
ORA-1109 signalled during: ALTER DATABASE CLOSE NORMAL...
ORA-00313: open failed for members of log group 1 of thread 1
ORA-00312: online log 1 thread 1: '/u01/oracle/oradata/beta/redo01.log'
ORA-27037: unable to obtain file status
ORA-00313: open failed for members of log group 2 of thread 1
ORA-00312: online log 2 thread 1: '/u01/oracle/oradata/beta/redo02.log'
ORA-27037: unable to obtain file status
ORA-00313: open failed for members of log group 3 of thread 1
ORA-00312: online log 3 thread 1: '/u01/oracle/oradata/beta/redo03.log'
ORA-27037: unable to obtain file status
```

Querying the `alert.log` file up to this phase is useful just to see the contents of the file and look for basic `ORA-%` strings. This could also be achieved by using the `alert.log` link in the **Enterprise Manager** (**EM**).

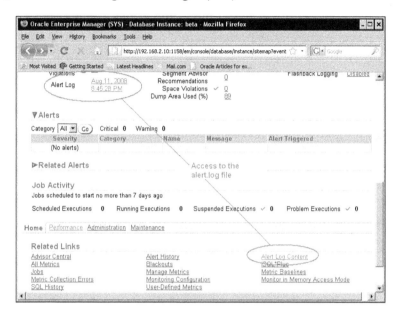

The `alert.log` file can be queried by means of the EM, but as this can only be viewed from the EM in an interactive mode, you can only rely on the preset alerts.

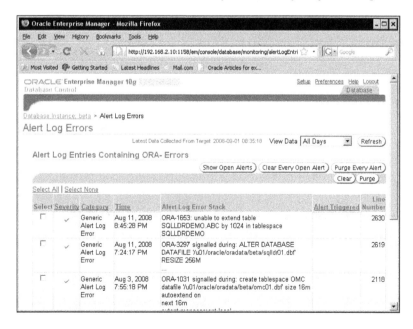

If further automatic work needs to be done, then it is useful to do some more work with the alert analysis tool. A temporary table can be used to store the contents of the ALERT_LOG table, along with an extra TIMESTAMP column, so it can be queried in detail in an EM-like manner.

```
create global temporary table TMP_ALERT_LOG (
    LINE_NO           NUMBER(6),
    TIMESTAMP         DATE,
    TEXT_LINE         VARCHAR2(512)
)
on commit preserve rows;
```

A bit of PLSQL programming is necessary so the ALERT_LOG file can be modified and inserted into the TMP_ALERT_LOG, (enabling further queries can be done).

```
declare
cursor
  alertLogCur is
  select ROWNUM,  TEXT_LINE
  from   ALERT_LOG;
currentDate       date;
altertLogRec      ALERT_LOG.TEXT_LINE%TYPE;
testDay           varchar2(10);
begin
currentDate := sysdate;
for alertLogInst in alertLogCur loop
  -- fetch row and determine if this is a date row
  testDay :=  substr(alertLogInst.text_line, 1, 3);
  if testDay = 'Sun' or
    testDay = 'Mon' or
    testDay = 'Tue' or
    testDay = 'Wed' or
    testDay = 'Thu' or
    testDay = 'Fri' or
    testDay = 'Sat'
  then
    -- if this is a date row, it sets the current logical record date
    currentDate := to_date( alertlogInst.text_line, 'Dy Mon DD HH24:
    MI:SS YYYY');
  end  if;
  insert into TMP_ALERT_LOG
  values(
    alertLogInst.rownum,
    currentDate,
    alertLogInst.text_line
  );
end loop;
end;
/
```

As the contents of the alert.log end up in a temporary table, more than one DBA can query it at the same time, or restrict the DBA's accessibilities. There is no need to manage the purge and maintenance of the table after the session has ended, it can be indexed and there is little overhead by means of this procedure. More over, as this is a temporary object, minimum redo log information is generated.

Once the external ALERT_LOG and the temporary ALERT_LOG tables have been created, it is possible to perform, not only filters by date (provided by Enterprise Manager) but also any query against the alert.log file.

```
SELECT TIMESTAMP, TEXT_LINE
FROM TMP_ALERT_LOG
WHERE TIMESTAMP IN (
    SELECT TIMESTAMP
    FROM TMP_ALERT_LOG
    WHERE TEXT_LINE LIKE 'ORA-%'
)
AND TIMESTAMP BETWEEN SYSDATE-30 AND SYSDATE
ORDER BY LINE_NO;
```

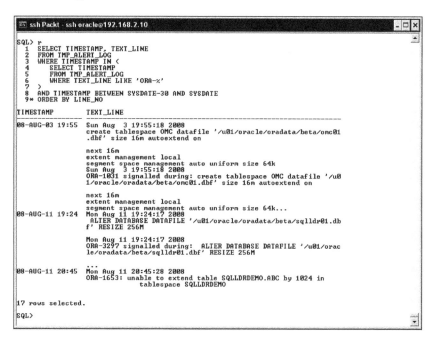

Further treatment can be done on this concept to look for specific error messages, analyze specific time frames and perform drill down analysis.

This procedure can be extended to read the trace files or any other text file from the database.

Reading the listener.log from the database

One particular extension of the above procedure is to read the `listener.log` file. This file has a specific star-delimited field file format which can be advantageous, and eases the read by means of the Loader driver.

The file format is as follows:

```
21-JUL-2008 00:39:50 * (CONNECT_DATA=(SID=beta)(CID=(PROGRAM=perl)(HOS
T=alpha.us.oracle.com)(USER=oracle))) * (ADDRESS=(PROTOCOL=tcp)(HOST=1
92.168.2.10)(PORT=8392)) * establish * beta * 0
21-JUL-2008 00:39:56 * (CONNECT_DATA=(SID=beta)(CID=(PROGRAM=perl)(HOS
T=alpha.us.oracle.com)(USER=oracle))) * (ADDRESS=(PROTOCOL=tcp)(HOST=1
92.168.2.10)(PORT=8398)) * establish * beta * 0
21-JUL-2008 00:40:16 * service_update * beta * 0
21-JUL-2008 00:41:19 * service_update * beta * 0
21-JUL-2008 00:44:43 * ping * 0
```

The file has a format that can be deduced from the above data sample:

```
TIMESTAMP * CONNECT DATA [* PROTOCOL INFO] * EVENT [* SID] * RETURN
CODE
```

As you can see this format, even though it is structured, it may have a different number of fields, so at loading time this issue must be considered.

In order for us to map this table to the database, we should consider the variable number of fields to have the External Table created. We'll create a temporary table so that this doesn't create an additional transactional overhead.

Now, let's create an External Table based on this format that points to:
$ORACLE_HOME/network/log

```
create directory NETWORK_LOG_DIR
as '$ORACLE_HOME/network/log';
```

Now, let's create the External Table:

```
create table LISTENER_LOG (
   TIMESTAMP          date,
   CONNECT_DATA       varchar2(2048),
   PROTOCOL_INFO      varchar2(64),
   EVENT              varchar2(64),
   SID                varchar2(64),
   RETURN_CODE        number(5)
)
organization external (
   type   ORACLE_LOADER
   default directory NETWORK_LOG_DIR
```

```
access parameters (
  records delimited by NEWLINE
  nobadfile
  nodiscardfile
  nologfile
  fields terminated by "*" LDRTRIM
  reject rows with all null fields
  (
     "TIMESTAMP" char date_format DATE mask "DD-MON-YYYY HH24:MI:SS
",
     "CONNECT_DATA",
     "PROTOCOL_INFO",
     "EVENT",
     "SID",
     "RETURN_CODE"
  )
)
location ('listener.log')
)
reject limit unlimited;
```

The structure of interest is specified above, so there will be several rows rejected. Seeing as this file is not fully structured, you will find some non formatted information; the bad file and the log file are not meaningful in this context.

Another application of the LISTENER_LOG External Table is usage trend analysis. This query can be issued to detect usage peak hours.

```
SQL> select to_char(round(TIMESTAMP, 'HH'), 'HH24:MI') HOUR,
  2        lpad('#', count(*), '#') CX
  3  from     listener_log
  4  group by round(TIMESTAMP, 'HH')
  5  order by 1;
HOUR   CX
-----  -----------------------------------------------------
14:00  ###
15:00  #########################
16:00  ######################
17:00  ####################
18:00  ####################
19:00  ##############
```

Reading the listener.log file this way allows the DBA not only to keep track of the listener behavior, but also it allows a security administrator to easily spot hacking attempts.

Let's find out who is trying to access the database with `sqlplus.exe`.

```
SQL> select timestamp, protocol_info
  2  from listener_log
  3  where connect_data like '%sqlplus.exe%'
  4  /

TIMESTAMP            PROTOCOL_INFO
------------------- -----------------------------------------------------
01-SEP-2008 14:30:37  (ADDRESS=(PROTOCOL=tcp)(HOST=192.168.2.101)
                                                          (PORT=3651))

01-SEP-2008 14:31:08  (ADDRESS=(PROTOCOL=tcp)(HOST=192.168.2.101)
                                                          (PORT=3666))

01-SEP-2008 14:31:35  (ADDRESS=(PROTOCOL=tcp)(HOST=192.168.2.101)
                                                          (PORT=3681))
```

The use of External Tables to analyze the `listener.log` can be used not only to have an in-database version of the `listener.log` perform periodic and programmatic analysis of the listener behavior, but also to determine usage trends and correlate information with the audit team so that unauthorized connection programs can be easily and quickly spotted. Further useful applications can be found by reading the `listener.log` file. There are two fields that must be further parsed to get information out of them, but parsing those fields goes beyond the scope of this chapter. The structure that the analysis should consider is detailed next:

Connect String

1. **SID**: The Database Oracle SID, which is populated if the connection was performed by SID, otherwise it is NULL.

2. **CID**: It contains two subfields, **PROGRAM** and **HOST**

3. **SERVER**: This field indicates the connection type, either dedicated or shared

4. **SERVICE_NAME**: This field is populated when the connection is performed by a Service instead of **SID**.

5. **COMMAND**: The command issued by the user.

6. **SERVICE**: Present only when listener commands are issued.

7. **FAILOVER_MODE**: In **Real Application Clusters** (RAC) environments this field is used if the client performed a connection due to a failover. It shows the failover mode used.

Protocol

1. **PROTOCOL**: Indicates the used to perform the connection; this will be TCP most of the times.

2. **HOST**: This is the client's IP Address.

3. **PORT**: The port number of the oracle server used to establish the connection.

Mapping XML files as External Tables

XML has become a de facto information exchange format, which is why oracle has included the **XML Database (XDB)** feature from 9.2.0. However, it requires the data to be actually loaded into the database before it can be processed. An External Table allows the user to take a quick look at the contents of the external file prior to performing any further processing.

In this example an External Table is created out of an XML file. This file is read by means of a CLOB field, and some further XDB commands can be issued against the external XML file to extract and view data.

Let's create the external XML file first:

```
create table EMPLOYEES_XML (xmlFile CLOB)
organization external (
  type ORACLE_LOADER
  default directory EXTTABDIR
  access parameters (
    fields (xmllob char terminated by ',')
    column transforms (xmlFile from lobfile(xmllob))
  )
  location('employees.dat')
)
reject limit unlimited;
```

The `employees.dat` file contains the file name of the XML file to load as an external CLOB file. This file, for the purpose of the demo, contains the file name: `employees.xml`.

Now the file can be queried from the database as if it was a regular table with a single XML column.

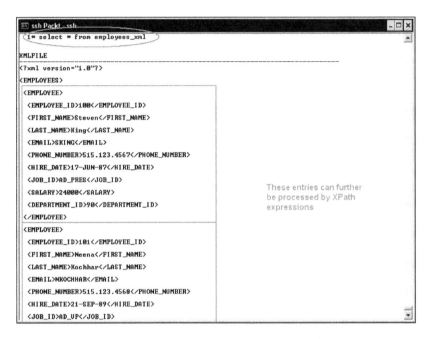

Dynamically changing the external reference

When managing External Tables, there should be an easy way to redefine the external source file. It is enough to change the External Table properties by means of an ALTER TABLE command. Let's create a stored procedure that performs this task by means of a dynamically generated DDL command. This procedure, named Change_ External_Table redefines the location property. Using a stored program unit is a flexible way to perform this task.

```
create procedure change_external_table
( p_table_name in varchar2
, p_file_name in varchar2
) is
begin
execute immediate 'alter table '
|| p_table_name
|| ' location ('''
|| p_file_name
```

```
||  ''')' ;
exception
when others
then
raise_application_error(sqlcode,sqlerrm) ;
end ;
/
```

Oracle 11g External Table enhancements

External Tables work the same in 10g and in 11g, so there are no differences when working with these two versions. When working with Data Pump External Tables, and one single row proves defective, the data set reading operation is aborted. An enhancement in this 11g release prevents the data load aborting, thus saving reprocessing time.

Summary

Managing data with External Tables is a means not only for mapping external flat files as regular (but limited) tables inside the database, but also a tool to more efficiently perform administrative tasks such as programmatically processing database log files such as the `alert.log` or the `listener.log` files. It can be used to easily view external XML formatted files from inside the database without actually loading the file to the database. It can also be used as a means of unloading data in temporary external storage to exchange data among different Oracle versions. This particular feature allows the user to easily build an Oracle Datamart that allows the pre-formatting and summarization of data from the source, enabling it to be directly inserted into the target data warehouse.

The different uses an External Table has allows the user to take full advantage of external flat files and have them loaded to the database in a very easy and convenient way. There are limitations with External Tables, such as the lack of indexes, the full table scans operations that must be performed even if a single row is to be accessed, the lack of security for the flat files, and the lack of transactional control, but certainly the advantages this concept offers overcome its disadvantages. The flexibility to manage data in different ways makes it the default choice for data exchange operations.

Recovery Manager Advanced Techniques

Recovery Manager is a powerful tool. It can easily and efficiently perform the day to day "must-do" backup tasks.

As time goes by databases become bigger and bigger. There almost seems to be a competition to break the storage world record, where just one decade ago it was amazing to hear about databases that had broken the Gigabyte limit. Today the limit is at the Terabyte range, and in a few more years it won't be surprising to find databases storing Petabytes or more.

Considering this growth, unless technology radically changes the speed to store and retrieve data, it becomes more and more important to choose the right backup strategy.

Today the term **User Managed Backup** (**UMB**) is less frequently used in the oracle communities and the reasons are obvious. UMBs are not reliable, and must backup the complete datafile, even if there are many blank blocks. A UMB cannot detect block corruptions at backup time. This may result to a redundant backup. Considering the database size and the backup and restore maintenance windows, the UMB is becoming an obsolete backup technique.

Recovery manager can deal with today's databases, it can proactively detect block corruptions, it can perform incremental backups, it allows backup compression, it can use transparent data encryption to provide secure backup environments, and it won't perform a useless backup.

In this chapter, we will be looking at methods to administer the Recovery Manager and to optimize the backup task. This will include backup multiplexing, configuration of a recovery catalog, performing backup in compressed mode, enabling backup compression, and the compression algorithms. We will also be looking the process of performing an intra-file parallel backup, reducing the performance impact of performing a backup, cloning a database on the fly, using Recovery Manager to migrate a database to a different platform, and finally, migrating the database to an ASM environment.

Recovery Manager basics

Recovery Manager (**RMAN**) is a tool that efficiently and reliably performs backup, restoration, and recovery tasks on Oracle Databases. It can be used from a **Command Line Interface** (**CLI**) or from the Enterprise Manager Web Console. It is still available in 10g from the Enterprise Manager Java Console. However, its usage is discouraged as this console has become obsolete and it is no longer available in 11g.

RMAN is a utility that works in a client-server fashion when launched in CLI mode, or in a three-tier fashion when launched from the EM Console. It commands actions from the client side and the entire backup and restore operations take place on the server side using the server storage resources. The database to be managed is known as the **TARGET** database. RMAN may optionally use a database to keep track of the backups. This database is known as the **recovery catalog** database, and is an independent database that stores information about the backup operations for different databases. This database shouldn't reside on the same server as the target database, and this database must have its own backup strategies. It is a good practice to perform the RMAN operations using a recovery catalog database, as this not only provides longer backup records, leveraging the target database control file from storing this information, but it can also be used to store frequently used RMAN scripts.

The backups can be stored on a server-side attached disk system, or if available, they can be stored on tape. A certified tape unit must be configured properly and for it to properly work with the RMAN script, a third party must supply the **Media Management Library** (**MML**).

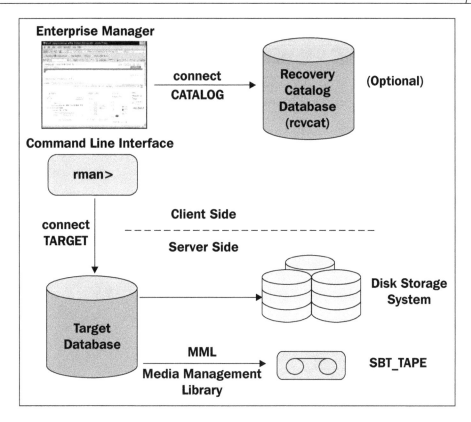

Getting started with a Recovery Manager session

Archivelog mode is mandatory if you wish to get the most out of any backup and recovery strategy. Archivelog mode is required not only to perform an online backup but also to unleash the power of all of the recovery strategies. For OLTP databases, the archivelog mode is necessary.

Both in 10g and in 11g databases a flash recovery area is, if selected at creation time, defined to store the archivelog files.

Let's configure the archivelog mode for our demo database:

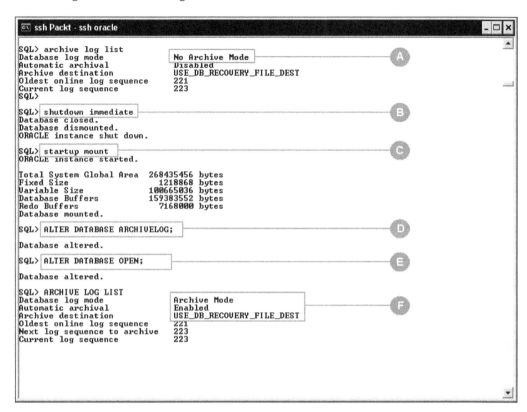

This database is currently working in **No Archive Mode** (**A**). In order for it to be configured in Archivelog mode, first it must be shut down in a consistent mode (**B**). This means that the shutdown mode must be normal, transactional, or immediate. The database cannot be shut down in abort mode as the datafiles must be consistent when Archivelog mode is enabled. Once stopped, the database must be mounted (**C**) and the **ALTER DATABASE ARCHIVELOG** command issued (**D**). Afterwards the database can be opened (**E**) and it will be in Archivelog mode (**F**) and ready for online backups.

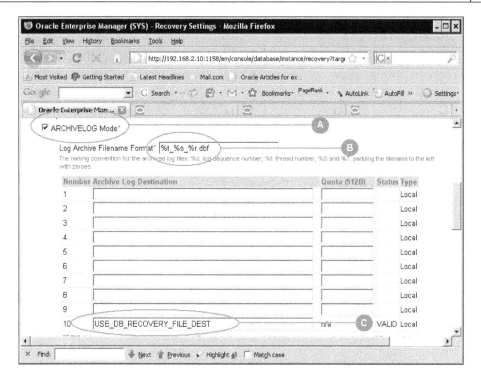

The database is now in **Archivelog Mode (A)**, and it takes the default **%t_%s_%r.dbf (B)** file format for the archivelog files (this format will be explained later in this chapter), which will be located at the flash recovery area (**C**).

The flash recovery area can be used to store the archivelog files as well as the RMAN backups, and it should be frequently monitored to make sure it will always have enough free space for the daily production environment. If it ever suffers a resource shortage and the free space is not enough to store the archivelog files, then database activity will be frozen until the flash recovery area is freed again.

The **Flash Recovery Area** is configured by means of two parameters, the DB_RECOVERY_FILE_DEST and DB_RECOVERY_FILE_DEST_SIZE. They specify the physical location of the flash recovery area and the maximum allocated space for it. The default maximum size is set at 2 Giga bytes, which will most likely be insufficient for a production environment.

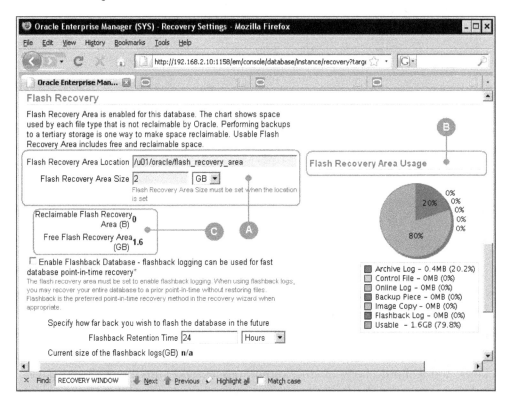

Now let's configure the RMAN environment:

```
$ rman target username/password@targetDatabase catalog rcatuser/password@
RecoeryCatalogDatabase
```

During the RMAN session's start, shutdown or incomplete recovery operations may take place. The user that connects to the target database must have the SYSDBA role granted. If the user connects locally at the server, where the target database resides and OS authentication is enabled, then it is enough to specify target as the target connect, it is assumed the ORACLE_SID environment variable has been properly specified.

RMAN stores the configuration in the control file. The command to display the current configuration is shown next:

```
RMAN configuration parameters are:
CONFIGURE RETENTION POLICY TO REDUNDANCY 1; # default
CONFIGURE BACKUP OPTIMIZATION OFF; # default
CONFIGURE DEFAULT DEVICE TYPE TO DISK; # default
CONFIGURE CONTROLFILE AUTOBACKUP OFF; # default
CONFIGURE CONTROLFILE AUTOBACKUP FORMAT FOR DEVICE TYPE DISK TO '%F'; #
default
CONFIGURE DEVICE TYPE DISK PARALLELISM 1 BACKUP TYPE TO BACKUPSET; #
default
CONFIGURE DATAFILE BACKUP COPIES FOR DEVICE TYPE DISK TO 1; # default
CONFIGURE ARCHIVELOG BACKUP COPIES FOR DEVICE TYPE DISK TO 1; # default
CONFIGURE MAXSETSIZE TO UNLIMITED; # default
CONFIGURE ENCRYPTION FOR DATABASE OFF; # default
CONFIGURE ENCRYPTION ALGORITHM 'AES128'; # default
CONFIGURE ARCHIVELOG DELETION POLICY TO NONE; # default
CONFIGURE SNAPSHOT CONTROLFILE NAME TO '/u01/oracle/oracle/
product/10.2.0/db_1/dbs/snapcf_beta.f'; # default
```

The SHOW ALL command output is explained next.

```
export ORACLE_SID=ORCL
$ rman target /
RMAN> SHOW ALL;
```

- **RETENTION POLICY**: Since Oracle 9i Rel. 1, RMAN can specify the retention period for a backup. Once the retention period has expired the backup is considered obsolete and it can be purged. The retention policy specifies this retention period with one out of two mutually exclusive policies. It can specify that the backup will be retained for an explicit period given that the **RETENTION POLICY** is configured to a **RECOVERY WINDOW OF n days**. It can also specify a given number of redundant backups (**REDUNDANCY n**), which means that after **n+1** backups, the oldest backup from this series is considered obsolete and RMAN can get rid of it.

- **BACKUP OPTIMIZATION**: This directs RMAN to not backup datafiles which have not changed since the last backup operation. This option can be overridden any time if the **FORCE** modifier is used at backup time.

- **DEFAULT DEVICE TYPE**: When issuing an RMAN backup or restore operation, a device channel should be specified, otherwise RMAN will use the device specified with this parameter.

- **CONTROLFILE AUTOBACKUP**: This option specifies whether an automatic copy of the controlfile and spfile will be taken each time a backup or a structure change takes place.

- **CONTROLFILE AUTOBACKUP FORMAT**: By default this is set to %F, which specifies that backups should be made in the oracle managed file format. If no path is specified, by default this file is stored in the flash recovery area, in a directory created by RMAN, which is named after the sysdate and the backup format. The path where the controlfile auto-backup is stored can be seen by issuing a simple list backup command.

The next screen shot shows the **LIST BACKUP (A)** command issued to display recently taken backups and the automatically generated **controlfile backup (B)**.

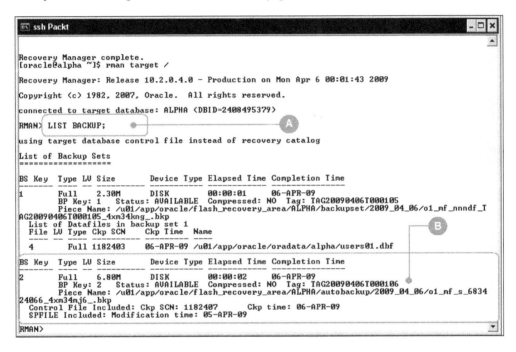

- **DEVICE TYPE DISK**: This parameter is used to configure specific channel limits.

- **DATAFILE BACKUP COPIES**: This specifies the number of multiplexed backups to be generated. By default, it will only generate one single backup.

- **ARCHIVELOG BACKUP COPIES**: Just like the datafile backup copies parameter, this parameter configures the number of multiplexed archivelog backups to be performed.

- **MAXSETSIZE**: This parameter limits the maximum size for a backup set. The parameter value is by default specified in bytes. Don't set it unless you are sure you want to limit the backup set size. If the backup space requirements exceed this limit the backup operation is aborted.

- **ENCRYPTION**: This parameter specifies whether the backup will use the **Transparent Data Encryption** (TDE) facility. This feature is only available in the Enterprise Edition, from 10g Rel. 2 and later. It requires a properly configured TDE facility.

- **ENCRYPTION ALGORITHM**: The DBA can specify which particular encryption algorithm will be used to encrypt the RMAN backups.

- **ARCHIVELOG DELETION POLICY**: This parameter defines when the archivelog files are eligible for deletion. This policy applies to all archivelog destinations. By default this option is turned off. This makes RMAN consider archivelog files eligible for deletion when either it has already been backed up at least once or if the archivelog files have already been transferred to their remote destinations (Data guard configurations). If the flash recovery area runs out of space, RMAN purges the archivelog files if it determines that the archivelog files are eligible for deletion based on the previously stated criteria.

The options this parameter can hold are `BACKED UP integer TIMES TO DEVICE TYPE` and for a data guard configuration other options are: `APPLIED ON STANDBY` and `SHIPPED TO STANDBY`. The `BACKED UP integer TIMES TO DEVICE TYPE` command specifies that the archivelog files won't be eligible for deletion unless *n* archivelog backups have been taken, this option can always be overridden by the RMAN **FORCE** option.

- **SNAPSHOT CONTROLFILE NAME**: The snapshot controlfile is a consistent copy of the controlfile that recovery manager automatically creates during a backup operation. By default, it is stored in the `$ORACLE_HOME/dbs/sncf$ORACLE_SID.ora` file (for Unix like environments) or the `%ORACLE_HOME%\database\SNCF%ORACLE_SID%.ORA` file on Windows environments.

- **COMPRESSION ALGORITHM**: This parameter is available starting with 11g; it declares the compression algorithm to be used by RMAN to produce zipped backups. It utilizes the **BZIP2** algorithm by default.

If a parameter configuration is to be set to its default value then the **CLEAR** keyword must be used along with the `CONFIGURE` command:

```
CONFIGURE RMAN PARAMETER CLEAR;
```

If you want to verify the setting of a particular `rman` parameter, then issue the SHOW command:

```
SHOW RMAN PARAMETER;
```

The `SHOW ALL` command shows all currently set `rman` parameters.

To show the CLEAR command, in the following example, some rman parameters are modified and then set back to their default values:

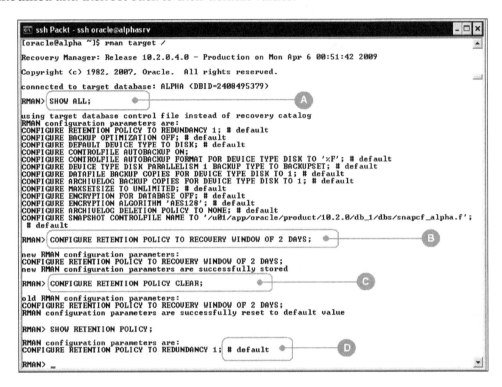

The **SHOW ALL** command displays all the current parameter values (**A**). The next command configures the recovery window (**B**) changing it from 1 redundant backup (default value) to **2 days**. Afterwards the CLEAR command is applied on the recently modified parameter (**C**), and finally it shows its original value (**D**).

Format masks used by recovery manager

You can use the following format masks for the files generated by recovery manager.

Format Mask	Description
%a	Specifies the activation ID of the database
%c	Specifies the copy number of the backup piece within a set of duplexed backup pieces
%d	Specifies the name of the database
%D	Specifies the current day of the month from the Gregorian calendar
%e	Specifies the archived log sequence number

Format Mask	Description
%f	Specifies the absolute file number
%F	Combines the **Database ID (DBID)**, day, month, year, and sequence into a unique and repeatable generated name
%h	Specifies the archived redo log thread number
%I	Specifies the DBID
%M	Specifies the month in the Gregorian calendar in MM format
%N	Specifies the tablespace name
%n	Specifies the name of the database, padded on the right with n characters to a total length of eight characters
%p	Specifies the piece number within the backup set
%s	Specifies the backup set number
%t	Specifies the backup set timestamp
%T	Specifies the year, month, and day in the Gregorian calendar
%u	Specifies an eight-character name constituted by compressed representations of the backup set or image copy number
%U	Specifies a system-generated unique filename (this is the default setting)

What happens in a user-managed online backup?

There are two ways to perform a backup; the **offline backup** and the **online backup**: The first one is performed when the database has been cleanly shutdown (normal, immediate or transactional). The second one is performed when the database is open.

The offline database backup does not require the database to be in archivelog mode; meanwhile the online database backup requires the database to be in archivelog mode. An online backup is usually preferable to an offline backup, as an online backup does not require the database to be shutdown.

For the DBA to be able to perform a recoverable online backup the database must be in archivelog mode. The backup can be performed either as a user managed backup or an RMAN managed backup. When the backup starts, Oracle issues a checkpoint operation against the datafile, this flushes all target related database blocks to the datafiles belonging to the tablespace; afterwards the datafile header is frozen.

The next query is used to display the datafile header after the ALTER TABLESPACE
BEGIN BACKUP command is issued.

```
SQL> select file#         "FileNo",
  2    status             "Status",
  3    checkpoint_time     "ChkptTime",
  4    checkpoint_change# "ChkptChg",
  5    checkpoint_count    "ChkptCnt",
  6    fuzzy               "Fuzzy"
  7* from v$datafile_header

   FileNo Status  ChkptTime    ChkptChg    ChkptCnt Fuz
---------- ------- ---------- ---------- ---------- ---
        1 ONLINE  29-10:1944   13326323         361 YES
        2 ONLINE  29-10:1944   13326323         324 YES
        3 ONLINE  29-10:1944   13326323         361 YES
        4 ONLINE  29-10:1532   13287836         362 YES
        5 ONLINE  29-10:1944   13326323         323 YES
        6 ONLINE  29-10:1944   13326323         274 YES
        7 ONLINE  29-10:1944   13326323         270 YES
```

Every datafile on this database has the same checkpoint, except for the datafile
related to the tablespace, which is currently in hot backup mode. This tablespace can
be monitored on the V$BACKUP dynamic view.

```
SQL> SELECT FILE#, STATUS, CHANGE#, TIME
  2* FROM V$BACKUP

   FILE# STATUS      CHANGE# TIME
---------- ---------- ---------- ----------
        1 NOT ACTIVE           0
        2 NOT ACTIVE           0
        3 NOT ACTIVE           0
        4 ACTIVE        13287836 29-10:1532
        5 NOT ACTIVE           0
        6 NOT ACTIVE           0
        7 NOT ACTIVE           0
```

Myths related to the online backup method

There are many myths related to the online backup feature, one relates to the amount of redo information, and another widely spread myth has to do with the datafile activity. There is additional information stored in the online redo log the first time a data block is changed when in hot backup mode. Afterwards only the regular log entries are recorded. The reason why this is the only extra information generated has to do with the second fact, the datafile has normal read/write activity, except for its header which remains frozen during the hot backup session. Once the backup starts it reads the database blocks, but there are two IO levels: that of the database block and that of the OS block, which happen to have different sizes.

The following diagram shows how the fractured block issue is produced during a user managed online backup. If the backup operation reads an oracle block and in the middle of the operation, the **RDBMS** requests a write operation, the datafile backup will read an inconsistent database block. If the additional redo information was not generated then a fractured block issue would be raised, and the recovery process would not be possible. The datafile header remains frozen as a milestone telling to the recovery process where it has to start. During the recovery process, the fractured blocks are repaired and the recovery transaction is performed until the limit established during the recover session.

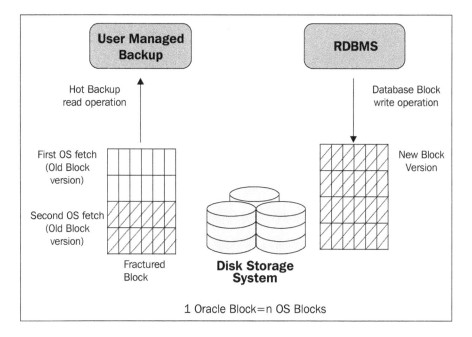

Recovery Manager has a fractured block management system that is comparatively better. It performs a consistent database block backup by reading a number of OS blocks equivalent to multiples of database blocks.

Configuring a multiplexed backup

This allows the user to specify more than one backup path. Let's configure two specific parameters, datafile backup copies for device type disk, and a couple of **channels** for **disk IO**.

```
RMAN> CONFIGURE CHANNEL DEVICE TYPE DISK FORMAT 'D:\HOME\ORACLE\BACKUP\
RMAN\%U.BUS', 'D:\HOME\ORACLE\BACKUP2\RMAN\%U.BUS';
RMAN> CONFIGURE ARCHIVELOG BACKUP COPIES FOR DEVICE TYPE DISK TO 2;
RMAN> CONFIGURE DATAFILE BACKUP COPIES FOR DEVICE TYPE DISK TO 2;
```

Once the path is configured let's backup the database:

```
RMAN> backup database;
Starting backup at 23-OCT-08
allocated channel: ORA_DISK_1
channel ORA_DISK_1: sid=146 devtype=DISK
channel ORA_DISK_1: starting full datafile backupset
channel ORA_DISK_1: specifying datafile(s) in backupset
input datafile fno=00001 name=D:\ORACLE\PRODUCT\10.2.0\ORADATA\ALPHA\
SYSTEM01.DBF
input datafile fno=00003 name=D:\ORACLE\PRODUCT\10.2.0\ORADATA\ALPHA\
SYSAUX01.DBF
input datafile fno=00005 name=D:\ORACLE\PRODUCT\10.2.0\ORADATA\ALPHA\
EXAMPLE01.DBF
input datafile fno=00002 name=D:\ORACLE\PRODUCT\10.2.0\ORADATA\ALPHA\
UNDOTBS01.DBF
input datafile fno=00004 name=D:\ORACLE\PRODUCT\10.2.0\ORADATA\ALPHA\
USERS01.DBF
channel ORA_DISK_1: starting piece 1 at 23-OCT-08
channel ORA_DISK_1: finished piece 1 at 23-OCT-08 with 2 copies and tag
TAG20081
023T121900
piece handle=D:\HOME\ORACLE\BACKUP\RMAN\03JTS65L_1_1.BUS comment=NONE
piece handle=D:\HOME\ORACLE\BACKUP2\RMAN\03JTS65L_1_2.BUS comment=NONE
channel ORA_DISK_1: backup set complete, elapsed time: 00:01:46Finished
backup at 23-OCT-08

Starting Control File and SPFILE Autobackup at 23-OCT-08
piece handle=D:\ORACLE\PRODUCT\10.2.0\FLASH_RECOVERY_AREA\ALPHA\
```

```
AUTOBACKUP\2008_

10_23\01_MF_S_668866848_4J1DMKHS_.BKP comment=NONE

Finished Control File and SPFILE Autobackup at 23-OCT-08
```

Now, let's backup the archivelog files:

```
RMAN> backup archivelog all delete input;
Starting backup at 23-OCT-08
current log archived
using channel ORA_DISK_1
channel ORA_DISK_1: starting archive log backupset
channel ORA_DISK_1: specifying archive log(s) in backup set
input archive log thread=1 sequence=2 recid=1 stamp=668709676
input archive log thread=1 sequence=3 recid=2 stamp=668709684
input archive log thread=1 sequence=4 recid=3 stamp=668866560
input archive log thread=1 sequence=5 recid=4 stamp=668867197
channel ORA_DISK_1: starting piece 1 at 23-OCT-08
channel ORA_DISK_1: finished piece 1 at 23-OCT-08 with 2 copies and tag
TAG20081023T122637
piece handle=D:\HOME\ORACLE\BACKUP\RMAN\05JTS6JU_1_1.BUS comment=NONE
piece handle=D:\HOME\ORACLE\BACKUP2\RMAN\05JTS6JU_1_2.BUS comment=NONE
channel ORA_DISK_1: backup set complete, elapsed time: 00:00:09
channel ORA_DISK_1: deleting archive log(s)
archive log filename=D:\ORACLE\PRODUCT\10.2.0\FLASH_RECOVERY_AREA\ALPHA\
ARCHIVEL
OG\2008_10_21\01_MF_1_2_4HWM3NT8_.ARC recid=1 stamp=668709676
archive log filename=D:\ORACLE\PRODUCT\10.2.0\FLASH_RECOVERY_AREA\ALPHA\
ARCHIVEL
OG\2008_10_21\01_MF_1_3_4HWM42SJ_.ARC recid=2 stamp=668709684
archive log filename=D:\ORACLE\PRODUCT\10.2.0\FLASH_RECOVERY_AREA\ALPHA\
ARCHIVEL
OG\2008_10_23\01_MF_1_4_4J1DBGSV_.ARC recid=3 stamp=668866560
archive log filename=D:\ORACLE\PRODUCT\10.2.0\FLASH_RECOVERY_AREA\ALPHA\
ARCHIVEL
OG\2008_10_23\01_MF_1_5_4J1DYD7F_.ARC recid=4 stamp=668867197
Finished backup at 23-OCT-08
Starting Control File and SPFILE Autobackup at 23-OCT-08
piece handle=D:\ORACLE\PRODUCT\10.2.0\FLASH_RECOVERY_AREA\ALPHA\
AUTOBACKUP\2008_
10_23\01_MF_S_668867208_4J1DYSBD_.BKP comment=NONE
Finished Control File and SPFILE Autobackup at 23-OCT-08
```

This configuration has created a duplex backup destination. This is useful when more than one backup is required in a production environment. The duplex backup must be specified outside the flash recovery, otherwise an ORA-19806 will be raised.

Configuring the RMAN recovery catalog

Using a recovery catalog is not mandatory, but using one will free the controlfile from the overhead of keeping track of backups, allowing a longer backup history. It avoids a single point of failure, and allows the DBA to securely store backup information in a central repository.

Storing the backup information in the RMAN repository, also allows the DBA to create and store recovery manager scripts.

The repository is created as a regular schema on a regular Oracle database. The repository isn't a super database, able to rescue other databases and capable of rescuing itself; suitable backup strategies must be provided for it so it can be restored and recovered in case of failure.

The procedure to create the RMAN repository is outlined next:

1. Create a database whose purpose will be that of storing the backup information. Even though the overhead of managing the backup information is not meaningful, it doesn't mean it is advisable to create the recovery repository on an existing database. I would not recommend it. This should be an independent database responsible for watching over the other databases.
2. Create a regular tablespace; this will be used to store the recovery catalog schema objects.
3. Create a regular user in the recovery catalog database and assign catalog administrative privileges to it. Assign the previously created tablespace to it as its default tablespace. This user can have the database default temporary tablespace as its temporary tablespace.
4. Make sure the connectivity to this database has been properly setup.
5. Open a recovery manager session and connect to the recovery catalog database as the recovery catalog owner.
6. Issue the command to create the recovery catalog.
7. Connect to each target database and have it registered against the recovery catalog.
8. From this point on, the backup environment can call on this site to have all databases registered against it.

For the purposes of the demonstration, a regular database has been created and it has been configured.

Now, let's follow the previous procedure and let's have our environment registered against the recovery catalog.

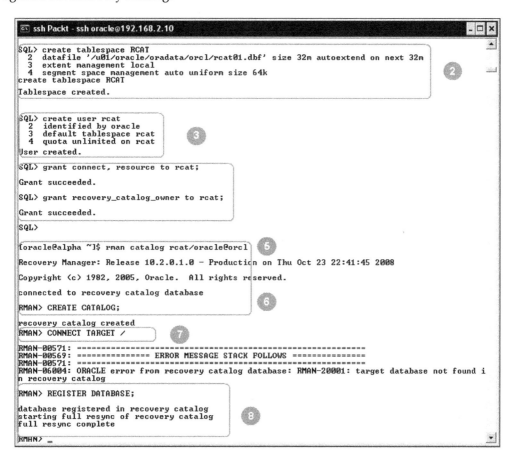

In the above demonstration, when trying to connect to the target database, an RMAN-06004 error shows up, the reason for this is that the database has not been registered yet against this repository.

It is important to note that the database to be registered has a unique database id, this information can be taken out of the V$DATABASE dynamic view.

```
SQL> select name, dbid from v$database;

NAME          DBID
---------     ----------
ORCL          1196669688
```

A cloned database won't have a unique DBID. If you register a cloned database and if the source database is already registered, then this cloned database will be misinterpreted as a new incarnation of the source database. Prior to registering a cloned database, you must run the **newdbid utility** (**nid**) against the cloned database.

A simple backup session

The backup command has a wide variety of options, for the purposes of this chapter we'll keep things plain and simple:

An information systems rule of thumb states:

> *No matter what, just make sure you have a valid backup for your environment*

So let's create a simple full database backup using the BACKUP DATABASE command, this will create a full backup of our database, and it will be useful to show the main basic backup and recover RMAN features.

```
RMAN> backup database;
Starting backup at 23-OCT-08
using channel ORA_DISK_1
channel ORA_DISK_1: starting full datafile backupset
... rman Backup progress log ...
channel ORA_DISK_1: backup set complete, elapsed time: 00:01:26
Finished backup at 23-OCT-08
```

Recovery manager only performs the backup on the database files, archivelog files, controlfile and spfile. It doesn't backup temporary datafiles and redo log files.

Now, let's assume there is a problem with some of our datafiles. Our production environment may risk being out of business if the failure compromises critical database files; the point here is what does critical mean in this context? From a purely Oracle technical point of view, a critical datafile is a file that must be consistent, available and online for the database to be up and running. The critical files are those related to the **SYSTEM, SYSAUX** and **UNDO** tablespaces. There are other files that hold the production data and other files such as the temporary datafiles. These can easily be troubleshooted.

Loss of critical datafiles: If a technically defined critical datafile is lost, there is no way to start the database, and the file must be restored and fully recovered for the database to be open.

Loss of non-critical datafiles: In this case, the database can be opened as long as the missing datafiles are declared offline. A recover operation can take place on the specific missing database files once they have been restored from a valid backup.

The recovery manager command used to perform the restore and recover operations are precisely RESTORE and RECOVER. They have a simple syntax. The emphasis in this book is on the RMAN features rather than the rman syntax.

Backup compression

If limited disk space is available, or a backup across a network environment imposes bandwidth restrictions, or if the backup is to be transported on media with a limited storage capacity, then a compressed backup is a good option.

Fast backup compression

The compressed backup can be directly configured as an option for the CONFIGURE CHANNEL command.

```
CONFIGURE DEVICE TYPE DISK PARALLELISM 1 BACKUP TYPE TO COMPRESSED
BACKUPSET;
```

Once the backup is performed, it will be done in a compressed format.

The compression can also be configured in a non-persistent way, it can be specified directly as a command option:

```
BACKUP AS COMPRESSED BACKUPSET DATABASE PLUS ARCHIVELOG;
```

In order for the DBA to recover from a compressed backup, they just need to issue the regular RESTORE/RECOVER commands. There are no specific parameters required to recover from a compressed backup set.

Let's take a look at the backup with compression enabled:

```
RMAN> BACKUP AS COMPRESSED BACKUPSET DATABASE PLUS ARCHIVELOG;

Starting backup at 23-OCT-08

current log archived

allocated channel: ORA_DISK_1

channel ORA_DISK_1: sid=149 devtype=DISK

channel ORA_DISK_1: starting compressed archive log backupset...

channel ORA_DISK_1: starting compressed full datafile backupset...

channel ORA_DISK_1: backup set complete, elapsed time: 00:00:03

Finished backup at 23-OCT-08

Starting backup at 23-OCT-08

current log archived

using channel ORA_DISK_1

channel ORA_DISK_1: starting compressed archive log backupset...

Finished backup at 23-OCT-08
```

The backup takes place just as any other regular RMAN backup. Now let's take a look at the generated fileset.

These are the files generated by a regular full database backup:

```
 980447232    o1_mf_annnn_TAG20081023T230825_4j2lktyv_.bkp
   7143424    o1_mf_ncsnf_TAG20081023T230936_4j2lpr9g_.bkp
    417792    o1_mf_annnn_TAG20081023T231218_4j2ls4bs_.bkp
1776123904    o1_mf_nnndf_TAG20081023T231221_4j2ls73t_.bkp
   7143424    o1_mf_ncsnf_TAG20081023T231221_4j2lwkc3_.bkp
     87040    o1_mf_annnn_TAG20081023T231416_4j2lwsom_.bkp
```

And these are the files generated with the compress option enabled:

```
   1383424    o1_mf_annnn_TAG20081023T235442_4j2o8mw3_.bkp
 318857216    o1_mf_nnndf_TAG20081023T235445_4j2o8p3d_.bkp
   1114112    o1_mf_ncsnf_TAG20081023T235445_4j2ofwk3_.bkp
     59392    o1_mf_annnn_TAG20081023T235738_4j2og3r3_.bkp
```

	No Compressed Backup	Compressed Backup
Backup set size	2,643 M	307 M
Backup pieces	6	4

In comparison with the regular backup set, the size of the compressed backup set is significantly smaller and less backup files were produced.

Improving data set compression with the ZLIB algorithm (11g only)

One new feature in 11g is more efficient compression, using the ZLIB Algorithm. In previous releases, RMAN used the BZIP2 algorithm for backupset compression; however, there was a CPU cost penalty involved. 11g introduced a ZLIB algorithm, which is less aggressive in terms of CPU usage. The user can decide which compression algorithm to use by setting a value to the **COMPRESSION ALGORITHM RMAN** configuration parameter.

The default value for the Compression algorithm in 11g is:

```
CONFIGURE COMPRESSION ALGORITHM 'ZLIB';
```

If you want to revert to the BZIP2 algorithm, just change the setting to reflect this:

```
CONFIGURE COMPRESSION ALGORITHM 'BZIP2';
```

If your system doesn't see the CPU compromised when performing a compressed backup you can consider this technique. If you are performing a backup against a tape device that also performs some sort of compression, don't mix both techniques, use either that of the tape or that of RMAN. Mixing both won't lead to a satisfactory result as you cannot compress an already compressed data set.

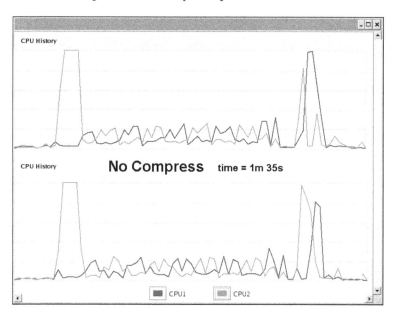

The two tests performed show the total time elapsed when the No Compress option was specified on the backup channel. All the tests were performed against the default general-purpose 11g database. The first and the last peaks have to do with the I/O activity related to the read datafile task and the write backup task; the backup activity takes around 1 minute 36 seconds and the CPU remains around 15% and 25% within this actual backup period.

Now let's activate the compressed backup feature, first with the **BZIP2** algorithm, next with the **ZLIB** algorithm:

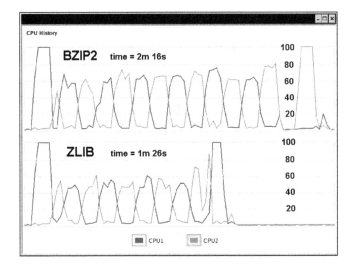

Here it can be observed, at first glance, the time it took to perform the backup with the **BZIP2** algorithm and the amount of CPU required for each algorithm. When the **BZIP2** algorithm was used, the CPU consumption was between 60% and 70%, and there were some peaks that consumed near 80% CPU. However, when using the **ZLIB** algorithm, the CPU consumption was between 50% and 60%, reaching some peaks that were for short periods of time between 70 and 80%.

The table below summarizes the results:

Compression algorithm	Elapsed time	CPU consumption	File size	Compression rate
No Compressed	95 s	15% - 25%	1,521 M	1
BZIP2	136 s	60% - 70%	252 M	0.17
ZLIB	86 s	50% - 60%	282 M	0.19

BZIP2 provides a marginally better compression rate at a higher CPU and time cost than the ZLIB algorithm.

Faster backups through intra-file parallel backup and restore operations (11g only)

When a parallel backup takes place there are several backup processes started. Each one is responsible for processing one file at a time. Oracle is aware that this strategy is fine for the current average database size, but this strategy soon may not be enough.

This scalable solution for backups is also known as the multi-section backup. Each datafile is divided into a defined number of sections, each section is defined as a contiguous range of database blocks, and each parallel process takes care of one section at a time, so several parallel processes manage a big database file at the same time.

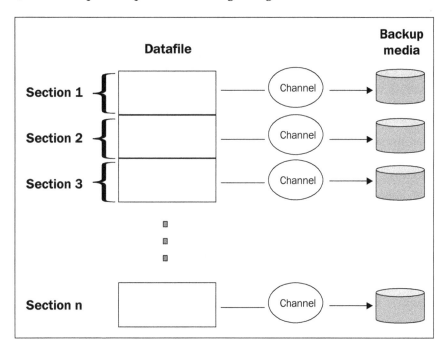

Let's issue the command to perform the multi section backup:

```
# One-off configuration of device type and parallelism.
CONFIGURE DEVICE TYPE sbt PARALLELISM 4;
CONFIGURE DEFAULT DEVICE TYPE TO sbt;

# Divides the tablespace in 512M sections.
RUN {
  BACKUP SECTION SIZE 512M TABLESPACE any_huge_TS;
}
```

Some issues you should keep in mind when performing this kind of backup:

- The file size should be bigger than the section size; otherwise RMAN won't use multi section backups

- A backup set always includes the whole datafile, regardless of whether it was produced by multi section backup or not

- If RMAN determines that more than 256 sections will be produced, then RMAN adjusts the section size to meet this maximum

- The last section size may be less or equal than the defined backup section

Block media recovery

Block media recovery is a powerful and very practical RMAN feature. This feature allows the DBA to recover from the dreaded `ORA-01578 ORACLE data block corrupted (file # <fileNo>, block # <blockNo>)` error. In order for RMAN to be successful in recovering from this error, some conditions must be met:

- The database must be in archivelog mode.

- You must have a full database backup. A level 1 incremental backup is not supported in this scenario because in a missing archivelog scenario the recovery process would fail.

- If flashback is enabled, RMAN can look for valid block copies, making the recovery process faster.

In the following example, some blocks were corrupted at datafile 5. The corruptions were created using the Unix command `dd`. When querying the database looking for data using a regular `SELECT` SQL command, the `ORA-01578` error shows up:

```
SQL> select * from employees;
select * from employees
             *
ERROR at line 1:
ORA-01578: ORACLE data block corrupted (file # 5, block # 84)
ORA-01110: data file 5: '/u01/oracle/oradata/beta/example01.dbf'
SQL> select * from departments;
select * from departments
             *
ERROR at line 1:
ORA-01578: ORACLE data block corrupted (file # 5, block # 56)
ORA-01110: data file 5: '/u01/oracle/oradata/beta/example01.dbf'
```

At this point, a dbv command is issued from the command line prompt to find out the status of datafile **5**. **DBV** here stands for **Database File Verifier**.

```
$ dbv file='/u01/oracle/oradata/beta/example01.dbf'
DBVERIFY - Verification starting : FILE = /u01/oracle/oradata/beta/
example01.dbf
Page 16 is marked corrupt
Corrupt block relative dba: 0x01400010 (file 5, block 16)
Bad header found during dbv:
Data in bad block:
 type: 67 format: 7 rdba: 0x0a545055
 last change scn: 0x0000.0006d15a seq: 0x1 flg: 0x06
 spare1: 0x52 spare2: 0x52 spare3: 0x0
 consistency value in tail: 0xd15a0601
 check value in block header: 0xcb3b
 computed block checksum: 0xe446
```

Several other pages were found to be corrupt:

```
DBVERIFY - Verification complete
Total Pages Examined         : 12800
Total Pages Processed (Data) : 4405
Total Pages Failing   (Data) : 0
Total Pages Processed (Index): 1279
Total Pages Failing   (Index): 0
Total Pages Processed (Other): 1581
Total Pages Processed (Seg)  : 0
Total Pages Failing   (Seg)  : 0
Total Pages Empty            : 5515
Total Pages Marked Corrupt   : 20
Total Pages Influx           : 0
Highest block SCN            : 4860803 (0.4860803)
```

We already found out that there are problems with our database; it is time to have them fixed as soon as possible. If a user managed backup is available this would be the last option, as this is not reliable; if this datafile was already corrupt when the backup took place, the datafile backup would also be corrupt and this would lead us to a very complicated situation. RMAN detects the corruptions during a backup or a backup validate operation. In the following case, we issue the VALIDATE backup against datafile 5 to verify the datafile:

```
RMAN> backup validate datafile 5;

Starting backup at 26-OCT-08

allocated channel: ORA_DISK_1

channel ORA_DISK_1: sid=145 devtype=DISK

channel ORA_DISK_1: starting full datafile backupset

channel ORA_DISK_1: specifying datafile(s) in backupset

input datafile fno=00005 name=/u01/oracle/oradata/beta/example01.dbf

channel ORA_DISK_1: backup set complete, elapsed time: 00:00:01

Finished backup at 26-OCT-08
```

This command will fill up the V$BACKUP_CORRUPTION dynamic view. This information will be useful when RMAN builds up the block fix list:

```
SQL> SELECT FILE#, BLOCK#, MARKED_CORRUPT, CORRUPTION_TYPE
  2  FROM V$BACKUP_CORRUPTION;

   FILE#      BLOCK# MAR CORRUPTIO
---------- ---------- --- ---------
        5          16 YES CORRUPT
        5          56 YES CORRUPT
        5          72 YES CORRUPT
        5          84 YES CORRUPT
        5         112 YES CORRUPT
```

This information can also be gathered from the V$DATABASE_BLOCK_CORRUPTION dynamic view. We have the file number as well as the specific block number to repair. Now there are two options to carry out this task:

1. Issue the BLOCKRECOVER DATAFILE file# BLOCK block# command, listing each corrupted block.
2. Issue the BLOCKRECOVER CORRUPTION LIST command, this will read the information from the views mentioned above to build the target block list. This option is easier than the first one when there are several blocks to fix.

The following `rman` command reads the corruption list and performs the block recovery process without prompting the user for each individual block:

```
RMAN> BLOCKRECOVER CORRUPTION LIST;
Starting blockrecover at 26-OCT-08
using channel ORA_DISK_1
channel ORA_DISK_1: restoring block(s)
channel ORA_DISK_1: specifying block(s) to restore from backup set
restoring blocks of datafile 00005
```

More restore/recovery information is displayed:

```
    media recovery complete, elapsed time: 00:00:10
    Finished blockrecover at 26-OCT-08
```

The problem is solved and the information recorded in the V$DATABASE_BLOCK_ CORRUPTION dynamic view is automatically cleared once the problem is solved.

Backup duration and throttling

Performing a database backup is a task that consumes large amount of resources. If the production system worked from nine to five, Monday to Friday, then we would easily be able to find a maintenance window, which could be used to schedule the costly backup operation. But what about a 24x7 system where it is very hard to find a maintenance window where the backup task must fiercely compete with other processes to gain access to CPU and I/O resources to achieve the task? The answer, so far, is simple, the backup must be done, whatever the price to be paid.

Oracle 10g introduced a nice feature that allows the DBA to launch the backup task reducing system resource consumption. It allows the DBA to control the backup duration so that the backup may take longer but it will also consume fewer system resources.

In the following example a backup operation takes place. As you can see — the first run shows the amount of CPU consumed by the regular backup operation against the time that operation takes to complete. On the second run, the duration has been configured so that the workload against the database is minimized. The backup operation takes longer, but the advantage of it is the reduced performance impact. This can be seen in the example below:

Regular backup:

```
RMAN> BACKUP DATABASE;
```

Backup duration and throttling:

```
RMAN> BACKUP
2>      DURATION 0:10
3>      MINIMIZE LOAD
4>      DATABASE;
```

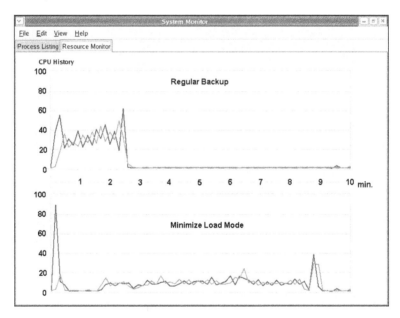

Database cloning

Cloning a test or development environment after the backup has been taken from the production environment is a very good opportunity to test if the backup will serve its purpose. This is not the only time when a database clone is required, there are several other scenarios, such as providing a fresh environment for developers and pre-production environments, manually setting up a disaster recovery site, upgrade preparation, and performance and stress testing, to name just a few.

Database cloning procedure

Let's assume we have a **Source Database** named SRCDB and the target database, named CLONEDB. A Unix like environment is assumed, but this can be implemented on Windows as well, just be aware of the particular Oracle implementation on a Windows platform (orapwd file name, service creation, path format).

When performing the clone process, two channels must be open, one for the target database, and the second one for the auxiliary database. The auxiliary connection performs the heavy part of the clone process, this will open a session at the cloned database and it will perform the restore/recover operations required at the auxiliary site. The clone database may reside either on the local host or on the remote hosts. In most cases, due to storage capacity or other factors, the clone database will reside remotely, so it is important to consider where the backup is located at the remote site; the same paths must be used and the backup must be transferred to the auxiliary site. If using a tape based backup, the auxiliary site must have access to the tape device; it is possible to use **Network File System** (**NFS**) to have access to the backup too.

The clone procedure is shown below:

1. Start by creating a password file for the **Cloned** (CLONEDB) instance:

   orapwd file=/u01/app/oracle/product/10.2.0/db_1/dbs/orapwCLONEDB password=password entries=10

2. Configure the connectivity (tnsnames.ora and listener.ora). Properly identify the database at the tnsnames.ora and have the instance manually registered against the listener.ora files, both files located at the $ORACLE_HOME/network/admin directory.

3. Manually register the database against the listener (listener.ora):

```
(SID_DESC =
  (ORACLE_HOME = /u01/app/oracle/product/10.2.0/db_1)
  (SID_NAME = CLONEDB)
)
```

4. Add the target CLONEDB to the tnsnames.ora:

```
CLONEDB =
  (DESCRIPTION =
    (ADDRESS_LIST =
      (ADDRESS = (PROTOCOL = TCP)(HOST = myhost.mydomain.com)(PORT
= 1521))
    )
    (CONNECT_DATA =
      (ORACLE_SID = CLONEDB)
    )
  )
```

5. Reload the listener:

```
$ lsnrctl reload
```

6. Next, create an `init.ora` file for the cloned database. In case the same database file paths cannot be used on the auxiliary host, either because it is the same source host or because those paths are not reproducible on the target, then proper values for DB_FILE_NAME_CONVERT and LOG_FILE_NAME_CONVERT are required.

```
DB_NAME=CLONEDB

CONTROL_FILES=(/u02/oradata/CLONEDB/control01.ctl,
               /u02/oradata/CLONEDB/control02.ctl,
               /u02/oradata/CLONEDB/control03.ctl)

# Convert file names to allow for different directory structure.
DB_FILE_NAME_CONVERT=(/u02/oradata/SRCDB/,/u02/oradata/CLONEDB/)
LOG_FILE_NAME_CONVERT=(/u01/oradata/SRCDB/,/u01/oradata/CLONEDB/)

# block_size and compatible parameters must match those of the
source database
DB_BLOCK_SIZE=8192
COMPATIBLE=10.2.0.1.0
```

7. Connect to the cloned instance:

```
ORACLE_SID=CLONEDB; export ORACLE_SID
sqlplus /nolog
conn / as sysdba
```

8. Create an SPFILE based on the `init.ora`:

```
CREATE SPFILE FROM PFILE='/u01/app/oracle/admin/CLONEDB/pfile/
init.ora';
```

9. Start the database in NOMOUNT mode:

```
STARTUP FORCE NOMOUNT;
```

10. Connect to the TARGET, CATALOG, and AUXILIARY databases. In this code snippet, the clone database process is performed using the catalog database, but it is not required, it can be performed with or without a recovery catalog. At the auxiliary site, using RMAN, three connections are open, one for the **Source Database (SOURCEDB)**, another for the **Catalog** database (**RCAT**), and one more for the **cloned database (CLONEDB)**:

```
ORACLE_SID=CLONEDB; export ORACLE_SID
rman TARGET sys/password@SRCDB CATALOG rman/rman@RCAT AUXILIARY /
```

11. Recovery Manager provides the DUPLICATE command to perform the clone operation. The cloned database can either be completely recovered up to the last redo entry available or it can be cloned to a point in time, this would be equivalent to an incomplete recover operation at the auxiliary site. The two cases are shown below:

    ° First case, clone the database in complete recovery mode:

    ```
    DUPLICATE TARGET DATABASE TO CLONEDB;
    ```

    ° Second case, clone the database up to a defined point in time in the past using an incomplete recover:

    ```
    DUPLICATE TARGET DATABASE TO CLONEDB UNTIL TIME 'SYSDATE-2';
    ```

At the end of this point, the process is finished; the newly created CLONEDB database is ready to be used as an independent new database.

The DUPLICATE command will take care of the final details. It will create the controlfile for the cloned environment, restore all datafiles and manage the auxiliary instance. As an additional task, it will open the database with the resetlogs option and it will create a new DBID for the cloned database, except for the DUPLICATE ... FOR STANDBY case.

Database cloning on the fly (11g only)

As you have seen, Oracle 10g required the database to have a backup, and some manual preparation must be done prior to the clone process execution. Starting with 11g the DBA is leveraged from some tasks. With 11g, it is no longer required to have the target spfile created, this can be created on the fly, and there is no need to have a pre-existing backup from the source database. RMAN reads the original database files the same way it reads the datafiles for a backup operation and transfers the on-the fly backup to the auxiliary database using an inter-instance network connection. RMAN utilizes an in-memory rman script to perform the cloning tasks at the auxiliary location. Some preparation at the destination site must be still performed prior to the clone process; the cloned environment must be already identified with a password file, which holds the same password as that defined at the source site.

The following diagram illustrates the clone on the fly procedure using the **DUPLICATE ... FROM ACTIVE DATABASE** command. Intermediate files are not required to clone the database.

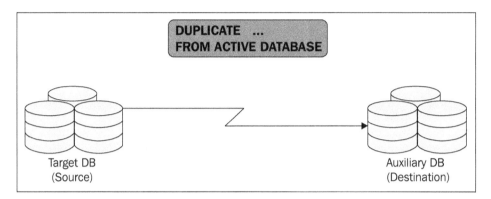

The command modifier used to perform the task is **FROM ACTIVE DATABASE**, which makes RMAN aware of both the **Auxiliary DB (Destination)** and the **Target DB (Source)**. The source database can either be in archivelog or no-archivelog mode.

When this operation takes place, the DBA should be aware of the required resources at the source database, CPU, I/O and bandwidth, so there may be some overhead involved during the clone operation. You have seen from previous topics the amount of resources consumed by a regular backup operation.

When the clone operation takes place, it may be possible that the destination site doesn't have the same paths used at the source database, so it is required to specify the DB_FILE_NAME_CONVERT and the LOG_FILE_NAME_CONVERT, which directs RMAN as to where the database files (at the destination) are to be created. These parameters as well as many other parameters can be specified as arguments at the time the DUPLICATE command is issued. This feature allows the DBA to save time issuing the ALTER SYSTEM commands at the destination instance.

```
DUPLICATE TARGET DATABASE
    TO CLONEDB
    FROM ACTIVE DATABASE
    SPFILE
        PARAMETER_VALUE_CONVERT   '/u01','/u02'
        SET LOG_FILE_NAME_CONVERT '/u01','/u02'
        SET DB_FILE_NAME_CONVERT  '/u01','/u02'
        SET SGA_MAX_SIZE 512M
        SET SGA_TARGET 400M;
```

The `PARAMETER_VALUE_CONVERT` is used to avoid specifying each path related parameter, this parameter doesn't define the `LOG_FILE_NAME_CONVERT` or `DB_FILE_NAME_CONVERT` parameters.

Inter-platform database migration

When performing an inter-platform migration operation, due to natural OS incompatibilities, the most commonly used method is a regular export/import (exp/imp or the Data Pump version). This approach happens not to be a scalable solution. The amount of data to transfer is directly proportional to the time taken to complete. Day by day databases are growing larger and the maintenance windows are becoming narrower, so a logical data transfer may leave us in a very uncomfortable situation. If the database is 10g Release 1 or higher, the DBA can take advantage of the inter-platform transportable tablespace feature. The total amount of time it takes to have the database migrated to the target platform is equal to the time it takes to prepare all tablespace metadata to be exported, plus the time it takes to copy the datafiles to the target platform, plus the time to apply the inter-platform datafile conversion, plus the time it takes to have the metadata imported.

The reason why a datafile belonging to a database created on HP-UX cannot be read on a database created on a Windows x32 platform, or a datafile belonging to a database on Linux cannot be read on Solaris is **Endianess**. Endianess is a term used in computing and refers to the byte ordering used to represent data. This term was coined after the Jonathan Swift's novel *The Gulliver's Travels* which depicts the conflicts between Lilliput and Blefuscu who discussed which side was the right one to crack the egg, the little end or the big end. Technically speaking, the big endian format defines that the most significant byte is stored at the memory location with the lowest address; the next byte value in significance is stored at the following memory location and so on. On the other hand, the little endian format states that the least significant byte value is at the lowest address, and the other bytes follow in increasing order of significance.

The procedure to transport a tablespace across platforms is as follows:

1. Make the tablespace read only.
2. Verify that you are working with a valid transportable set, that is non self-contained tablespaces or tablespaces containing objects belonging to SYS are not valid.
3. Extract the metadata with the `transport_tablespace` option.
4. Check out the source and target endian format, if those are compatible just proceed, otherwise use RMAN to perform the endian conversion either at the source or the target platform.

5. Transfer the datafiles to the target platform (if the DBA decides to perform the format conversion at the target platform, then the file transference must be performed first).

6. Import the tablespace metadata at the target database.

7. Make the tablespace read/write.

Some important points to consider when performing an inter-platform tablespace transportation are:

- The source and target database character sets must be the same
- The source and target platforms must have the same Endianess, if this is not the case; it is when RMAN must perform the endianess conversion.
- The tablespace name must be unique at the target database and the data must be self-contained. If the tablespace is not unique, then it must be renamed.

Let's create a regular locally managed tablespace on a windows platform. The goal is to have this tablespace migrated to a server running under a Linux operating system:

```
SQL> create tablespace MIGRATE_TO_UNIX_TS
  2   datafile 'C:\ORACLE\PRODUCT\10.1.0\ORADATA\ALPHA\MIGRATE_TO_UNIX_
TS_01.DBF' size 64m
  3   extent management local
  4   segment space management auto uniform size 64k;
Tablespace created.
SQL> create table system.where_are_you_from(
  2      Question          varchar2(40),
  3      Answer            varchar2(80))
  4   tablespace MIGRATE_TO_UNIX_TS;

Table created.
SQL> select * from where_are_you_from;

QUESTION           ANSWER
---------------    --------------------------------
Version            Oracle Database 10g Enterprise
                   Edition Release 10.1.0.5.0 - Prod
OS Platform        Microsoft Windows IA (32-bit)
Endian Format      Little
SQL> exec dbms_tts.transport_set_check('MIGRATE_TO_UNIX_TS', TRUE);
SQL> SELECT *
  2   FROM transport_set_violations;
no rows selected
```

The next step is to set this tablespace in read-only mode and have the metadata exported:

```
SQL> alter tablespace MIGRATE_TO_UNIX_TS read only;
SQL> create directory DATA_PUMP_DIR
  2* as 'C:\Oracle\product\10.1.0\admin\alpha\dpdump';
SQL> grant read,write on directory data_pump_dir to public;
```

At the OS prompt the export Data Pump utility is invoked to generate a dump file containing the metadata required to perform the tablespace transportation:

```
C:\>expdp system/oracle dumpfile=MigrateToLinux directory=DATA_PUMP_DIR
transport_tablespaces=MIGRATE_TO_UNIX_TS

Export: Release 10.1.0.5.0 - Production on Tuesday, 28 October, 2008 2:57

Copyright (c) 2003, Oracle.  All rights reserved.

Connected to: Oracle Database 10g Enterprise Edition Release 10.1.0.5.0 -
Production
With the Partitioning, OLAP and Data Mining options
Starting "SYSTEM"."SYS_EXPORT_TRANSPORTABLE_01":  system/********
dumpfile=MigrateToUnix direct
ory=DATA_PUMP_DIR transport_tablespaces=MIGRATE_TO_UNIX_TS
Processing object type TRANSPORTABLE_EXPORT/PLUGTS_BLK
Processing object type TRANSPORTABLE_EXPORT/TABLE
Processing object type TRANSPORTABLE_EXPORT/TTE_POSTINST/PLUGTS_BLK
Master table "SYSTEM"."SYS_EXPORT_TRANSPORTABLE_01" successfully loaded/
unloaded
**********************************************************************
Dump file set for SYSTEM.SYS_EXPORT_TRANSPORTABLE_01 is:
  C:\ORACLE\PRODUCT\10.1.0\ADMIN\ALPHA\DPDUMP\MIGRATETOUNIX.DMP
Job "SYSTEM"."SYS_EXPORT_TRANSPORTABLE_01" successfully completed at
02:58
```

During a regular transportable tablespace operation, the next step is to have the related datafile(s) copied to the target platform, but in this case, it is not possible, as these are two different platforms. So there it is when RMAN comes to the rescue. The goal of RMAN is to transform the endianess from the source OS to the target OS, and this operation can take place either at the source or at the target platform.

```
# Conversion on a Windows source host to a Solaris destination file.

CONVERT TABLESPACE my_tablespace
  TO PLATFORM 'Solaris[tm] OE (32-bit)'
  FORMAT='C:\Oracle\Orastage\TransportSet\%U';

# Conversion on a Solaris destination host from a Windows source file.

CONVERT DATAFILE=
    '/Oracle/Orastage/TransportSet/SourceDatafile01.dbf',
    '/Oracle/Orastage/TransportSet/SourceDatafile02.dbf'
  FROM PLATFORM 'Microsoft Windows IA (32-bit)'
  DB_FILE_NAME_CONVERT
    '/Oracle/Orastage/TransportSet','/u01/oradata/TARGETDB';
```

Once this is done, just proceed with the regular metadata import operation, so the tablespace is adopted at the target database and the inter-platform transportable tablespace operation gets done.

```
[oracle@alpha ~]$ impdp system/oracle dumpfile=MIGRATETOUNIX.DMP
directory=DATA_PUMP_DIR trans
port_datafiles=/u01/oracle/oradata/gamma/MIGRATE_TO_UNIX_TS_01.DBF
Import: Release 11.1.0.6.0 - Production on Tuesday, 28 October, 2008
3:06:19
Copyright (c) 2003, 2007, Oracle.  All rights reserved.
Connected to: Oracle Database 11g Enterprise Edition Release 11.1.0.6.0 -
Production
With the Partitioning, OLAP, Data Mining and Real Application Testing
options
Master table "SYSTEM"."SYS_IMPORT_TRANSPORTABLE_01" successfully loaded/
unloaded
Starting "SYSTEM"."SYS_IMPORT_TRANSPORTABLE_01":  system/********
dumpfile=MIGRATETOLINUX.DMP di
rectory=DATA_PUMP_DIR transport_datafiles=/u01/oracle/oradata/gamma/
MIGRATE_TO_UNIX_TS_01.DBF
Processing object type TRANSPORTABLE_EXPORT/PLUGTS_BLK
Processing object type TRANSPORTABLE_EXPORT/TABLE
Processing object type TRANSPORTABLE_EXPORT/TTE_POSTINST/PLUGTS_BLK
Job "SYSTEM"."SYS_IMPORT_TRANSPORTABLE_01" successfully completed at
03:06:39
```

Migrate to and from an ASM environment

RMAN is the only available method to migrate from and to ASM environments. ASM is an efficient and reliable storage mechanism that first appeared in 10g Rel. 1. There are two ways to backup an ASM environment, one is by means of a low level disk dump, which performs a complete raw device dump and does not allow the DBA to select individual storage structures such as tablespaces or datafiles; the other method is by means of Recovery Manager. Today, ASM seems pretty complex and abstract for several DBAs, but once it is setup and is up and working, it is seamless to work with it, and it is quite the same as if it was a regular storage unit with tablespaces and datafiles. The flash recovery area, redologs, backups, and datafiles live in there and are managed just like any other regular database file.

The database could have been created in an ASM environment since the very beginning, but what about if this was not the case? Is there a means to move datafiles inside an ASM storage unit? Or is there a way to take a datafile out of an ASM environment and convert it into a regular datafile without recreating the physical structure. The answer is RMAN, which, by the way, is the only available method to backup and restore individual datafiles.

This code snippet performs the migration of not only a datafile, but also the whole database from a regular environment to an ASM storage unit. The commands are launched from an `rman` prompt:

```
# Start nomount to perform controlfile level operations.
STARTUP NOMOUNT;
# The controlfile is copied from its current position
# to the DiskGroup inside the +ASM instance
RESTORE CONTROLFILE FROM '/u01/oracle/oradata/orcl/control01.ctl';
# The database can be mounted now
ALTER DATABASE MOUNT;
# This operation will perform the database copy
# to the +DiskGroup destination
BACKUP AS COPY DATABASE FORMAT '+DiskGroup';
# This command updates the controlfile and declares
# that the official database files are those recently copied
SWITCH DATABASE TO COPY;
# Renames all redolog files to logfiles inside the ASM
# this command must be issued for each existing redo log file

SQL "ALTER DATABASE RENAME '/u01/oracle/oradata/rdo01.log' to
'+DiskGroup';
# This opens the database and creates a new redolog file set
# inside the ASM
ALTER DATABASE OPEN RESETLOGS;
```

```
# Don't forget about the temporary datafiles, rman doesn't
# manage the temporary datafiles, so the DBA must be aware
# of this prior to releasing the database to production.
# Finally get rid of the old temporary datafiles
SQL "ALTER TABLESPACE TEMP ADD TEMPFILE";
SQL "ALTER DATABASE TEMPFILE '/u01/oracle/oradata/temp01.dbf' DROP;
```

The old database files at the regular file system can now be removed. At this point the database has been migrated to the ASM environment. If the DBA wants to manage a hybrid environment, then it is possible to use the COPY command to manage individual database files.

General backup advices

As previously stated, no matter what, you must always have a valid backup. A backup is protection for a company's most valuable asset, its data. Throughout the years, I have heard thousands of Halloween tales related to loss of data. Some good advice is listed next. The following is not a complete set of best practices, and the DBA should always make sure to have a tested backup/recovery procedure to be efficient and effective in restoring data, in case of failure.

- Always check the backup output log.
- The validity of a backup should never be taken for granted.
- If possible, periodically use your backup to replicate the production environment on a test or development environment to verify it can be used to recover the production environment in case of failure.
- Watch out for scheduled backups that are synchronized with other file processing routines. More than one backup has been rendered corrupt after a batch zip assumed it had ended at a specified pont in time. If the backup is to be processed further, then the Oracle 10g/11g scheduling mechanism should be used, this allows the DBA to create asynchronous tasks and program OS activities.
- Before any major change or any maintenance task that compromises data, a backup should be performed.
- Periodically verify that the recovery procedures meet the maintenance windows agreed with the users.

- Never deploy a new application to a production environment unless it has been thoroughly tested in a development environment.

- Consider a replicated site, a data guard of some sort for your production environment, in case of failure at the primary site you'll always have a plan B where your production will continue uninterrupted.

- Create a scaled down copy of your production environment where you can put to the test all possible failure scenarios, it is very important to keep in good shape by practicing different recovery techniques and make sure that in case of a real failure you are prepared to apply the right recovery strategy in the least possible time.

- After each backup, make sure you have a doubled backup copy at a remote location; this will ensure that in case of site failure you can always have a second valid copy of your data.

- Keep the backup media stored in a physically safe place.

Summary

When the production data, the most company's valuable asset, is involved—checking the status of the backup procedures, verifying those will take back our database safe and sound, measuring both, time it takes and space it requires are some of the common tasks a DBA must perform.

Thinking today of the old, de facto deprecated, User Managed Backup concept is equivalent to taking our database back to the 7.3 prehistoric ages. Since Recovery Manager first appeared as a new feature back in 8.0, it has never stopped evolving. Release after release, Oracle has continuously developed new features, improving it and making it more user friendly. Starting with Oracle 9i, RMAN has introduced a set of new features that has turned this tool into the default choice to perform backup and recovery strategies. Oracle is always improving this tool and making it more efficient. Both in 10g and 11g there are several features oriented to make the backup and recovery session more productive, and more manageable.

It is an absolute must to make sure you have a valid procedure to bring back to life your database in case of failure, but it is equally important to know how to perform this procedure in the most efficient way. This chapter has focused more on the RMAN features that provide efficiency and manageability rather than on the command syntax. RMAN is a very extensive topic, and when addressing it there are never enough pages, but the chosen topics and the way they were explained here had the purpose of hopefully making you aware that there are always more efficient ways to perform must-do tasks.

5

Recovery Manager Restore and Recovery Techniques

Once a backup has been taken the second part of the process is to perform the restore or recover operation. This is an operation no one wants to have to undertake, but you must be prepared to do so if it is required. This chapter deals with the recovery tasks from the recovery manager point of view.

All the scenarios assume that you have a database in archivelog mode and a valid backup which was taken using recovery manager. The database used to perform the demonstrations is a regular general purpose database created with the DBCA. The scenarios are performed with the SYSDBA role because this role can manage the Oracle instance and it can perform incomplete recovery operations.

Oracle database recovery

There are two situations when a database recovery process will be required, one is after an instance failure, and the other is after a media failure. The recovery process takes information from the redo log files or the archivelog files as required and applies the changes found there against the datafiles. The applied changes depend on each individual datafile, and they range from the last applied change against the datafile to the last **System Change Number** (**SCN**) recorded at the control file.

The recovery process will read the transactions and it will apply all the recorded changes against the datafiles, the changes are from either committed or uncommitted transactions. During the first recovery phase all changes stored in either the archive log files or the redo log files are applied against the datafiles (this is known as rolling forward). During the second recovery phase all uncommitted transactions are rolled back. The recovery process ends when all the changes have been applied against the database files or if the DBA explicitly defined a point where the recovery process must stop, then the recovery process will end when the recovery manager reaches that point.

The `controlfile` is a critical file during the recovery process as this file contains the information that marks the transactional point the database must reach to perform a complete recovery process.

Instance failure

An instance failure happens when the database did not receive the last checkpoint before the instance was shutdown, leaving the datafiles in an inconsistent state. This can happen when a `SHUTDOWN ABORT` command is issued or when the host is abruptly shutdown after a power failure and there was no way to properly shutdown the database with a `SHUTDOWN NORMAL | IMMEDIATE | TRANSACTIONAL` command. At startup time Oracle realizes there is a difference between the SCN information stored in the controlfile and the SCN information recorded at the datafile headers. Once the difference has been stated the **System Monitor Background Process (SMON)** starts an automatic instance recovery process by reading the missing transactions from the redo log files and applying them against the datafiles requiring them. This process does not require DBA intervention and it does not require the database to be in **archivelog** mode. Once all the transactions have been applied the database is automatically opened by the instance.

Media failure

A media failure happens when a datafile gets corrupted or lost. This requires the DBA to take a valid backup and restore the missing datafile or datafiles to their original location (if possible) or to a different location. The last applied transaction found in the restored datafiles comes from the backup time, which most probably is far away from the range stored at the redo log files, so it is required to read the missing transactions from the `archivelog` files. At this point the startup process will be stopped thus letting the DBA know that a database recovery process is required.

 If the database is not in Archivelog mode then it is not possible to apply a database recovery process and in the best case scenario the only information that will be restored will be from the last valid offline backup time.

In the following image a recovery process takes place:

1. The first step restores the missing datafiles from a valid backup.

2. At this point all physical structures are available but there are missing changes, so a recovery process is required.

3. Once the process is finished the database is open.

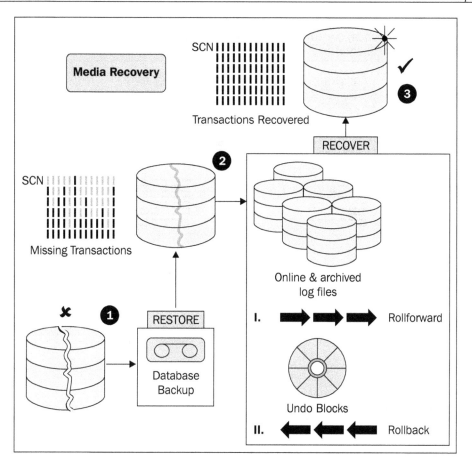

Complete recovery

The following image depicts the complete recovery process. In a complete recovery all pending changes are applied against the database files. The recovery goal is determined after the information stored in the `controlfile`.

1. In a complete recovery scenario only the missing or corrupt datafiles need to be restored.

2. The recovery process aims to recover the inconsistent datafiles.

3. Once the process is finished the database is open.

The log sequence number (the monotonically increasing number that counts the number of log switches) continues from the last sequence number.

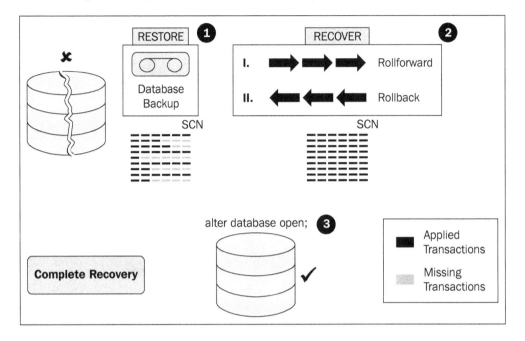

Incomplete recovery

In an incomplete recovery process the applied changes are behind the maximum change number recorded at the control file. The process requires the DBA to restore all data files (temporary files are not considered) from a valid backup. All other physical structures remain unchanged.

 Don't touch the `controlfile` and the redo log files as they identify the highest possible SCN to which the restore may be performed.

The process requires the DBA to define the recovery goal. This can be specified in terms of a timestamp, a System Change Number, or a specific log switch number. Once the recovery process has reached the recovery goal it is stopped and the database is opened with the RESETLOGS option. The log switch number is reset to 1 and it is recorded as a new database incarnation. The database changes that were made between the recovery goal and the last database SCN will be lost forever.

Before an incomplete recovery process takes place it is advisable to have a valid backup so you can rollback the scenario just in case things don't work as expected.

> In particular, some DBAs will make an additional copy of all online redo logs as these files store critical information used during recovery.

You must be aware that the control file contents are modified after the process is finished. You must have a control file backup so that the scenario can be restored to its initial state just as if nothing had happened.

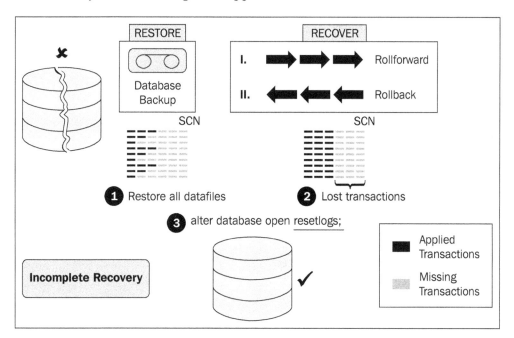

An incomplete recovery process is required when you want to take the database back to a point in time to undo a critical change that cannot be undone in any other way. It is also required if a missing archive log prevents a complete recovery from completing, or if a backup control file is used.

In RMAN there are three ways to define the target point in time for an incomplete recover, by means of the sequence log switch number, the SCN, or by time stamp.

Syntax	Description
UNTIL TIME = 'date string'	Specifies a time as an upper limit. RMAN selects only files that can be used to recover up to but not including the specified time.
UNTIL SCN = integer	Specifies an SCN as an upper limit. RMAN selects only files that can be used to recover up to but not including the specified SCN.
UNTIL SEQUENCE = integer THREAD = integer	Specifies a redo log sequence number and thread as an upper limit. RMAN selects only files that can be used to recover up to but not including the specified sequence number.
	The THREAD parameter makes sense in RAC environments.

The following examples are rman commands used to perform an incomplete recover:

Incomplete recover defined by timestamp:

```
RMAN> RESTORE DATABASE UNTIL TIME "TO_DATE('10/04/09','MM/DD/YY')";
```

Incomplete recover using a redo log switch number:

```
RUN{
    SET UNTIL SEQUENCE 9876 THREAD 1;
    RESTORE DATABASE;
    RECOVER DATABASE;  # recovers through log 9875
    ALTER DATABASE OPEN RESETLOGS;
    }
```

In this example an incomplete recover utilizes the SCN as the recovery
goal definition:

```
RUN{
    RESTORE DATABASE;
    RECOVER DATABASE UNTIL SCN 123456;  # recovers through SCN 123455
    ALTER DATABASE OPEN RESETLOGS;
}
```

Loss of data files

When a media loss occurs it can hit either critical or non-critical data files or a
combination of both. In the event of media loss several Oracle storage structures
may be compromised, this includes redo log files, control files and temporary files
also. Non critical database files are all database file except those that belong to the
SYSTEM, SYSAUX, and UNDO tablespaces. The critical data files are those that belong to
the SYSTEM, SYSAUX, and UNDO tablespaces. The procedure to recover from a loss of
datafiles, either critical or non-critical is quite the same, the difference comes after the
database possibility to be open with the damaged data files offline and perform the
recovery process when the database is open.

Queries used to diagnose data files

There are two basic queries that are frequently used to diagnose problematic data
files. The first one is used to display the information in the data file header. The
second one is used to display the data files requiring to be recovered.

Datafile Header: The data file header stores vital information used by the SMON
background process at start-up time to determine if the data file is consistent or
not. This information includes the SCN. If the database received its last checkpoint
before the Oracle instance was shutdown then the SCN will be consistent, otherwise
the SCN won't match that stored in the control file and this will alert SMON. By
querying the datafile header you will know if the datafile is or is not consistent. The
following query is used to query the datafile header:

```
col FILE_NAME for a45
col TIMESTAMP for a9
col FILE#     for 9999

select D.FILE#,
       D.NAME   FILE_NAME,
       H.CHECKPOINT_CHANGE#,
```

```
        to_char( H.CHECKPOINT_TIME, 'HH24:MI:SS') TIMESTAMP
from    V$DATAFILE D, V$DATAFILE_HEADER H
where   D.FILE# = H.FILE# ;
```

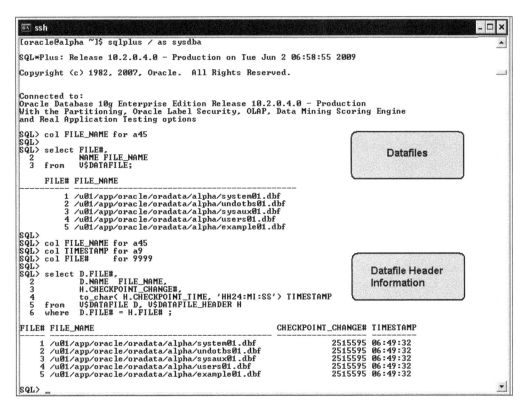

Recover File: The inconsistent datafiles are reported at the V$RECOVER_FILE dynamic view. It is important to query this view since at startup time, after SMON has determined that there are data files that required to be manually recovered, a message will be displayed showing only the first inconsistent data file. The complete list of inconsistent data files is shown with the following query:

```
col FILE#     for 9999
col FILE_NAME for a45
col ERROR     for a25

select D.FILE#,
       D.NAME    FILE_NAME,
       R.ERROR
from    V$RECOVER_FILE R, V$DATAFILE D
where   R.FILE# = D.FILE#;
```

```
ssh Packt - ssh oracle@alphasrv                                    _ □ ✕

SQL> col FILE#      for 9999
SQL> col FILE_NAME for a45
SQL> col ERROR      for a25
SQL>
SQL> select D.FILE#,
  2          D.NAME    FILE_NAME,
  3          R.ERROR
  4    from   U$RECOVER_FILE R, U$DATAFILE D
  5    where  R.FILE# = D.FILE#;

FILE# FILE_NAME                                     ERROR
----- --------------------------------------------- -------------------------
    4 /u01/app/oracle/oradata/alpha/users01.dbf     FILE NOT FOUND
    5 /u01/app/oracle/oradata/alpha/example01.dbf   FILE NOT FOUND

SQL>
```

Loss of a non-critical datafile

From the Oracle perspective a non critical file is a file that does not prevent the database from being opened if it is taken off line. Certainly, the DBA must assess how critical a datafile is from the business' perspective. However, technically speaking Oracle can be operational if a non-critical datafile is damaged.

When a non-critical datafile is missing, the procedure to bring back the database to the open state and fully recovered is as follows:

1. Try to open the database. As at least one datafile is missing the Oracle instance won't open the database and an error will be displayed.

2. Identify the missing data files.

3. Proceed to restore the previously identified data files from a valid backup.

4. At this point it is up to the DBA to put offline the restored datafiles and open the database or just proceed to the recover process

5. Recover the datafile or datafiles.

6. If the database was open before the recover process was executed on the problematic data files then just put online the recovered data files. Otherwise, if the database was left in a mount state then proceed to open the database once the recover process is finished.

In the following scenario, a non-critical datafile has been lost. Two datafiles belonging to the USERS and EXAMPLE tablespaces are deleted on purpose. This will create an error at startup time. When a datafile is missing, only the first missing datafile is reported in the SQL prompt. So, we need to find out the complete list of missing datafiles. A query is issued to find all problematic datafiles.

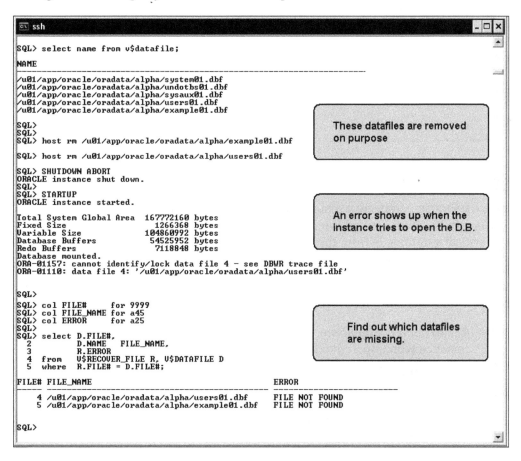

A recovery manager session is opened to proceed with the recovery process. This will show that there are two non-critical datafiles missing, so the recovery process can take place while the database is open.

A new rman session is started. rman is directed to restore the missing data files from the backup media. As these data files are not critical for the database to be open the datafiles are set offline, the database is open and the recovery process can take place while the database is in a productive state. Then rman determines which one is a suitable backupset for the restore and recovery operations.

You must remember that critical and non-critical is an adjective qualified from the Oracle perspective, not from the production environment point of view, so you must assess if you can afford to partially enter into production with the remaining data structures.

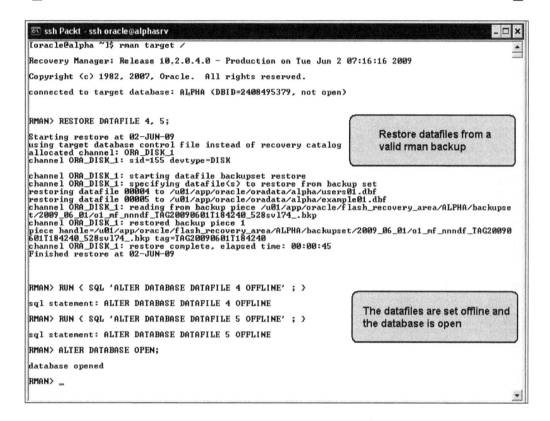

At this point, the database has entered into production, the users can start opening sessions in the database. The recovery process takes place at this point. It is enough to issue the recover command from the `rman` prompt. The recover process takes place only at the datafile level, it points to the specific datafiles that are offline.

In the image the RESTORE procedure is shown, it is not a requirement to open the database. You only have to put the missing datafiles offline. The missing datafiles can be restored and recovered after the database is open.

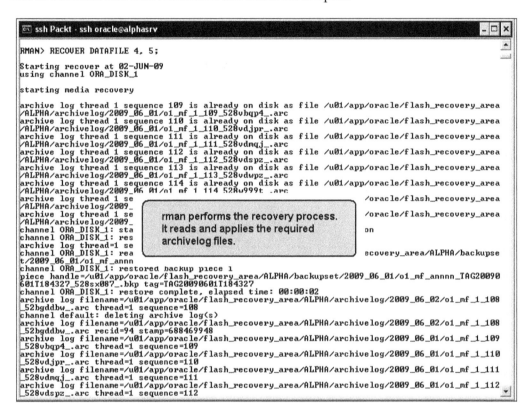

The last step in this recovery process is to put back online the recovered datafiles:

```
SQL> ALTER DATABASE DATAFILE 4 ONLINE;

SQL> ALTER DATABASE DATAFILE 5 ONLINE;
```

In the next image the datafiles are set online and the status is verified from the V$DATAFILE_HEADER dynamic view. There it can be seen that there are no more datafiles listed in the V$RECOVER_FILE view, this means all missing datafiles have been recovered and there are no further recover actions to be performed.

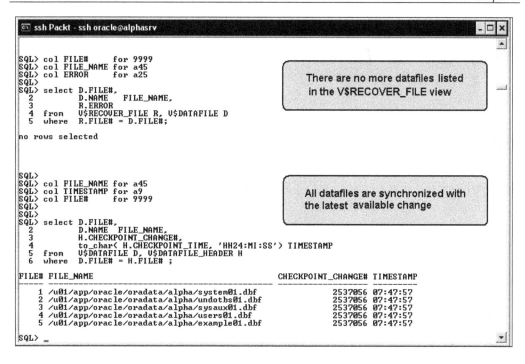

Loss of a temporary datafile

Temporary tablespaces are never backed up. They are not considered as part of a backup strategy. A temporary datafile can always be recreated if required. Its information is not considered critical for database recovery purposes.

Starting 10g Rel. 2 at database open time Oracle automatically rebuilds the missing temporary datafiles.

In the following scenario, the user used for demonstration purposes is SYS connected as SYSDBA. The temporary datafile configuration is that of the default database created with the DBCA assistant.

Originally, the datafile is physically located in the directory reported by the V$TEMPFILE dynamic view (**A**). A query explicitly requiring sort segments is issued (**B**). In the middle of the sort operation from another OS session the temporary datafile is physically removed and some errors are displayed on the screen letting the user know that some temporary datafiles are missing (**C**).

If the temporary datafile is lost then the database operations requiring temporary segments will be interrupted and an ORA-01565 and ORA-27037 errors will be displayed.

It is confirmed that the file has been physically removed from the file system (**D**).

The datafile belonging to the temporary tablespace TEMP is lost. In this scenario it is enough to bounce the Oracle instance for this issue to be corrected. Oracle automatically recreates the missing temporary datafile at startup time (**E**). This can be confirmed by taking a look at the file system. The temporary datafile has been recreated at its original location (**F**).

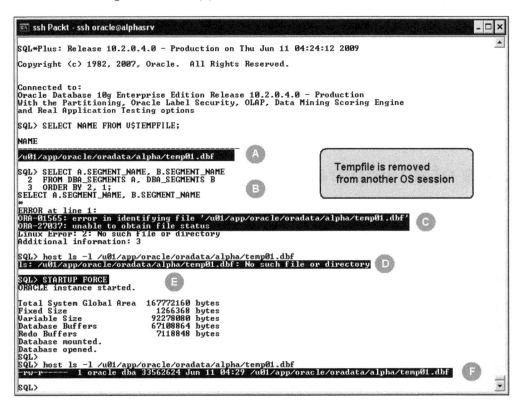

Managing temporary datafiles

In the previous scenario the database was shutdown to force the temporary datafile creation at startup time. This means that the database's availability was compromised while the shutdown or startup procedure took place.

In the following scenario it was not needed to restart the database. It was enough to simply create a new temporary datafile (**G**) and get rid of the lost datafile definition (**H**).

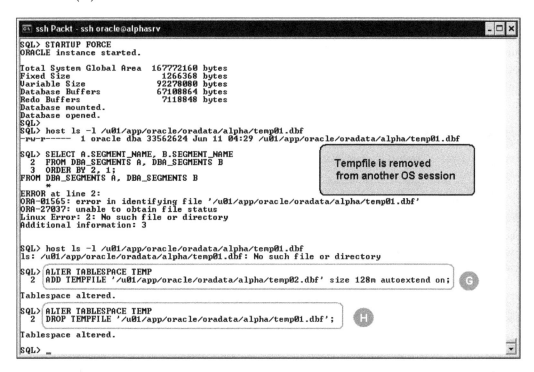

Loss of a critical datafile

The critical datafiles must be online in order for the oracle instance to be able to open the database. If a critical datafile is lost then a recovery operation must be performed so the database can be opened.

When a critical database file is lost, the procedure to bring the database back to business is as follows:

1. Try to open the database, the procedure will stop the database at the mount point and the error message will show the missing datafile or datafiles.

2. Verify at the V$RECOVER_FILE how many other datafiles are missing besides the one reported in the previous error.

3. Issue the restore command. This will restore the correct datafile from the backup media.

4. As the database won't allow the datafile to be set offline a recover operation must take place.

Once the complete recovery process is finished, to alter the database status so it gets to the open state. At this point the recovery process is finished and the database is taken back to its production state.

In the next example three critical datafiles are lost. For demonstration purposes the datafiles belonging to the SYSTEM, SYSAUX and UNDO tablespace were deleted on purpose. When the DBA tries to open the database an ORA-01157 error is displayed letting the DBA know that there is a problem with datafile 1. This is not the only datafile missing, so a query against the V$RECOVER_FILE view is required to find out how many other datafiles are missing.

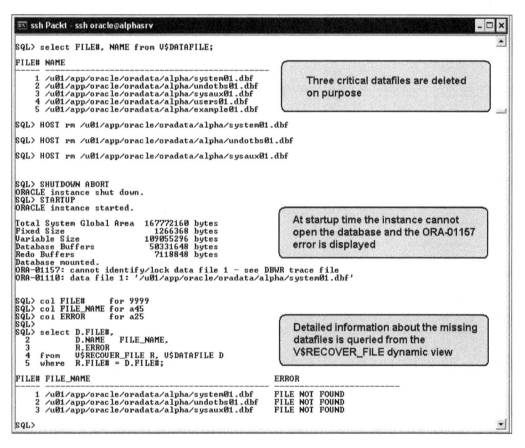

A look at the related `alert<SID>.log` file, will show information about the missing datafiles too.

```
ALTER DATABASE OPEN

Tue Jun  2 10:13:05 2009
Errors in file /u01/app/oracle/admin/alpha/bdump/alpha_dbw0_28543.trc:
ORA-01157: cannot identify/lock data file 1 - see DBWR trace file
ORA-01110: data file 1: '/u01/app/oracle/oradata/alpha/system01.dbf'
ORA-27037: unable to obtain file status
Linux Error: 2: No such file or directory
Additional information: 3

Tue Jun  2 10:13:05 2009
Errors in file /u01/app/oracle/admin/alpha/bdump/alpha_dbw0_28543.trc:
ORA-01157: cannot identify/lock data file 2 - see DBWR trace file
ORA-01110: data file 2:   '/u01/app/oracle/oradata/alpha/undotbs01.
dbf'
ORA-27037: unable to obtain file status
Linux Error: 2: No such file or directory
Additional information: 3

Tue Jun  2 10:13:05 2009
Errors in file /u01/app/oracle/admin/alpha/bdump/alpha_dbw0_28543.trc:
ORA-01157: cannot identify/lock data file 3 - see DBWR trace file
ORA-01110: data file 3: '/u01/app/oracle/oradata/alpha/sysaux01.dbf'
ORA-27037: unable to obtain file status
Linux Error: 2: No such file or directory
Additional information: 3
ORA-1157 signalled during: ALTER DATABASE OPEN...
```

Three critical datafiles are missing, so it is not possible to open the database unless these files are completely recovered.

A critical database file cannot be set offline, and the database cannot be opened until the datafile is completely recovered.

In this recovery scenario, rman performs the restore and the recovery operation of the missing datafiles. Once they are completely recovered the database is open and the recovery process finishes.

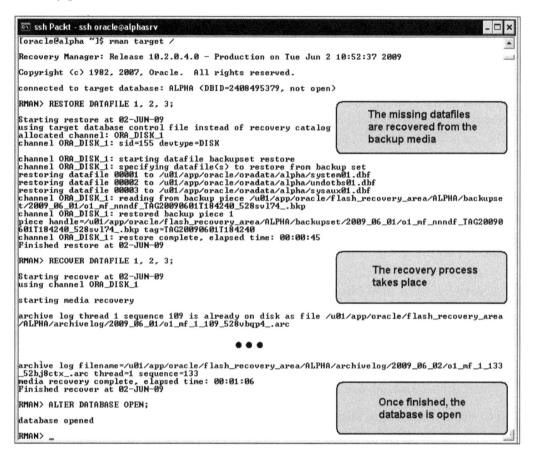

Loss of redo log files

The redo log files are written by the background process **Log Writer** (**LGWR**) with the information stored at the log buffer. If the log files are not available the process gets stuck, the transactional activity in the database is frozen and an error message is written to the alert.log file (ORA-00313: open failed for members of log group ## of thread ##), as shown in the next screenshot.

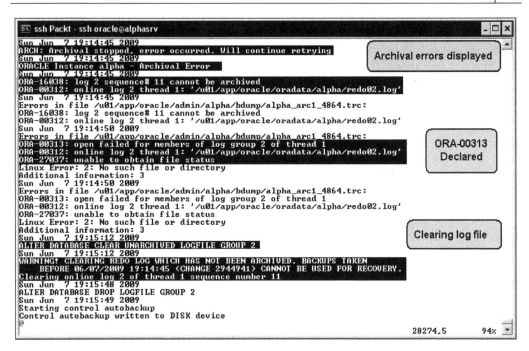

When a loss of redo log files occurs there are two different scenarios which depend on the status of the lost redo log. If the lost redo log had the status of inactive it is not critical. It is just enough to logically remove the group and rebuild it. On the other hand, if the status of the lost redo log file was CURRENT, then the situation may get complicated as the CURRENT status means the redo log was at that time written by the LGWR process, and the **DB Writer (DBWR)** process had not yet synchronized the datafiles by writing the dirty blocks from the DB buffer cache to the datafiles.

The query used to monitor the redo logs is:

```
col GROUP# for 99999
col STATUS for A8
col MEMBER for A40

select    F.GROUP#,
          SEQUENCE#,
          L.STATUS,
          MEMBER
from      V$LOGFILE F, V$LOG L
where     F.GROUP# = L.GROUP#
order by GROUP#
/
```

These scenarios are detailed in the next sections.

Loss of the inactive redo log group

In this scenario, it is assumed that there are three redo log groups with no multiplexed members. The loss of an inactive redo log group means all the available members of an inactive group are lost or corrupt.

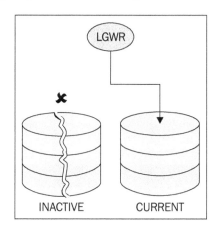

The problem will be noticed when the LGWR tries to perform the log switch and it tries to make the broken redo log group **CURRENT**. The redo log group does not physically exist, so the transactional activity is frozen and an error starts to show up in the alert.log file.

```
ORA-00313: open failed for members of log group 1 of thread 1
ORA-00312: online log 1 thread 1: '/u01/app/oracle/oradata/alpha/
redo01.log'
ORA-27037: unable to obtain file status
Linux Error: 2: No such file or directory
Additional information: 3
logfile 1 open failed:313
*** 2009-06-03 05:40:23.138 21373 kcrr.c
```

The missing redo log group makes the database stop all transactional activity until the redo log group gets cleared. The redo log group cannot be archived, so the information previously stored there will be lost. The command issued to clear the redo log group is:

```
SQL> ALTER DATABASE CLEAR UNARCHIVED LOGFILE GROUP 1;
```

The number evidently depends on the log group number reported in the `alert.log` file. After the command has been issued, Oracle automatically recreates the redo log file and it continues as if nothing has happened. You don't need to shutdown and re-open the database, and the normal users activity is resumed.

 You must be aware that since the `CLEAR UNARCHIVED` option was issued an archived log file is missing, thus creating a gap. You must perform a complete backup as soon as possible. Otherwise you will face an incomplete recovery scenario due to missing archivelog files.

Loss of the current redo log group

This scenario is similar to the previous one. The main difference here is that the lost redo log is the one marked as CURRENT. This is a very serious situation as this means the information that was currently being written by the LGWR is lost, the changes were not written to the archivelog destination yet and there is no way this can be retrieved elsewhere. In this scenario you will face an incomplete recovery situation and you will loose the data stored at that time in the current redo log group.

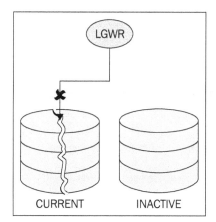

In the case of the loss of the current redo log, the procedure involves an incomplete recover scenario. You should be aware that all the changes recorded in the redo log do not longer exist, they used to be at the redo log buffer, and they were flushed when the entries were written to this redo log file.

In the following scenario there were several transactions applied against the database. After the commit is confirmed, all the changes are recorded at the **CURRENT** redo log group. The **CURRENT** redo log group is lost. At this point an incomplete recovery takes place. There may still be transactional activity at the database, but sooner or later all the transactional activity will be frozen.

Once the database is not able to handle any more transactions all transactional activity will be stuck until the situation that prevents the redo entries from being stored in the redo log files is corrected. In the meantime all attempts to login to the database will be greeted with this error message:

```
[oracle@alpha ~]$ sqlplus scott/tiger
SQL*Plus: Release 10.2.0.4.0 - Production on Fri Jun 5 23:48:09 2009
Copyright (c) 1982, 2007, Oracle.  All Rights Reserved.
ERROR:
ORA-00257: archiver error. Connect internal only, until freed.
Enter user-name:
```

 At this point the first reaction the DBA may have is to shut down the instance. In this kind of scenario this will lead to a definite loss of data.

In the following scenario the CURRENT redo log file is lost after a high transactional activity.

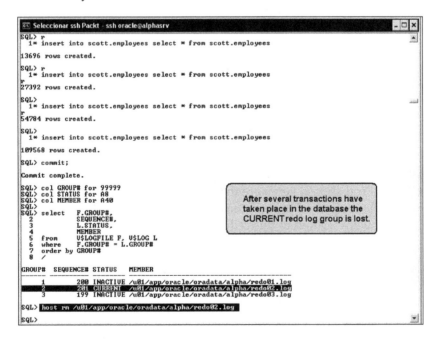

As soon as the database gets frozen and the ORA-00257 error is displayed the DBA performs a **shutdown abort** (**A**) against the database. When the DBA tries to open the database (**B**) the errors ORA-00313, ORA-312 and the error ORA-27037 are displayed; these errors mean that there is a missing redo log that contained information required to perform the instance recovery (**C**). By taking a look at the original directory where the redo log file was supposed to be found the DBA confirms that the redo log file has disappeared (**D**).

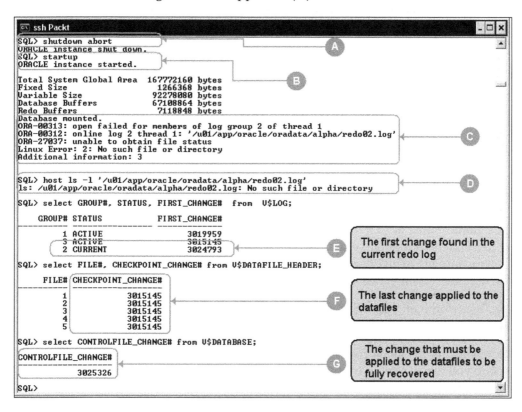

Three queries are performed to show why it is not possible to recover information and why the loss of a CURRENT redo log file implies an incomplete recovery operation. In the first query (**E**) the change number ranges are retrieved from the redo log files:

```
select  GROUP#,
        STATUS,
        FIRST_CHANGE#
from    V$LOG;
```

By the time the Oracle instance was shut down the change number recorded at the datafiles (**F**) so far can be retrieved with this query:

```
select FILE#,
CHECKPOINT_CHANGE#
from V$DATAFILE_HEADER;
```

There is a third query that finds out the last change the database should have to be considered consistent (**G**), this information is the change number recorded at the control file.

```
select CONTROLFILE_CHANGE#
from   V$DATABASE;
```

The following table describes the scenario faced by the database

Change Number	Value
Change Number from the `controlfile`	3025326
Change Number from the redo logs	3024793
Last Change applied against the datafiles	3015145

The datafiles must be at the change number 3025326, which was in the missing redo log file. Oracle cannot make up this information and there is no way to recover it, so an incomplete recovery process must be started by the DBA and all the changes stored in the missing redo log will be lost.

After an incomplete recovery you must get a full database backup as soon as possible. This will be your new restore point after the reset logs operation.

Before starting the incomplete recovery you must make sure you have a valid backup you can use to undo the incomplete recovery just in case something does not work as expected.

A `rman` session is started. The `rman` command shown in the following image performs three operations:

- Defines the point where the incomplete recovery process will be (**H**)
- Performs the restore operations (**I**)
- Performs the recovery process bound to the condition defined in the first bullet (**J**)

The `rman` code used to execute the recover process follows:

```
RUN{
    SET UNTIL SEQUENCE=201;
    RESTORE DATABASE;
    RECOVER DATABASE;
    }
```

The first clause defines the point where the recovery manager process will be stopped (**201**), which is the redo log number of the lost log file. The second clause performs the restore operation (all datafile) and the last clause will execute the recover process bound to the constraint defined in the first clause.

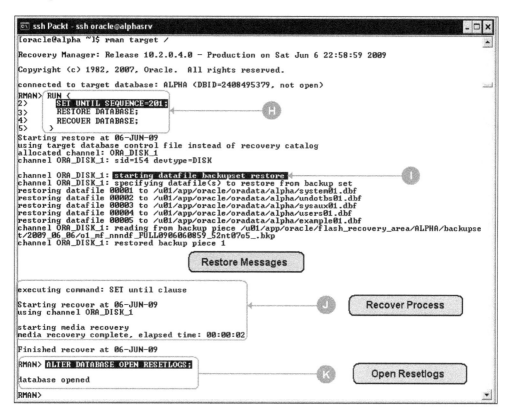

Once the process has finished an ALTER DATABASE OPEN RESETLOGS command is issued, this resets the log switch number to 1 and it starts a new database incarnation.

When the incomplete recover process has finished you must take a full database backup as soon as possible, this will be your lifeboat in case something happens shortly after resetting the log sequence.

Test restore

A production environment cannot be conceived without a backup policy. Not having a backup compromises overall productivity directly or indirectly related to the database. It is pretty evident that your job and that of the people responsible for the operation will be compromised as well. Performing a backup is a must do task in all production environments, but testing the backup doesn't seem to be as important for some corporations. Testing a backup is as important as performing the backup itself.

A useless backup is equivalent to not having a backup at all. At the least, it wastes time that could have been used to formulate alternate strategies.

When asked about a backup policy most declare they have one implemented. On the other hand, when asked about a test policy, very few hands are raised. Then, what is the acid test for every backup? Most of the times the answer is: it is required after a real life failure scenario. The reason why most people don't implement a test policy is because of a lack of resources. It is very difficult for some companies to have a duplicated environment to test the backup each time a new backup is taken. The `rman` test restore feature is a convenient way to validate the backup will work as expected when needed. The test restore `rman` command performs the restore cycle without actually restoring the database

In the following scenario a retention policy of three redundant backups is defined. A test restore is performed against each backupset.

The command issued to test each backupset is:

```
RESTORE VALIDATE DATABASE FROM TAG='Tag name';
```

If the backup is valid then it will show a **validation complete** message.

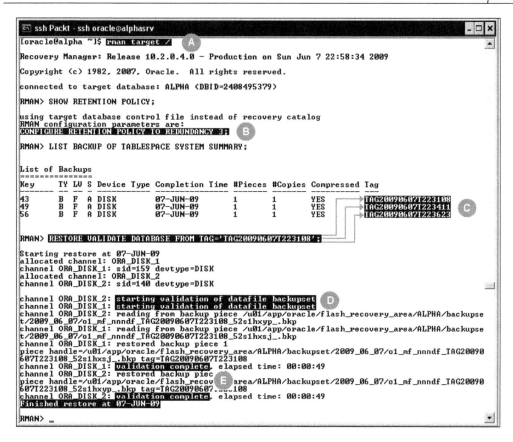

Once an `rman` session is started (**A**) the retention policy is displayed (**B**) as well as the backup summary information (**C**). The test backup is performed against each backupset. The outcome from the first backup test shows the message **starting validation of datafile backupset** (**D**). `rman` will read the backupset and will simulate a database restore operation. Once the process is finished it shows the **validation complete** (**E**) message. This means the backup is sound, and it is considered valid for recovery purposes. The complete test for each backupset is not shown in the image, but it is enough to replace the tag name in the restore command.

Crosscheck command

The crosscheck command is used to validate the physical backup is located where rman thinks it is. `rman` stores the backup information either in the `controlfile` or in the `rman` repository. If a restore operation needs to be carried out, `rman` determines the best suitable backupset and archivelog files required to successfully perform the recover process. If the backup is not where it is supposed to be then there will be problems.

In the following scenario `rman` validates the backup sets:

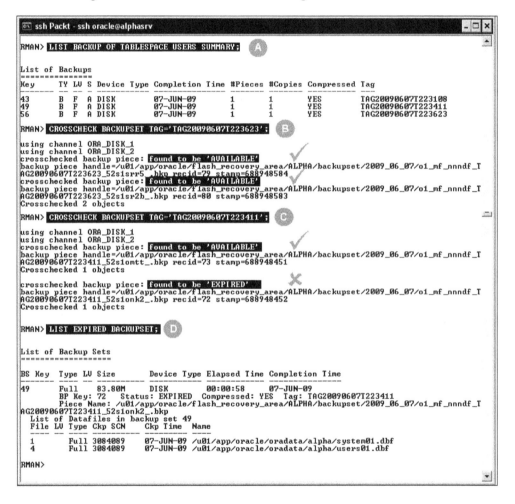

There are three backupsets, this can be queried using the LIST BACKUP command (**A**):

```
LIST BACKUP OF TABLESPACE USERS SUMMARY;
```

This is only to find out the backupset tag where a particular tablespace was stored. Afterwards, the CROSSCHECK command is issued against a particular backupset (**B**). In the first case the validation was successful for all backup pieces involved (all backup pieces were marked as **AVAILABLE**).

```
CROSSCHECK BACKUPSET TAG='Tag Name';
```

On the second execution of the CROSSCHECK command, a backup piece is missing, so it doesn't pass the CROSSCHECK test and it is marked as **EXPIRED** (**C**).

A final query is issued to find out which tablespaces are compromised after the EXPIRED backup pieces.

Nologging considerations

The nologging option is advantageous from the performance perspective, but from the recover perspective if it is not properly managed this will lead to sever errors. Nologging means no changes are recorded in the redo log files, so there is no way the information can be retrieved from the redo or archive mechanism in case of need.

In the following scenario an index is created using the **NOLOGGING** option.

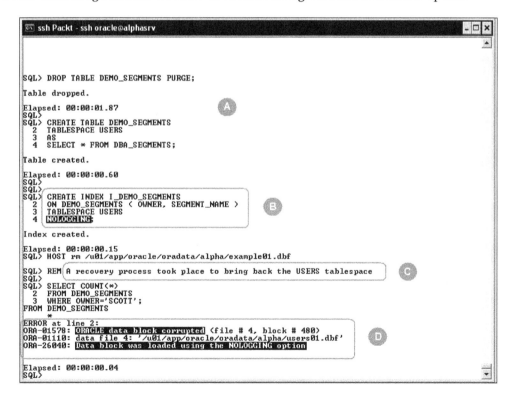

The first step prepares the scenario. A demonstration table is created. It uses a conventional path to create the table using a **Create Table As Select (CTAS)** syntax (**A**). Then the index is created (**B**), this command utilizes the NOLOGGING clause. This will only record information about the object creation. Data dictionary information is always recorded, but it won't record the changes on the data blocks, thus provoking data corruption.

An error is created on purpose (**C**). The datafile related to the **USERS** tablespace is removed, thus requiring a recovery process to be started. The commands issued to bring back the USERS tablespace are regular rman commands:

```
RUN{
    SQL 'ALTER TABLESPACE USERS ONLINE' ;
    RESTORE TABLESPACE USERS;
    RECOVER TABLESPACE USERS;
    SQL 'ALTER TABLESPACE USERS ONLINE' ;
    }
```

Once the process has finished, a query against the demonstration table is issued. According to the execution plan this query utilizes the index, not the table.

Query:

```
SELECT COUNT(*)
FROM DEMO_SEGMENTS
WHERE OWNER='SCOTT';
Execution Plan:
SELECT STATEMENT
    SORT AGGREGATE
            INDEX RANGE SCAN (I_DEMO_SEGMENTS)
```

The I_DEMO_SEGMENTS index was created using the NOLOGGING clause and it was at the recently recovered USERS tablespace. As no other precautions were taken, the index is rendered corrupt.

The error displayed is:

```
ORA-01578: ORACLE data block corrupted (file # 4, block # 480)
ORA-01110: data file 4: '/u01/app/oracle/oradata/alpha/users01.dbf'
ORA-26040: Data block was loaded using the NOLOGGING option
```

These errors are apparently due to a corrupt block. This is not the result of a physical corruption, but a data block that was loaded using the NOLOGGING option (ORA-26040). The recover process tried to recreate the index but as it had no data stored in the recover structures there was no way this task could successfully insert data into the index, even though rman reported a successful recover process (it was successful in terms of the available changes applied).

> Take a backup after a NOLOGGING statement or utility execution; otherwise your data will be corrupted after a recover operation.

Summary

The restore operation may take place under several conditions, such as the accidental loss of datafiles, media failure or a complete host failure, just to name a few cases. The scenario may end up in a loss of a critical or non-critical datafiles, a loss of the redo log (current or inactive), or a combination of such scenarios. You must always be prepared to face whatever critical situation comes up.

There are some pieces of advice you should keep in mind; practice the use of recovery manager, and get familiar with the syntax. Even if you have an application built on top of rman to perform the backup or recover operations you must know the nuts and bolts that make it work. Build a database that represents your production environment and practice different recovery scenarios on it, this will keep your recovery skills sharp and ready to be used any time.

Most botched recoveries can be attributed to human error. Make sure your backups are valid and usable. Consider including a test backup policy in your production environment. If you are using a tape to store your backups ensure your devices are periodically maintained and keep track of the used tapes. When planning your backup strategies keep in mind the *Safety First* principle and never take anything for granted. There are thousands of horror tales related to backup systems and failed recover scenarios.

The next chapter will address session management. It will guide the reader on how to diagnose, troubleshoot, and monitor sessions. Database sessions are what keep the database moving.

6
Session Management

Previous chapters have focused on using a single utility to improve your data management. This chapter will be slightly different. Here, we will look at several different tools and techniques for managing sessions in the database.

Users are very important to a DBA in many ways, but first they are the reason why there is need for a DBA. Users (either real or their electronic counterparts) are what keep the database in motion. Managing sessions means the DBA must monitor, tune and troubleshoot the entire outstanding user's activity in the oracle instance. We have different faces of database activity throughout the day, and over weeks, months, and years. It looks like the same data behaving differently throughout a given period, so there will be moments when the database is reported to be *slow*, there will be times when the database apparently will *hang*, and there will be other times when the database's performance will look *normal* from the user's perspective. What is the reason why the database's performance changes?

Monitoring, diagnosing, and troubleshooting sessions involve several tools and techniques; specific sections of Enterprise Manager are focused on session management, as we will see throughout this chapter. The exposed tools behave the same on Unix like and Windows environments; except the troubleshooting last resource, killing the session, which has specific behaviors on Windows platforms due to the specific architecture implementation, and we will have to deal with it by using the orakill tool.

In this context the user session can either be a session generated by a real user or by a program directed to perform some activity against the database. This session can be connected either in dedicated or shared mode.

User sessions in a dedicated server architecture

When a user requests a remote connection to the database it must first contact the listener. The listener redirects the request to the Oracle Instance. This will spawn a new Oracle Server Process, which from now on will be the process who will interface the user with the database; if the connection to the database is local to the machine, it may be established across the network or by **Inter-Process Communication (IPC)**, and the Oracle server process will be spawned too. This Oracle server process will be assigned to the user for the whole time the user remains attached to the database. The new user session will be assigned a Serial Number and a Session Id. These are the numbers used to uniquely identify a user connected to the database. The serial number guarantees that session-level commands are applied to the correct session objects in case a new session is started with the same SID. A user session can be initially monitored with the V$SESSION dynamic view.

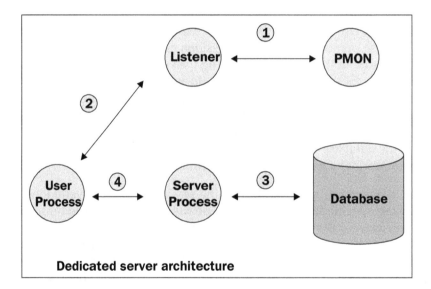

Dedicated server architecture

The **PMON** background process registers the Oracle instance against the **Listener** (in a self registration configuration), **PMON** registers information about dedicated server processes with the **Listener**. A **User Process** starts a connection against the Oracle instance by looking for the **Listener**, the **Listener** redirects the user process to the oracle **Server Process** and the dialog will be conducted from now on between the oracle server process and the user process. For each active connection in a **Dedicated Server Architecture** there will be one oracle **Server Process** on the host machine.

The connection through a dedicated server is the most widely used connection mode in most Oracle databases.

Instance self registration process

Starting with Oracle 8i, Oracle introduced the instance self registration process. This allows a running instance to contact the local listener and register itself against it. This mechanism is a convenient way to simplify listener configuration.

Assuming the listener is started prior to the Oracle instance, PMON will look for the listener located on the default 1521 port. In a few seconds the listener will have acknowledged the Oracle instance and it will be able to contact users with the Oracle instance. If the listener is not configured to listen on its default 1521 port then the LOCAL_LISTENER parameter must explicitly specify where the local listener is.

To do this, create a new entry in the tnsnames.ora file; this entry specifies the listener address. Set the value of the LOCAL_LISTENER instance parameter to that of the previously declared entry.

tnsnames.ora file entry:

```
LISTENER1525 =
    (DESCRIPTION =
            (ADDRESS_LIST =
                    (ADDRESS =
                            (PROTOCOL = TCP)
                            (HOST = HostName)
                            (PORT = 1525)
                    )
            )
    )
```

LOCAL_LISTENER instance parameter:

LOCAL_LISTENER = LISTENER1525

Define the INSTANCE_NAME and SERVICE_NAMES parameter in the server parameter file (spfile).

```
instance_name = orcl
service_names = ( orcl.oracle.com, finance, payroll )
```

An oracle instance must have only one instance name, but it can have several service names.

The instance must be up and running for the listener to maintain its registration, as soon as it is shutdown the registration information is removed from the local listener. The instance doesn't require reaching the **Mount** state to start the registration process, it is enough to have it started.

Once it is configured the Oracle instance will take at most 60 seconds to register itself against the listener, after it has registered itself it will update its status every 10 minutes.

You can issue the `lsnrctl` services listener command to display the instance registration information. If everything is successful, then the user can reach the Oracle instance through the listener; else an **ORA-12514** error is displayed.

Blocking sessions

When two or more different sessions compete for the same row simultaneously, Oracle will immediately raise the lock enqueue mechanism, which lets one process at a time modify the row. The lock will be released once the transaction is finished (after a commit or rollback command is issued). The first process that takes the row locks it, meanwhile the other processes will have to wait. If this wait time is visible to the user then it can be misinterpreted as a slow performance problem.

Blocking sessions are issues that should be solved at the program level, but in the mean time it is the DBA's responsibility to detect them and fix them. A blocking session may be normal during production time, this is not the real problem. Oracle is prepared to queue sessions, the real problem begins when a session hangs and leaves the other session indefinitely waiting for the row lock to be released.

Blocking sessions can easily be detected with **Enterprise Manager**. Besides the intermittent phone calls the DBA will receive because of the sudden slow performance, the DBA can determine there are hung sessions by using the information shown by Enterprise Manager.

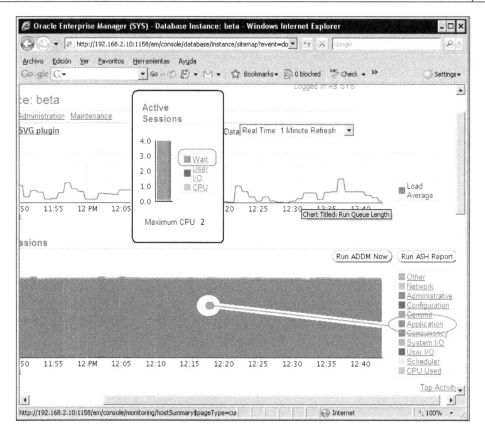

On the Enterprise Manager front page the **Active Sessions** graph can be seen. When looking at the performance tab, you will see that there are several sessions waiting and also what the session is waiting for. Here, the **Application** event is the most common outstanding event in the system. A lot of waits due to the **Application** event means that the currently running applications leave their sessions on the lock enqueue mechanism.

Clicking on the **Top Activity** link, will take the DBA to the processes details page. The reason why the system is slow is that there are several sessions waiting for the same row to be freed. The sessions may remain waiting there forever.

Optimistic versus pessimistic locking

Both optimistic and pessimistic locking will produce the same effect; the difference will be seen at the time the data is being locked.

Optimistic Locking: In optimistic locking data is not locked when it is selected, it is locked with subsequent update operations. Before locking the data rows it must be verified that nobody else has already locked them.

```
UPDATE
SET val1 = new_val1,
    val2 = new_val2,
...
WHERE key = key_value;
```

Pessimistic Locking: This means that data will be locked when it is selected to make sure nobody else updates it in between. The SELECT ... FOR UPDATE command uses the pessimistic locking.

Pessimistic locking requires a database session to be maintained between the SELECT and the UPDATE operations. In web applications it is not guaranteed that a database session is maintained, so optimistic locking must be used.

Row lock contention monitoring

Once a process locks a row or a set of rows, other processes are prevented from changing the data rows. Oracle's enqueue mechanism can be monitored from the Enterprise Manager **Active Session Waiting: Application** window.

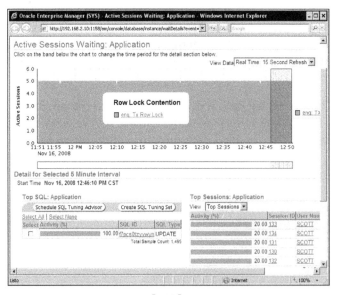

The culprit is discovered as **enq:Tx Row Lock Contention.** Meanwhile, the other processes just keep waiting. Now, it is time to correct this situation, either the user has to commit or rollback the pending transactions or the DBA will have to kill the user's session.

At the bottom of the page of the Enterprise Manager Performance Tab we find two links, one named **Blocking Sessions**, and a second one named **Hang Analysis**. Both can be used to monitor the blocking sessions; the first one is in character mode, and indented to show the session that caused the hang, meanwhile the Hang Analysis shows the hung sessions in graphic mode.

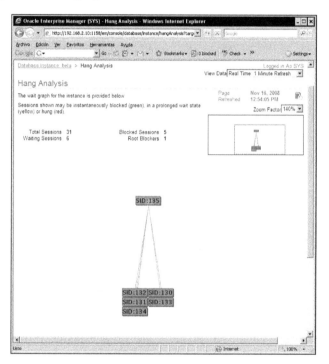

Looking at the graphical **Hang Analysis** tool it shows a graphical representation of the hung sessions. It shows the sessions in three colors; green, yellow, and red. Green is shown as soon as the blocking event is detected, and this status will remain for about 30 seconds, if the session remains blocked then it will change the status to prolonged wait (yellow), and if the event remains for another 30 seconds the status will be changed to hung (red).

Another convenient way to monitor the lock chain is the Blocking Sessions tool accessed from the OEM Performance page. Now let's take a look at the session details, to both evaluate the impact of the hung session and to proceed to kill the user session.

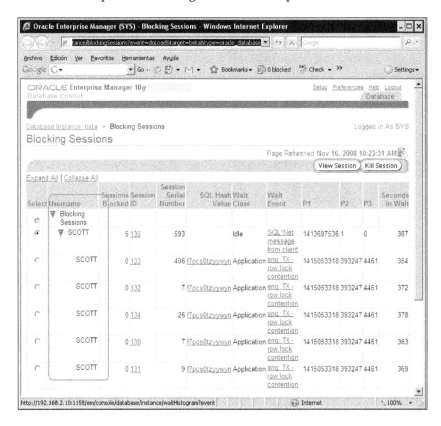

You can select the session to show its details either from the Hung Analysis or the Blocking Sessions. In this case you can click the **View Session** button. This will take you to the **session details** page, or you can directly proceed to kill the session. The session details will show you where the session comes from, when this was logged on the database, who the related OS user is, the name of the application that launched the session, and the reason why this session is maintained in a wait status.

If we are not successful in convincing the user to finish the transaction, then we'll have to kill the session. Once the session has been killed the PMON will issue a rollback action on behalf of the user and the locks held by the oracle server process will immediately be released.

When talking about users and sessions we regularly think of real users connected to the database from their applications. The real problem is that most of the modern applications use a three tiered architecture, and unless there is a means provided by the application to identify who the real user is and where it is connected from, the DBA cannot do much to phone the user and kindly ask him/her to finish the hung transaction.

On a three tiered architecture the problem is even worse. If the application tier doesn't provide a mechanism to detect and eliminate hung sessions, then in case of a connection failure between the application tier and the client tier, the database session may remain active and the locks might be held. If the user tries reconnecting it may attempt the same transactions against the same locked rows its last session left behind. This session will end up hung and the DBA will have to manually kill the blocking session.

Killing sessions

Enterprise Manager shows two options to get rid of a session, you must be aware of the behavior and the implications of the different options. When killing a session from enterprise manager, there are two options: **KILL IMMEDIATE** and **POST TRANSACTION**. On the first case the command issued is:

```
ALTER SYSTEM KILL SESSION 'SID,SERIAL#' IMMEDIATE;
```

And for the second option, the command issued is:

```
ALTER SYSTEM DISCONNECT SESSION 'SID,SERIAL#' POST_TRANSACTION;
```

When killing sessions in character mode there are more options:

```
ALTER SYSTEM KILL SESSION 'SID,SERIAL#' [IMMEDIATE];
```

KILL SESSION: This clause with no arguments instructs Oracle to terminate a session, rolls back any ongoing transactions and release locks, and it can partially recovery session resources. This marks the session status as KILLED, and this status remains until the user process issues any SQL command against the database. When this happens, the RDBMS replies with the **ORA-00028: your session has been killed** message and the session is definitely wiped off. If the session shows no further database activity, then the session may remain in **KILLED** status in the **V$SESSION** indefinitely until the client interacts with the database again.

IMMEDIATE: This option will mark the session as **KILLED** in the **V$SESSION** view. The difference between a regular **KILL SESSION** and an **IMMEDIATE KILL SESSION** is that this one will also leave the **KILLED** status for a while (about 30 seconds) then Oracle will definitely get rid of it. This option releases all session allocated resources. It rolls back pending transactions, and it will return control immediately. When a session is killed with the immediate option, it receives the **ORA-03113: end-of-file on communication channel** error message.

```
ALTER SYSTEM DISCONNECT SESSION 'SID,SERIAL#' [POST_TRANSACTION |
IMMEDIATE];
```

POST_TRANSACTION: This option leaves the user session alive, it allows the user to complete any transaction activity. As soon as the user issues either a commit or roll back command the session is disconnected.

IMMEDIATE: This simply kills the session. It releases all allocated session resources, sends the ORA-00028 error message to the user, and kills the Oracle server process. The **DISCONNECT IMMEDIATE** option behaves the same as the **KILL IMMEDIATE** option.

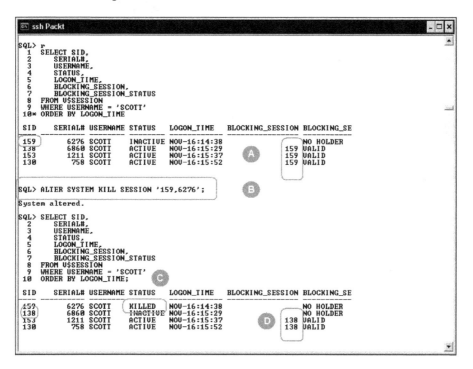

In the above image it can be seen there is a blocking session (**A**) whose SID is **159**, according to **V$SESSION** this is blocking three other sessions, **138**, **153**, and **130**. The DBA issues a simple **KILL SESSION** command (**B**), this kills the user session, but as there are no parameters specified to kill the session, the default behavior of this command will simply kill the session, the entry at the **V$SESSION** will remain there until somehow the oracle server detects some user activity so it can send the ORA-00028 error message. When monitoring the sessions, the **KILLED** status (**C**), as well as the new blocking session, session **138** (**D**), which was the next session in line on the enqueue mechanism, all killed sessions are reported in the alert<SID>.log file.

Deadlock handling

A deadlock occurs when two sessions competing for the same resources lock out one another while waiting for the resources to be released. Deadlock is an issue directly handled by Oracle; the DBA cannot do anything about it. As the root problem resides with the application logic, deadlock events should be reported to the development team.

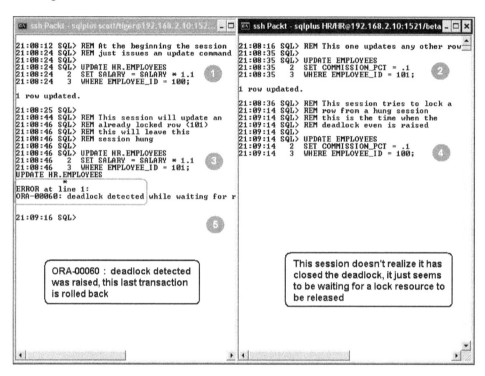

The above image shows the sequence that produces a Deadlock. All the time references of this particular example happened at 21 hours, so in the time reference will be shown in minutes/seconds.

1. At 08 minutes 24 seconds, the first session issues a transaction against a table.

2. At 08 minutes 35 seconds, the second session updates another row, different from the one chosen by the first session.

3. At 08 minutes 46 seconds, the first session tries to acquire a lock on the same row the second session is currently locking. The first session will be waiting for the lock on the row to be released, there is no error displayed on the screen so far.

4. At 09 minutes 14 seconds, the second session performs a transaction against the same row the first session originally locked, this closes the deadlock and an ORA-00060 error is raised on the first session. The second session doesn't realize this waits for the last resource to be released so it can continue its work. Oracle rolls back just the last transaction issued on the first session, hoping this session ends its current transaction.

5. Oracle's locking mechanism has prevented a deadlock to freeze both mutually locking transactions. This error is reported at the alert`<SID>.log` file, and a trace session file is also generated so the developers can analyze and correct the program logic to prevent this phenomenon from happening in the future.

Below is an excerpt from the `alert.log` file:

```
Sun Nov 16 21:07:07 2008
ORA-00060: Deadlock detected. More info in file /u01/oracle/admin/
beta/udump/beta_ora_21291.trc.
```

There it states that a secondary trace file details the recently detected deadlock problem. This trace file details the platform, the session where the deadlock was detected, the SQL command issued, and a warning message that reads:

```
The following deadlock is not an ORACLE error. It is a
deadlock due to user error in the design of an application
or from issuing incorrect ad-hoc SQL. The following
information may aid in determining the deadlock:
Deadlock graph:
```

Sniped sessions

Killing a hung session may be a good tactic, but it requires the DBA to constantly be monitoring the system or program a job that performs this task automatically. Another strategy could be to use the user profiles and declare a time out for a session. If a session ever issues a commit or roll back and if this is still alive, then the end user will perceive a "performance slow down", but it won't remain hung as previously shown. However, if the user never comes back, then there should be a mechanism that disconnects the user and wipes off its session.

When a profile time out is configured and a session exceeds its inactivity time, the session status is marked as SNIPED, this will hold this status until the user tries to issue any command against the oracle server, then the error message sent to the user is **ORA-02396: exceeded maximum idle time, please connect again**. As soon as a user session is marked as **SNIPED** the locks held by the user are released.

In the next example a user issues a transaction and holds the lock, when a second user tries to issue a transaction against the same row the first session has previously locked, it remains waiting for the resource to be released (**A**). We don't know when this will be, so a time out has previously been configured at the user's profile. Once its timeout has expired the session is marked as **SNIPED** (**B**) and the row control automatically goes to the next session waiting in line for the resource. As soon as the first session receives the ORA-02396 error message the session is definitely disconnected and it disappears from the V$SESSION view.

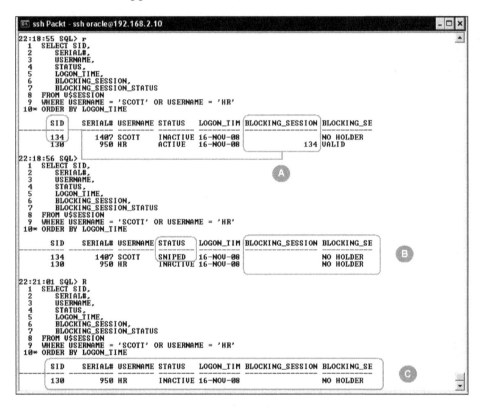

Now, what would happen if the original session never issues another command against the database? The SNIPED status would remain there indefinitely. If the DBA wants to completely wipe off the session from the V$SESSION view then they would need to kill the related OS process. It should be pointed out that killing an OS process means to kill the related Oracle Server Process, considering the user connected to the Oracle instance by means of a dedicated server process, and in Unix like environments this easily works as it is enough to identify the OS process and have it killed with a regular kill -9 OS command (this works for Unix like platforms only, Windows utilizes the orakill tool). This task can even be coded in a shell script and scheduled so it periodically checks and wipes off **SNIPED** sessions.

```
TEMPFILE=/tmp/$$.tmp
sqlplus system/system_password <<EOF
spool $TEMPFILE
select p.spid from v\$process p,v\$session s
where s.paddr=p.addr
and s.status='SNIPED';
spool off
EOF
for i in 'cat $TEMPFILE | grep "^0123456789"'
do
kill -9 $i
done
rm $TEMPFILE
```

Orakill

On Windows platforms the OS architecture is different; it works with threads. In Windows a process is defined as a container for address space and threads, the thread is the fundamental schedulable entity in the system. So there is no way to find a single Oracle server process at the OS in the way that we can on Unix like platforms, it simply doesn't exist as a session/OS process pair, the only process the DBA will find is a running `oracle.exe` process which embodies both the background and the user processes. A tool for Windows platforms to kill oracle processes from the OS prompt was specifically created by Oracle; the `orakill.exe` tool. In the next sequence a session has been marked as **SNIPED** on a Windows platform, and then the DBA may leave a task that periodically cleans up the **SNIPED** sessions.

```
Orakill Usage:  orakill sid thread
where sid    = the Oracle instance to target
thread = the thread id of the thread to kill
```

The `thread id` should be retrieved from the `spid` column of a query such as:

```
select spid, osuser, s.program from
v$process p, v$session s where p.addr=s.paddr
```

Orakill receives two arguments; the oracle instance name and the "OS PID". As Windows doesn't actually have a processes ID for the session process Oracle makes one up, and it can be queried from the `v$PROCESS` dynamic view. A kill SNIPED script is created, this queries the `v$PROCESS` view, takes the SPID, and it passes this value as argument to the `ORAKILL.exe` tool.

Let's assume some sessions remain SNIPED:

```
SQL> select username, sid, status from v$session
  2  where status='SNIPED';
USERNAME                              SID STATUS
------------------------------ ---------- --------
HR                                    132 SNIPED
HR                                    158 SNIPED
```

An SQL script to search and kill SNIPED session is created. This SQL script (killSniped.sql) is launched from an oracle session. This script dynamically creates several calls to the ORAKILL tool with the proper parameters.

```
store set sqlsettings.sql replace
set pagesize 0
set feedback off
set trimspool on
set termout off
set verify off
spool killSniped.bat
select 'orakill &1 '|| spid
from v$process p, v$session s, v$instance i
where p.addr=s.paddr
and s.status='SNIPED';
spool off
host killSniped
@sqlsettings
host del killSniped.bat
host del sqlsettings.sql
```

Launch killSniped from the OS:

```
C:\>sqlplus / as sysdba @killSniped orcl
C:\>orakill orcl 3340
Kill of thread id 3340 in instance orcl successfully signalled.
C:\>orakill orcl 2812
Kill of thread id 2812 in instance orcl successfully signalled.
```

You can check it from the `v$session`:

```
SQL> select username, sid, status from v$session
  2  where status='SNIPED';
no rows selected.
```

The SNIPED sessions have been wiped off.

Services

Services are the single most important tool available to perform instance consolidation. In this context, a service refers to the name by which a client can connect to the instance, this is configured by the `SERVICE_NAMES` instance parameter, and it defaults to `DB_UNIQUE_NAME.DB_DOMAIN` if defined.

Connecting through services in an RAC environment is useful to have shifted the service across instances depending on availability and scalability. Using services in a single instance is not frequently seen. Most DBA's configure the default service and even more, there are DBA's who simply ignore this parameter and configure connections to the database by means of TNS entries compatible with Oracle 8.0 using the Oracle SID instead of the Oracle Service.

In single instance environments sessions can be tuned by services. There are other session management tools like Resource Manager, which can provide different resource allocation emphasis based on the service the user defines to connect to the database, rather than the user itself.

In order to configure services in an Oracle environment, the dynamic `SERVICE_NAMES` instance parameter must be configured.

In this example the `SERVICE_NAMES` parameter has been configured so the instance can be reached by four different names:

```
SQL> SELECT VALUE FROM V$PARAMETER
  2  WHERE NAME = 'service_names';
VALUE
------------------------------------------------
beta, humanresources, sales, orders
```

From this point on each user will connect to the database by means of the following services: `beta`, `humanresources`, `sales`, or `orders`.

The listener has been configured to accept the services, which can be verified by means of the lsnrctl services command:

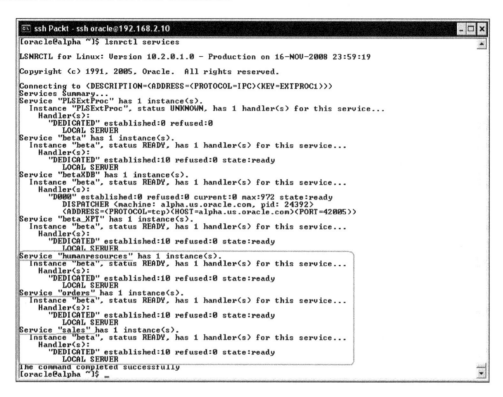

Each session can be connected by means of a different service name. In the next example we are connecting three different sessions, each one to a different service:

```
SQL> select sid, serial#, username, service_name
  2  from v$session
  3* where username in ('HR','SH','OE')
     SID    SERIAL# USERNAME   SERVICE_NAME
---------- ---------- ------   ---------------- --
     132      3713 OE         orders
     134      2210 HR         humanresources
     138      8125 SH         sales
```

Connecting users using services adds another identification dimension and allows the DBA to selectively allocate resources based on services. This can be achieved using Resource Manager.

Resource Manager

Resource Manager is a tool that provides the DBA more control over the resource allocation; this circumvents problems with inefficient OS resource allocation. The OS allocates CPU resources based on OS priorities, Oracle processes have the same priority against the OS scheduler, so it doesn't matter if you launch a CPU consuming task, this process may become a CPU hog. As a DBA there is nothing to do from the OS side as it is not advisable to change the process priority of any Oracle process.

Other problems that may be found at the OS level are:

- An excessive amount of context switching, resulting in an overhead when a high number of OS processes is found.

- Inefficient scheduling from the OS side: It may reschedule an Oracle server process while it holds latches, resulting in a reduction in the latch hit ratio.

- Inadequate resource allocation: This happens because from the OS point of view all processes are the same, and processes consuming a high amount of OS resources will be treated the same as any other process in the OS.

- The OS is not capable of controlling the degree of parallelism an Oracle process demands, resulting in an unbound resource allocation from a few processes that may create resource starvation for all the other concurrent process.

Resource Manager was created to address these issues, allowing the DBA to control specific Oracle resources from inside the instance; such as the degree of parallelism, the relative CPU consumption, the maximum amount of I/O, Undo resources, maximum number of sessions allowed to share a given resource, and execution and idle time.

Resource Manager Elements

Resource Manager comprises four main components:

1. Resource Consumer Group
2. Resource Plan
3. Resource Consumer Group Mapping
4. Resource Plan Directive

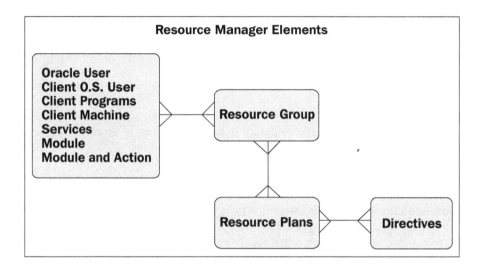

Element	Description
Resource Consumer Group	The group of users that share the same resource requirements.
Resource Plan	This is a plan that defines through directives how the instance resources will be allocated.
Resource Allocation Method	This is the policy or method used by Resource Manager to allocate resources. This is used by resource consumer groups and plans.
Resource Plan Directive	Directives are defined inside a Resource Plan and they define how resources are allocated to the individual resource consumer groups.
Resource Consumer Group Mapping	This defines the mapping between users and resources consumer groups.

At a given time a Resource Plan directs how resources are allocated.
The instance parameter used to define it is the dynamic RESOURCE_MANAGER_PLAN instance parameter.

`DBMS_RESOURCEMANGER` is the package used to administer, create and maintain the Resource Manager components. There are several data dictionary views where information about Resource Manager can be gathered.

Configuring resources assigned to users

You can map resources to database users, so that each user has a predetermined amount of resources allocated during its session. The steps to implement Resource Manager for database users are as follows.

- Create the database user and grant appropriate system and object privileges as required.

- Create the required Resource Consumer Groups.

- Map the users with the different Resource Consumer Groups. A user can belong to more than one Resource Consumer Group.

- Create the Resource Plans; each Resource Plan has different directives defined. The Resource Directives define how resources are allocated, they state the relative CPU emphasis, the active session pool with queuing, the degree of parallelism limit, the execution time limit, the undo pool and the idle time limit.

- Map the resources allocated to each Consumer Group through the Resource Plan directives.

- Once the Resource Manager infrastructure has been properly defined, use the `RESOURCE_MANAGER_PLAN` instance parameter to define which plan rules. You can use `DBMS_SCHEDULER` to define the time frame where a given Resource Plan is active.

This section only outlines the procedure to start allocating resources through Resource Manager to the database users. Most production applications don't work with database users, they rather use the application schema user as the only identifiable user in the database and it becomes difficult to find out who the real user is and the amount of resources to allocate to each user, a more practical approach in this case is to use the consumer group switching feature. The consumer group switching feature allows a user to change the consumer group it was originally attached at connect time to a different consumer group depending on its actual resource consumption profile. Another alternative to deal with this situation is to use the Resource Consumer Groups mapped to Services, which is described in more detail in the next section.

Configuring resources assigned to services

It was previously stated that Services introduce a new tuning dimension even in a single instance configuration. The procedure to allocate resources to database sessions connected to the Oracle instance through services is outlined next.

1. Create a database user and grant system and object privileges as required.
2. Define the different service names the instance uses to register against the listener configuring the SERVICE_NAMES instance parameter.
3. Verify the listener properly identifies all the service names associated to the Oracle instance.
4. Configure the tnsnames.ora entries that define which specific service will be used to get connected to the Oracle instance.
5. Create the Resource Consumer Groups.
6. Map the service names against the different Consumer Groups as required.
7. Create the Resource Plans and define the directives as required.
8. Define the value of the RESOUCE_MANAGER_PLAN instance parameter.
9. Test and Monitor.

Creating the database user

For the purpose of this demonstration the **SCOTT** demo user will be used, this user only requires the default privileges. The user **SCOTT** may need to be unlocked and its password may need to be reset.

```
SQL> ALTER USER SCOTT
  2   IDENTIFIED BY TIGER
  3   ACCOUNT UNLOCK;
```

Service names definition

The Oracle instance is defined with a unique name known as the **global name**. The global name is used as the default service name the instance will use to register itself against the listener. The SERVICE_NAMES instance parameter is used to define all the service names that can be used to access the instance.

```
SQL> ALTER SYSTEM
  2   SET SERVICE_NAMES = 'alpha, datawarehouse, sales';
```

The names defined here will be registered against the listener at most within the next 10 seconds.

Listener verification

Once the service names have been redefined, just issue an `lsnrctl status` or an `lsnrctl services` command, this will list all the service names defined in the previous step.

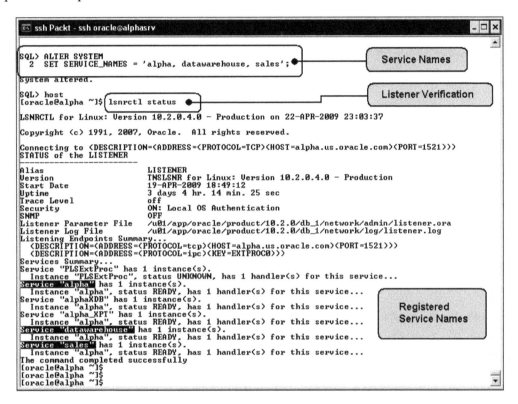

TNS entry configuration

There must exist one TNS connection descriptor for each previously defined service, so that the users can use it to specify which service it will use to connect to the Oracle instance.

```
ALPHA =
  (DESCRIPTION =
    (ADDRESS = (PROTOCOL = TCP)(HOST = alpha)(PORT = 1522))
    (ADDRESS = (PROTOCOL = TCP)(HOST = alpha)(PORT = 1521))
    (CONNECT_DATA =
      (SERVER = DEDICATED)
      (SERVICE_NAME = alpha)
    )
  )
```

```
SALES =
  (DESCRIPTION =
    (ADDRESS = (PROTOCOL = TCP)(HOST = alpha)(PORT = 1522))
    (ADDRESS = (PROTOCOL = TCP)(HOST = alpha)(PORT = 1521))
    (CONNECT_DATA =
      (SERVER = DEDICATED)
      (SERVICE_NAME = sales)
    )
  )

DATAWAREHOUSE =
  (DESCRIPTION =
    (ADDRESS = (PROTOCOL = TCP)(HOST = alpha)(PORT = 1522))
    (ADDRESS = (PROTOCOL = TCP)(HOST = alpha)(PORT = 1521))
    (CONNECT_DATA =
      (SERVER = DEDICATED)
      (SERVICE_NAME = datawarehouse)
    )
  )
```

In this example the same SCOTT database user can use three different connect descriptors to establish a connection to the database; each service will be later configured and mapped against a determined plan so that each connection has specific resource allocation.

Session 1: $ sqlplus SCOTT/TIGER@ALPHA

Session 2: $ sqlplus SCOTT/TIGER@SALES

Session 3: $ sqlplus SCOTT/TIGER@DATAWAREHOUSE

Once the users are connected through the different services this can be monitored on the V$SESSION dynamic view.

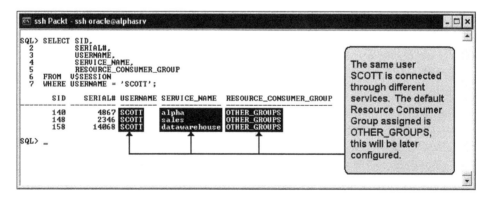

As no Resource Consumer Group has been defined, the one used is the default OTHER_GROUPS, this is the default Consumer Group all the users belong to.

Resource consumer group creation

Throughout the next topics, Enterprise Manager will be used to configure Resource Manager. Specific commands can be obtained by clicking on the **Show SQL** button any time prior to issuing the command.

At the **Administration** tab there is a section that is used to configure Resource Manager. It can see in the following screen shot.

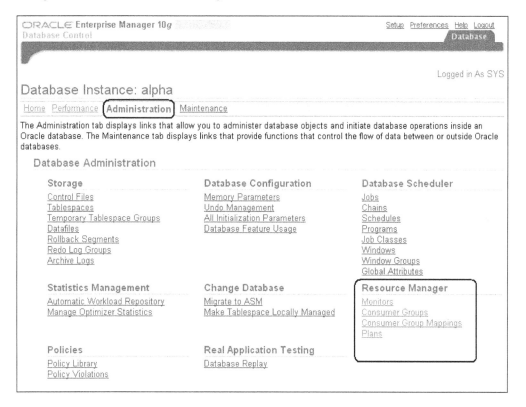

Click on the **Consumer Groups** link, there you will find a button that creates the groups. By clicking on the **Create** button a new window appears where the name of the group (**Consumer Group**) and an optional documentation text (**Description**) can be entered. The scheduling policy is the resource allocation method for distributing CPU among sessions in the consumer group. The default is ROUND_ROBIN, which uses a round-robin scheduler to ensure that sessions are fairly executed. You can change it to RUN_TO_COMPLETION; this scheduling method specifies that sessions with the largest active time are scheduled ahead of other sessions.

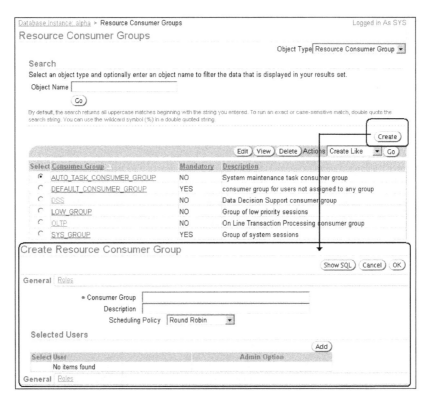

Service mapping

Each service is mapped against a specific Resource Consumer Group; this allows the user that connects through a given service to be automatically mapped against a Consumer Group. The user must have the Resource Consumer Group granted; otherwise the user will be mapped against the DEFAULT_CONSUMER_GROUP, no matter which service it used to gain access to the database.

In order for the user to be granted permissions with the consumer group, the permissions can be set either in the User configuration section in Enterprise Manager, or using the DBMS_RESOURCE_MANAGER.GRANT_SWITCH_CONSUMER_GROUP stored unit.

```
BEGIN
    dbms_resource_manager_privs.grant_switch_consumer_group(
        grantee_name   => 'SCOTT',
        consumer_group => 'DSS',
        grant_option   => FALSE
    );
END;
BEGIN
    dbms_resource_manager_privs.grant_switch_consumer_group(
        grantee_name   => 'SCOTT',
        consumer_group => 'OLTP',
        grant_option   => FALSE
    );
END;
```

The service mapping is configured by clicking on the Consumer Group Mappings link in the Resource Manager Section. Once the screen appears, you will see that you can map a Consumer Group with several objects, such as database users, OS client users, OS client programs, services, client machines, modules and modules and actions.

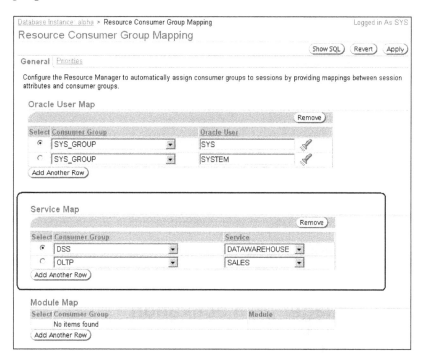

In the above example the service **DATAWAREHOUSE** is mapped against the DSS Consumer Group, meanwhile the **SALES** service is mapped against the **OLPT** Consumer Group.

Resource plan definition

In this stage of development the plan directives are defined. You can edit the directives by clicking on the edit action menu in the Consumer Group listing. Directives associated with a Consumer Group are CPU emphasis, maximum degree of parallelism, session pool (used to limit the maximum number of concurrent users belonging to a specific consumer group), undo pool, maximum execution time, consumer group switching and idle time.

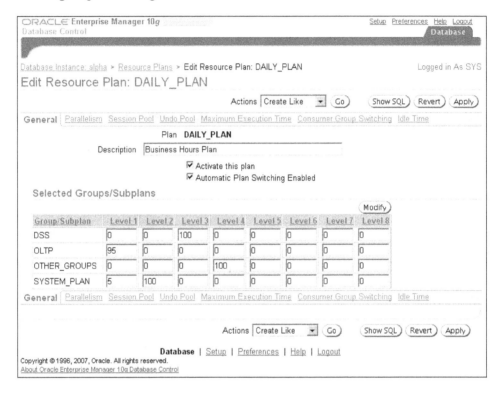

This is the last step in configuring the Resource Manager elements. The next step activates a specific plan.

Resource manager plan activation

There are several places where the plan can be activated, it can be done from the Resource Plans window, the Resource Manager monitor or directly from the SQL*Plus command line.

If you are using SQL*Plus CLI, and connected as a privileged user issue the `ALTER SYSTEM` command:

```
SQL> ALTER SYSTEM
  2   SET RESOURCE_MANAGER_PLAN = ActivatedPlan;
```

The activated plan indicates the plan that rules the current instance:

The DBMS_RESOURCE_MANAGER package can be used too to achieve the same result.

```
SQL> begin
  2   DBMS_RESOURCE_MANAGER.SWITCH_PLAN ('ActivatedPlan');
  3   end;
  4   /
```

You can use the DBMS_SCHEDULER package to perform plan activation at specific points in time, this is useful to allow a daily plan to be active during working hours and a maintenance plan active during off hours.

Testing and monitoring

Two tests are performed to show the different emphasis achieved once Resource Manager does its work. During the first scenario the **SCOTT** user is connected through two different services, the **sales** and the **datawarehouse** services. The active plan was originally **OLTP**, which simulates an environment where the users that entered the database through the **datawarehouse** service are relegated to a lower CPU priority. On the second scenario the plan is switched to an off hours plan, in this plan the directives the users that entered the database through the **datawarehouse** service automatically have a higher CPU priority.

Three sessions are open, each session gets access through a different service, thus the resource allocated for each connection are different and the CPU emphasis each session will experiment will depend on the currently active plan. Each session performs the same workload starting at the same time so they compete for the same resources within the same time frame.

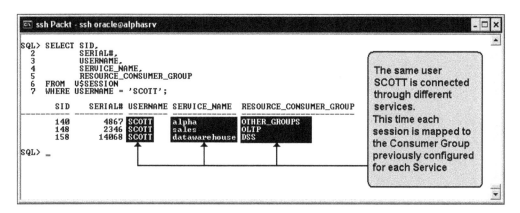

Scenario 1: **DAILY_PLAN** is active. In this scenario all users connected through the **sales** service are favored and automatically receive more CPU emphasis. The number of CPU yields and the wait time are higher for users that gain access through the **datawarehouse** service.

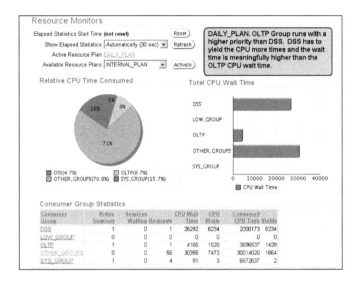

Scenario 2: The instance switches to the **NIGHTLY_PLAN**. In this scenario all users connected through the **datawarehouse** service are favored and automatically receive more **CPU** emphasis. The number of CPU yields and the wait time are higher for users that gain access through the **sales** service.

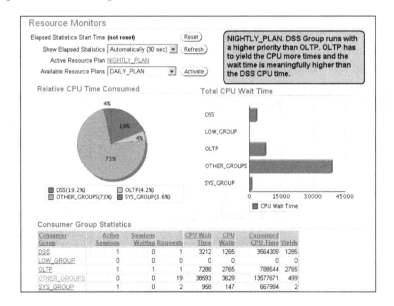

Throughout these scenarios it was evident the advantage of controlling resource allocation to the different database sessions through the service mapping. This is particularly useful when there is no way to distinguish a session user in the database. Once it was configured it becomes easy to access as the application only has to change the connection descriptor to get into the database through an specific service. When this concept is extended to the RAC environment the tuning possibilities get multiplied as this allows a better workload balance, a dynamic node allocation, and it allows the DBA to better comply with the service level agreements.

Active Session History (ASH)

Let's assume there was an outstanding user activity, the performance was reported to be slow, but there is no more activity on the database, how would the DBA be able to identify what the problem **was**? The only possible way is by means of a tool that is able to generate a report of the past user activity, the Active Session History Report, known also as ASH.

You can view the Active Session History Report via the Performance tab. At the **Average Active Sessions** section you should see a button named Run ASH Report, clicking this will take you to the ASH report time frame specification, once the period of time has been set, the report can be generated.

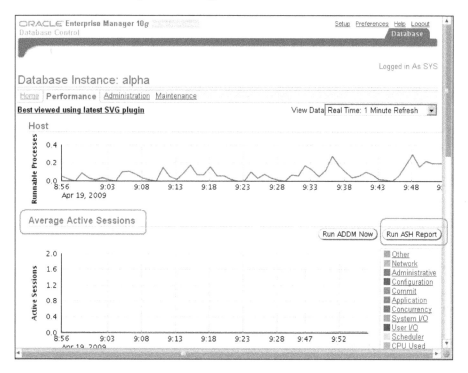

Here you can see the time frame specification and the report header, for your convenience the report can be saved in HTML format for further analysis.

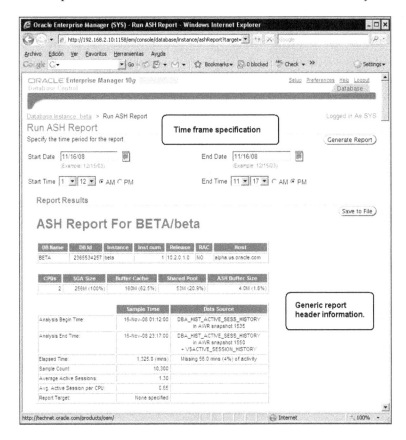

The Active Session History report is produced out of several AWR tables, the AWR takes a periodic activity snapshot and it stores the information for a given period of time, seven days by default. The DBA views that can be used to read the historical information from the AWR are listed with this query.

```
SELECT table_name
FROM dictionary
WHERE table_name like 'DBA/_HIST/_%' ESCAPE '/'
ORDER BY table_name;
```

The V$ACTIVE_SESSION_HISTORY view provides sampled session activity in the instance. Active sessions are sampled every second and are stored in a circular buffer in SGA. An active session is defined as a session connected to the database that is waiting for an event that does not belong to the Idle wait class.

The reported information belongs only to the active sessions. Using the ASH enables you to examine and perform detailed analysis on both current data in the V$ACTIVE_SESSION_HISTORY view and historical data in the DBA_HIST_ACTIVE_SESS_HISTORY view.

The ASH report can be obtained not only from enterprise manager, but also from the SQL*Plus command line. There is an SQL script that performs this task, and it can be directed to write the report to either a text file or an HTML file.

You can use the following script to generate the ASH report from a SQL*Plus prompt:

```
@?/rdbms/admin/ashrpt.sql
```

Actually, the ashrpt.sql script is just a launcher script that collects parameters and invokes the ahsrpti.sql script.

The main view where the ASH report is taken from is DBA_HIST_ACTIVE_SESS_HISTORY.

The character mode report interactively asks for some parameters; the kind of report output, the start of evaluation period defined in hours/minutes, the upper time limit and the ASH report name.

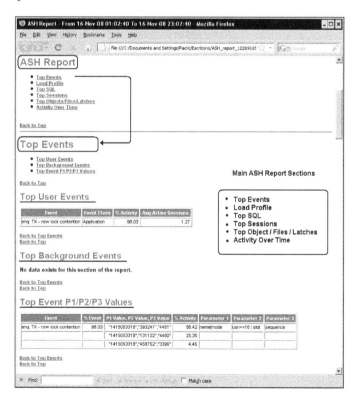

The report has seven main sections:

- **The report header**: A report summary that provides generic information.
- **Top Events**: The most outstanding events reported during the given period of time.
- **Load Profile**: This section reports which were the most active database services, the most outstanding clients and the top SQL command types issued.
- **Top SQL**: This is self explanatory, the most meaningful SQL statements.
- **Top Sessions**: This shows the most active sessions, it shows the session details ordered by the activity percentage, the reason why the event is considered a top session, and other session specific details. This section also includes a blocking sessions and a parallel query report section.
- **Top Object / Files / Latches**: This details which objects were used the most.
- **Activity Over Time**: This section summarizes the activity over the given period of time.

Session monitoring, the traditional way

Dynamic **v** dollar (v$) views have been historically used to perform session monitoring in character mode, this is useful when the DBA creates batch procedures or develops PLSQL programming to monitor the users activity.

The traditional views used to perform manual analysis and session analysis queries are:

- V$SESSION: This view lists information for each current session.
- V$SESSION_CONNECT_INFO: This view displays information about network connections for the current session.
- V$SESSION_CURSOR_CACHE: This view displays information on cursor usage for the current session.
- V$SESSION_EVENT: This view lists information on waits for an event by a session. If you see a value of zero on the TIME_WAITED and AVERAGE_WAIT columns, this means that the platform does not support the fast timing. If this is the case then set the TIMED_STATISTICS instance parameter to true.

- V$SESSION_LONGOPS: This view provides information about tasks that last more than 6 seconds. This view is useful to monitor the task progress. It is required to run on cost based optimizer and have the TIMED_STATISTICS or SQL_TRACE instance parameter to TRUE.

- V$SESSION_OBJECT_CACHE: This view displays object cache statistics for the current user session on the local instance.

- V$SESSION_WAIT: This view displays the resources or events for which active sessions are waiting. The columns **P1** and **P1RAW** have the same value, the difference is that the **PnRAW** columns display the value in hexadecimal format. If the WAIT_TIME column has a value of -2, this means that the platform does not support the fast timing mechanism and the TIMED_STATISTICS instance parameter must be set to TRUE.

- V$SESSION_WAIT_CLASS: This view displays the time spent in various wait event operations on a per-session basis.

- V$SESSION_WAIT_HISTORY: This view displays the last 10 wait events for each active session.

- V$SESSMETRIC: This view displays the last 10 wait events for each active session.

- V$SESSTAT: This view lists user session statistics. The statistic name associated with each statistic number (STATISTIC#) can be found in the V$STATNAME view.

- V$SESS_IO: This view lists I/O statistics for each user session.

- V$SESS_TIME_MODEL: This view displays the session-accumulated time for various operations.

- V$SES_OPTIMIZER_ENV Displays the contents of the optimizer environment used by each session.

You may refer to the Oracle documentation for further details on the column description of each view.

Summary

Oracle sessions are the living part of the database; they are the elements that keep performance views moving. Monitoring instance activity just provides an idea of the average database activity, but this information is not enough to enable the DBA to troubleshoot a particular peak, or to help them identify which user is issuing a resource consuming SQL statement. The monitoring tools provided by Oracle starting with 10g frees the DBA from the time consuming analysis task, and points the DBA to the root of the problem. Those tools not only show what the problem is, but they also categorize the different problems found by impact and provide a diagnostic and a solution.

Enterprise manager, and the session management sections are a complete set of productive tools that allow the DBA to quickly focus on what the problem is, even if this is a complex problem that otherwise would have taken the DBA a lot more time to find out where the root of the problem was.

7
Oracle Scheduler

When the lights go off at the office, the automated tasks take place. Scheduling tasks to be run at a given time is one of the most frequently performed activities in many companies. I would even go so far as to say in all companies.

There are a lot of tasks that must be executed at a specific time; day or night, weekdays, weekends, or holidays. Scheduling a task may not be new, this could be solved to a certain extent with the **Windows Scheduler** (on Windows platforms), or with the **cron utility** (Unix like systems). Although, you should be aware that these schedules assume your batch program is intelligent enough to not only perform a given task, but also to proceed with a plan B in case something is wrong. Your batch should also be intelligent enough to detect when an event is raised and proceed to trigger a sequence. This is just like expecting a file to arrive and you only know the estimated arrival time, but you are not certain about the exact time, and you cannot proceed with the rest of the tasks in a processing chain unless this file arrives.

The Oracle Scheduler is much more than just a Scheduler to program automatic tasks; this is a complete system that lets you schedule complex chains and make decisions based on the task's outcome. It allows you to specify maintenance windows, assign priorities, configure job classes, and more.

Oracle Scheduler concepts

A Scheduler should be able to be controlled with a minimum of two basic parameters, what you want to launch, and when you want to start launching it (plus how often this task should be launched). A good Scheduler has additional capabilities such as monitoring, repetition control, suspending, resuming, and cancelling tasks. In previous Oracle versions (8i to 9i) this was performed by means of the DBMS_JOB. The problem with this package was that the scheduling mechanism required you to provide a date expression, not quite readable when the scheduling was a bit more complex than usual. DBMS_JOB was not originally intended to be a Scheduler, it was simply designed to be a job initialization utility limited to jobs inside the database.

When dbms_scheduler was designed (it was originally derived from OEM's mgmt_jobs), Oracle had in mind a tool that could make the user's life easier. This tool was able to manage complex schedules, create scheduling patterns that could be reused, and launch different tasks seamlessly. You could create a Scheduler for a regular PLSQL task as well as an OS task that could be launched from the database server side, all without requiring the OS Scheduler. Sometimes, you may need to launch a task within a given time frame (maintenance window). During this maintenance window the task may require special attributes when scheduled, such as a specific priority, an emphasis on parallelism or other OS resources. There is the need to create a job pattern for those tasks that require similar scheduling parameters.

Then Oracle created the DBMS_SCHEDULER. This is a powerful tool that in a simple and elegant way handles complex schedules. In order for you to be able to manage the Scheduler, you should first get acquainted with some basic Oracle concepts.

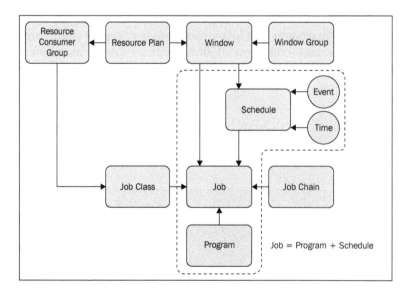

Program: **Program** and **Job** are two different concepts. Program relates to the metadata about what should be run; it specifies the program object, the program action, and the program type. A Job specifies when the program is to be executed, so the same program can be scheduled at different times and frequencies by different jobs. When working with programs, the program is meant to separate the *what* part of the job.

Schedule: The Schedule defines the point in time when a job is programmed to be executed, and how often the job will be executed (frequency). This could be just a onetime execution or a repetitive execution. For jobs to be scheduled at a later time, it specifies when the job will start executing, and for repetitive jobs it also specifies the start time and whether the job will run indefinitely or when the job schedule will expire. The schedule also specifies if a job will be executed when an event is raised. A schedule is also a database object. When working with simple jobs, the job can define what is going to be run and when it is going to be run. The Schedule is a means of separating the *when* part of the job.

Job: A Job is a user-defined task programmed to be run at a specific point in time, a job specifies what will be run and when it will be run. This task may be programmed to be run once or several times. The task could be a PL/SQL block. A job is a database object.

Job Classes: If you create several jobs that share the same attribute values, then those jobs could be included under the same job class. If a Job is assigned to a Job Class then the job inherits the attributes defined for that Job Class. All the jobs belong to a job class, if a job class is not specified at job creation time; the job automatically belongs to the DEFAULT_JOB_CLASS.

Window: A Window is a time frame used to redefine allocation resources among jobs. The Window is defined along with resource manager to specify resource allocation policies. The Window specifies the resource plan to be activated and each job class specifies which resource consumer group to map. The Windows may overlap in time, if this happens the Window with the higher priority is chosen over the Window with lower priority.

Window Groups: When a job is required to be scheduled on different windows, you can define several windows and then group them under a single name. Let's assume a maintenance job is chosen to be run when the workload is lower during weekends, nights and holidays. There are two regular windows—**Weekend**, and **Weeknight**, and several other windows, each one defining one holiday. All of these windows can be grouped under a Window Group named `Maintenance_Window`.

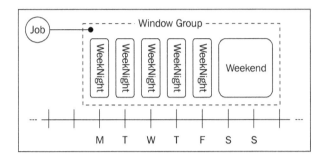

Resource Manager: The Resource Manager is a means of providing the DBA with more control over resource allocation. It specifies the amount of resources a process may use, it determines the degree of parallelism, the CPU emphasis, the maximum blocking time, and the maximum idle time, among other resources. In the Scheduler context, it specifies the resource limits for a Window or a Job Class. Resource Manager represents an entire subsystem of DBA resource control and is closely tied to Services (previously discussed). The Oracle Scheduler has been designed to integrate with that subsystem.

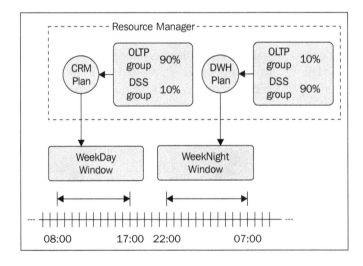

Job Chains: Scheduling a single task can be relatively easily done, it can be scheduled to be run at a specific point in time, or, as previously seen, it can be triggered after a specific event is raised. But when a task depends on other tasks to be completed before they can be scheduled, or if a task is to be conditionally scheduled, a complex shell script must be prepared.

Time Schedule: This is the most frequently used schedule. Normally the tasks are scheduled at a given point in time, which can occur once or on a repetition basis. A time expression is required to define when the task will be executed.

Event Schedule: A Job cannot only be scheduled by a time expression, but also by a non-deterministic situation. Assuming a file arrives around 2:00 a.m., but not at a precise point in time, if a chain process is waiting for this event to start just in time, then a regular schedule may either start too early or too late, and would not be a convenient way to schedule the file processing job. An event-based schedule is more suitable for this scenario, this way we will always know that a process chain won't start unless the required triggering condition is met.

An event-based schedule requires a queue specification and an event condition to be met.

Getting started with the Oracle Scheduler

There are a number of database privileges and properties that need to be set for a user to be able to access and utilize the Scheduler. Once the user has been granted the proper privileges they are ready to use the DBMS_SCHEDULER package.

Required privileges

In order for you to create a new job manager you must grant the SCHEDULER_ADMIN role.

```
GRANT SCHEDULER_ADMIN TO <username>;
```

This role provides a lot of power for a regular user, allowing the grantee to run any code. If this happens to be a regular user who will launch its own jobs, then it should be granted the CREATE JOB privilege. This allows the grantee to create jobs, schedules, and programs in its own schema.

```
GRANT CREATE JOB TO <username>;
```

If the user will be performing other management tasks besides creating jobs and schedules, then the DBA should grant the MANAGE SCHEDULER privilege. This allows the grantee to create, alter or drop windows, job classes, and windows groups, as well as manage the Scheduler attributes and purge the Scheduler log. These tasks are often performed by the DBA, so the database administrator should assess if the user really requires this privilege level.

```
GRANT MANAGE SCHEDULER TO <username>;
```

Let's create the Scheduler manager with the minimum privileges required to create basic objects and manage the Scheduler:

```
create user OSCHEDMGR
identified by ORACLE
default tablespace USERS
quota unlimited on USERS;

grant create table,
 create procedure,
 create sequence,
 manage scheduler
to OSCHEDMGR;
```

This code creates a regular user with minimum privileges to use dbms_scheduler to create jobs:

```
create user OSCHEDULER
identified by ORACLE
default tablespace USERS
quota unlimited on USERS;

grant
    create session,
    create table,
    create procedure,
    create sequence
    create job
to OSCHEDULER;
```

Scheduling our first job

In this example the user issues a Scheduler job by means of the DBMS_SCHEDULER.CREATE_JOB that is a stored procedure. The parameters required by the CREATE_JOB procedure depend on the version of the stored procedure used. CREATE_JOB is an overloaded procedure, there are six different versions of it, so when programming a task using this procedure, be sure to use the right parameter combination for the selected CREATE_JOB procedure.

This schedule task is composed of a simple database stored unit that updates a table at a specified time. First you must create the procedure, and then schedule it. At this stage this schedule doesn't include the program or the schedule concept to create the job, those are explicitly defined in one step. In a later example these will be created separately.

The parameters used in this example are explained next.

Creating the job

The jobs are created using the CREATE_JOB procedure. The following parameters are used in the example and are as shown in the screenshot:

JOB_NAME: Jobs are database objects and require a unique name that follows the standard Oracle object naming convention.

JOB_TYPE: There are several different kinds of jobs — programs (external OS commands or shell scripts), PL/SQL Blocks, Stored Procedures, executable programs, or chains.

JOB_ACTION: This refers to the procedure name to be executed.

REPEAT_INTERVAL: DBMS_SCHEDULER utilizes time expressions with a particularly simple syntax to define the job frequency. In the example, the job was specified to run every two minutes (FREQ=MINUTELY; INTERVAL=2).

START_DATE: The start date is defined with a timestamp using time zone data type. In the example, it is defined using the to_timestamp_tz function.

END_DATE: If this parameter is defined, it means the job will finish being scheduled at this point in time; otherwise it means the job will keep on running indefinitely.

JOB_CLASS: This parameter specifies the job class to which the job will be related. All jobs must belong to a job class. As it is not defined in this case, the job will belong to the DEFAULT_JOB_CLASS.

COMMENTS: This is a varchar2 column which is intended for the job creator to document what the job does.

AUTO_DROP: The job creator can specify whether or not the task will be automatically dropped after it is completed.

NUMBER_OF_ARGUMENTS: If the task to be launched requires arguments, this parameter specifies the number of arguments. The actual parameter values are not defined here; those are defined with the DBMS_SCHEDULER.SET_JOB_ARGUMENT_ VALUE procedures.

ENABLED: If there are no more parameters to be specified, the job can be enabled by setting the ENABLED value to TRUE. By default, this value is set to FALSE, so the job is created disabled.

This example schedules the LOG_ENTRY stored program unit, this is a simple user created procedure that obtains a sequence number and inserts a record into a log table. This is described next:

```
create table oscheduler.job_log(
    id      number(10),
    exec_time     date,
    what    varchar2(50))
tablespace users;

create sequence oscheduler.seq;
grant create procedure to oscheduler;

create or replace procedure oscheduler.ins_job_log_entry(
    log_info IN varchar2)
as
begin
    insert into job_log values(
            seq.nextval,
            sysdate,
            log_info
    );
    commit;
end;
/
```

This procedure requires an argument and a log info file. It also requires a special treatment when the procedure will be scheduled.

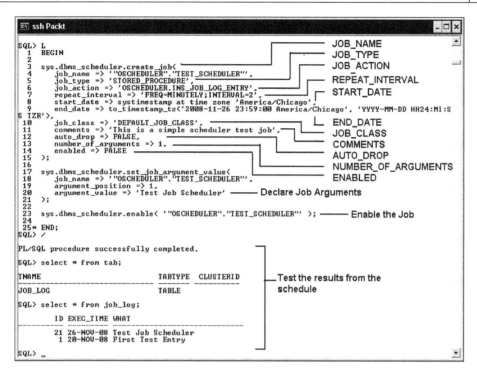

Specifying procedure arguments

In the above example, the job to be scheduled requires one argument, the argument is defined using the DBMS_SCHEDULER.SET_JOB_ARGUMENT_VALUE procedure. This requires three parameters, JOB_NAME, ARGUMENT_POSITION, and ARGUMENT_VALUE.

- **JOB_NAME**: This is the job name defined at job creation time.

- **ARGUMENT_POSITION**: The arguments are defined by position, this is a PLS_INTEGER value that specifies the parameter position.

- **ARGUMENT_NAME**: The argument can be defined not only by position, but also with the parameter name. In the case of PL/SQL procedures this refers to the parameter name defined at the PL/SQL program unit creation time.

- **ARGUMENT_VALUE**: This is the argument value, it is specified as a VARCHAR2 value. If the value is not a varchar2, then the procedure SET_JOB_ANYDATA_ARGUMENT_VALUE must be used instead.

Enabling the job schedule

Once the job has been properly created, then it is time to enable it, this is done using the DBMS_SCHEDULER.ENABLE procedure. The only argument it requires is the job name.

Using Enterprise Manager

Enterprise Manager is a convenient way to schedule a job, its interface is intuitive and user friendly. The Scheduler manager is found on the **Administration** tab in the **Database Scheduler** section. There you will find the Job definition section, the one first used to schedule a simple job (**Jobs**, **Schedules** and **Programs**), **Window Management** (**Windows**, **Window Groups**), Program definition (Programs), Job Classes, and Chains.

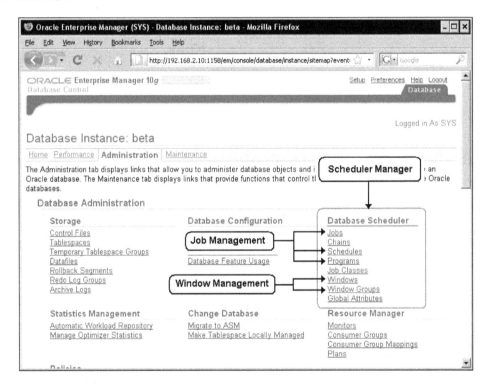

By clicking the Job definition section, the form to specify a simple job appears:

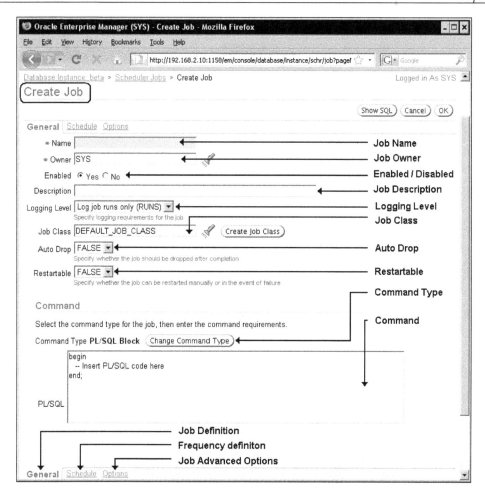

The kind of jobs that Scheduler accepts are Programs (specified Scheduler programs), PL/SQL anonymous blocks, stored procedures, executables (OS programs), and chains. The command type section will change the layout and the kind of arguments requested depending on the kind of command to schedule. The command used in the example was a simple PL/SQL stored unit with one parameter.

Once the job and job type has been defined, the next step is to define the schedule.

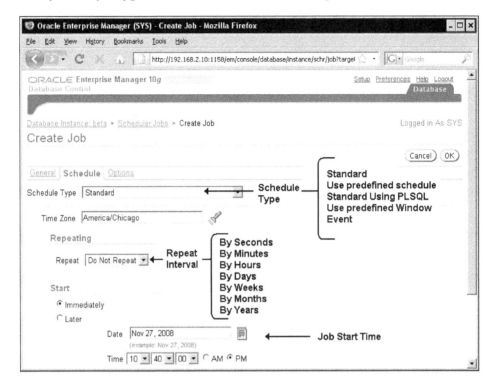

The Scheduler specifies when this job will be launched as well as the job frequency and the time this task will be programmed to start. The schedule type can be a standard Scheduler, an already defined schedule object, a standard PL/SQL, which means you will provide a time expression similar to the one used with DBMS_JOB, it can also be run within a predefined window, or an asynchronous schedule by means of the event scheduling. Each schedule type will change the form layout accordingly.

If a standard schedule is used, the repeating interval can be specified as a value from seconds to years. The repeating interval will also change the page layout depending on the kind of interval.

Finally, you can specify the time the job will be started; this can either be launched immediately or at a specific point in time.

Time expression syntax

Prior to DBMS_SCHEDULE, the way to specify the repeating interval with the DBMS_JOB was pretty complex, and not very easy to read. The time expressions were PL/SQL expressions that resulted in a rigid schedule pattern. The syntax used by the Scheduler time is far more flexible and powerful, and, among many other features, the richness of the time expressions is one of the Scheduler's strengths.

The repeat interval

The repeat interval goes from as little as seconds, to years. The frequency can be defined seconds, minutes, hours, days, weeks, months, and years.

The syntax used to write time intervals can be specified either using a regular schedule or a combined schedule.

```
repeat_interval = regular_schedule | combined_schedule
```

Regular schedule

The regular schedule is composed of three main sections — the **frequency definition**, the **interval**, and the **timing specification**.

```
regular_schedule =
        frequency_clause
        [";" interval_clause]
        [";" bymonth_clause]
        [";" byweekno_clause]
        [";" byyearday_clause]
        [";" bydate_clause]
        [";" bymonthday_clause]
        [";" byday_clause]
        [";" byhour_clause]
        [";" byminute_clause]
        [";" bysecond_clause]
        [";" bysetpos_clause]
        [";" include_clause]
        [";" exclude_clause]
        [";" intersect_clause]
        [";" periods_clause]
        [";" byperiod_clause]
```

```
Combined schedule = schedule_list
            [";" include_clause]
            [";" exclude_clause]
            [";" intersect_clause]
```

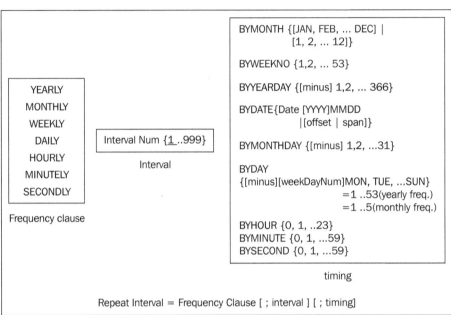

Frequency clause: This can be either a predefined frequency or a user defined frequency. The predefined frequencies are YEARLY, MONTHLY, WEEKLY, DAILY, HOURLY, MINUTELY, and SECONDLY. A task whose schedule is programmed with the clause FREQ=MINUTELY will wait for the next minute to start being scheduled.

In this example a task is programmed to run each minute, so the frequency clause is declared MINUTELY:

```
sys.dbms_scheduler.create_job(
job_name            => '"OSCHEDULER"."TEST_MINUTELY"',
job_type            => 'STORED_PROCEDURE',
job_action          => 'OSCHEDULER.INS_JOB_LOG_ENTRY',
repeat_interval     => 'FREQ=MINUTELY',
start_date          => systimestamp at time zone 'America/Chicago',
job_class           => 'DEFAULT_JOB_CLASS',
comments            => 'Test Minutely Scheduling',
auto_drop           => FALSE,
number_of_arguments => 1,
enabled             => FALSE);
```

Interval clause: The interval clause defines the time when the next occurrence of the schedule will take place; it ranges from 1 to 999 and its default value is 1.

Let's assume this scenario; if the user defines a schedule to occur HOURLY at an interval of three (hours, it uses the same unit as the frequency clause), starting at midnight with no ending clause defined, it means that the job will first run at 00:00 hours, and the next occurrence will be at 03:00 hours, next will be at 06:00, next will be at 09:00, and so on. In this example the time expression is:

```
'FREQ=HOURLY;INTERVAL=3'
```

Timing Specification: The individual timing clauses that define a timing expression are detailed in the table below.

BY{ * } clause	Syntax and Definition
BYMONTH	BYMONTH = { (JAN, FEB, ... DEC) | (1, 2, ... 12) }
	This specifies on which month or months the job is scheduled to be run. The syntax allows this time expression to be written either with numbers or with the month acronyms. Several months can be specified. Let's assume a task is scheduled to run in July, October and December; the time expression should be defined to run yearly, on the previously specified months, and its syntax would be: FREQ=YEARLY;BYMONTH=JUL,OCT,DEC
BYWEEKNO	BYWEEKNO = {1, 2, ... 53}
	This defines the Week number according to the ISO-8601 standard. A week starts on Monday and ends on Sunday, its value ranges from 1 to 52 (or 53 in a leap year). Parts of a week can be found on the previous year and parts of a week may be found on the next year. The BYWEEKNO is valid only on a YEARLY interval. According to the standard the week containing the first Thursday of the year is considered the week number one, for example on January 2004, the first day of the year was on Thursday, so this was considered the first week of the year, and it started on Monday 29th December 2003.

BY{ * } clause	Syntax and Definition
BYYEARDAY	`BYYEARDAY = {[minus] 1, 2, ..., 366}`
	The value of the year day ranges from 1 to 366, each year day is assigned a number and depending whether the year is or is not a leap year, the maximum value will range from 1 to 365 for the former and 366 for the later. In a regular year, the year day 59 corresponds to March 1 , meanwhile on a leap year the same year day corresponds to February 29
	When the value is preceded by a minus sign it means the day is counted from the last day of the year backwards. If the year day has a value of 20, it means it is the January 20, but if the value is -20, then the resulting date is December 11. `FREQ=YEARLY;BYYEARDAY=-20`
BYDATE	`BYDATE = {Date [YYYY]MMDD	[[+|-]offset	[+|-|^]` `span]}`
	This specifies a list of dates in the `YYYYMMDD` format. If the `YYYY` format mask is not included then it assumes the current year.
	The `BYDATE` specifier can be simplified using the span and offset modifiers, which will produce a set of consecutive dates. The expression `BYDATE=0201, 0202, 0203, 0204, 0205, 0206, 0207, 0208, 0209, 0210` can be simplified with the span modifier this way: `BYDATE=0201+9D`. The span modifier can be qualified with plus sign, which is an increasing date range starting with the given date, when it has the minus sign it stands for a monotonically decreasing date range starting with the given date, and if it has the circumflex sign, this means it is a range that spans n-days centered on the given date.
	The expression `BYDATE=0201+14D` is equivalent to a range of dates starting at 0201 and ending at 0215. This expression can also be written using the offset modifier this way: `BYDATE=0201+OFFSET:2W`

BY{ * } clause	Syntax and Definition
BYMONTHDAY	`BYMONTHDAY = {[minus] 1, 2, ..., 31}`
	The month day is the regular calendar day, it starts the first day of the month and it may end on the 28th, 29th, 30th, or 31st day of the month, depending on the specific month and year. If the month day includes a minus sign, this means that it counts backwards from the last day of the month, so a convenient way to refer to the last day of the month is with the expression `BYMONTHDAY= -1`.
BYDAY	`BYDAY = {[minus] [weekDayNum] MON, TUE, ... SUN}`
	`weekDayNum = {1 .. 53} (yearly)	{1 .. 5} (monthly)`
	The day refers to the week day ranging from MON to SUN, and the weekDayNum stands for the number of the week , which will span from 1 to 53 (in a yearly frequency) or from 1 to 5 (in a monthly frequency). So the 33rd Wednesday of the year can be expressed as:
	`FREQ='YEARLY'; BYDAY = 33 WED`
	Meanwhile the third Thursday of the month can be expressed as:
	`FREQ='MONTHLY'; BYDAY = 3 THU`
	If the BYDAY clause is preceded by the minus sign it means it will be counted backwards, so if you want to represent the last Friday of the year then you would use:
	`FREQ='YEARLY'; BYDAY = -1 FRI`
BYHOUR	`BYHOUR = {0, 1, ... 23}`
	This specifies the hour in a 24 hour format ranging from 0 (12:00 a.m.) to 23 (11 p.m.).
BYMINUTE	`BYMINUTE = {0, 1, ... 59}`
	This specifies the minutes past the hour the task will be scheduled, it ranges from 0 to 59. Its meaning is straightforward.
BYSECOND	`BYSECOND = {0, 1, ... 59}`
	This specifies the seconds past the minute the task will be scheduled, it ranges from 0 to 59. Its meaning is straightforward.

Combined schedule

The repeat interval can also be combined, and it can be seen as a set of points in time that can be intersected with other points in time, it can be included, excluded, or intersected. The repeated schedules are included only once in the resulting schedule.

```
combined_schedule = schedule_list [";" include_clause] [";" exclude_
clause] [";" intersect_clauseintersect_clause]
```

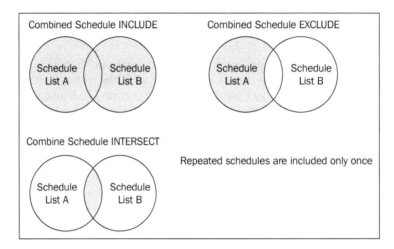

As previously shown on the diagram there are three ways to define a combined schedule. They are the `include`, `exclude` and `intersect` clauses.

Include: The `include` clause merges the resulting schedules from two or more named schedule lists. The repeated schedules are included only once. The `include` operation is equivalent to the Union set operator.

Exclude: This excludes the values in common with the schedule list A. The `exclude` clause is equivalent to the Minus set operator.

Intersect: The `intersect` clause is equivalent to the `intersect` set operator. This specifies an intersection between the calendaring expression results and the set of timestamps defined by one or more named schedules. Only the timestamps that appear both in the calendaring expression and in one of the named schedules are included in the resulting set of timestamps.

Exclude scenario

Let's assume this scenario, a process is scheduled to run on the first calendar day of the month at 08:00 a.m., except on January 1. Two schedules are created, one for January the first, and the second for the first day of each month.

In the following example `JAN_FIRST` is a schedule that resolves to the single date 01-JAN:

```
BEGIN
sys.dbms_scheduler.create_schedule(
    repeat_interval => 'FREQ=YEARLY;BYYEARDAY=1',
    start_date      => systimestamp at time zone 'America/Mexico_
                                                 City',
    comments        => 'Single date January 1st',
    schedule_name   => '"SYS"."JAN_FIRST"');
END;
```

This schedule resolves for the first day of each month except January 1st:

```
BEGIN
sys.dbms_scheduler.create_schedule(
    repeat_interval => 'FREQ=MONTHLY;BYMONTHDAY=1;BYHOUR=8;EXCLUDE=
                                                 JAN_FIRST',
    start_date      => systimestamp at time zone 'America/Mexico_
                                                 City',
    comments        => 'First day of the month',
    schedule_name   => '"SYS"."FIRST_MONTH_DAY_SCHED"');
END;
```

Both schedules can be queried from Enterprise Manager DB Control Console.

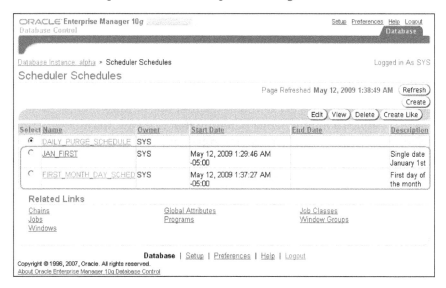

The resulting schedule will include the first day of each month, except January 1st. It must be pointed out that the FIRST_MONTH_DAY_SCHED schedule is defined to run at 08:00 a.m., meanwhile Jan 1 does not have a defined time.

 Excluded dates without a time component are treated as twenty four hour periods. All timestamps that fall on an excluded date are removed.

Considering the previously detailed expression:

```
FREQ=MONTHLY;BYMONTHDAY=1;BYHOUR=8;EXCLUDE=JAN_FIRST
```

All instances of the job are removed for Jan 01.

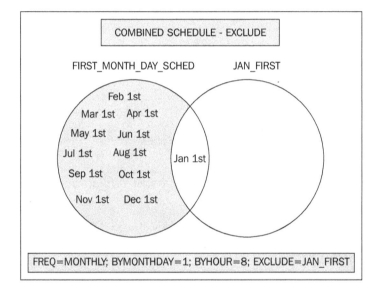

Include scenario

In this scenario two schedules are defined, the first one defines several holidays, and the second one defines a maintenance schedule that is meant to run every Sunday and on holidays. If a given date is both a Sunday and a holiday, the scheduled task is meant to run only once.

```
BEGIN
sys.dbms_scheduler.create_schedule(
    repeat_interval   =>
                'FREQ=YEARLY;
                BYYEARDAY=1,-286,-245,-241,-110,-107,-81,-60,-42,-7',
            start_date =>
                to_timestamp_tz('2009-05-12 America/Mexico_City',
                                            'YYYY-MM-DD TZR'),
    comments          => 'Company Holidays',
    schedule_name     => '"SYS"."HOLIDAYS"');
END;
/
```

This schedule is configured to run every Sunday, including holidays:

```
BEGIN
sys.dbms_scheduler.create_schedule(
    repeat_interval => 'FREQ=WEEKLY;BYDAY=SUN;BYHOUR=6;BYMINUTE=30;
                                            INCLUDE=HOLIDAYS',
    start_date      => systimestamp at time zone 'America/Mexico_
                                            City',
    comments        => 'Every Sunday and Holidays',
    schedule_name   => '"SYS"."EVERY_SUNDAY"');
END;
/
```

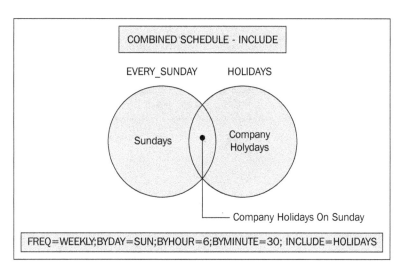

Intersect scenario

In this intersect scenario only the dates that are both a Sunday and the first day of the month will be displayed.

This schedule selects every Sunday:

```
BEGIN
sys.dbms_scheduler.create_schedule(
  repeat_interval => 'FREQ=WEEKLY;BYDAY=SUN',
  start_date      => systimestamp at time zone 'America/Mexico_City',
  comments        => 'Every Sunday',
  schedule_name   => '"SYS"."EVERY_SUNDAY"');
END;
/
```

The next scenario intersects the resulting timestamps from EVERY_SUNDAY with the first day of the month.

```
BEGIN
sys.dbms_scheduler.create_schedule(
  repeat_interval => 'FREQ=MONTHLY;BYMONTHDAY=1;INTERSECT=EVERY_
                                                  SUNDAY',
  start_date      => systimestamp at time zone 'America/Mexico_City',
  comments        => 'Every Sunday 1st during the year',
  schedule_name   => '"SYS"."EVERY_SUNDAY_1ST"');
END;
/
```

Only the common dates are selected by this schedule.

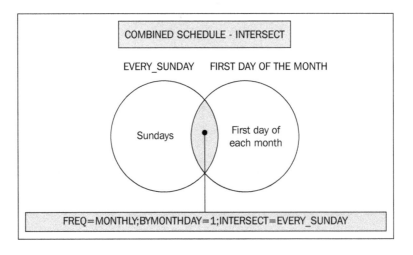

The resulting dates for the next five scheduled results are those shown in the below image:

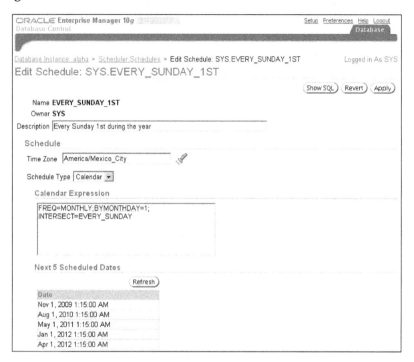

Time expression examples

The Oracle Scheduler time expressions are rich, flexible, and powerful. Once you get familiar with the basic syntax rules, you realize the syntax is pretty simple and straightforward. Let's take a look at some examples:

Schedule Requirement	Expression
Daily at noon	`FREQ=DAILY;BYHOUR=12;BYMINUTE=0;` `BYSECOND=0'`
Daily at midnight	`FREQ=DAILY;BYHOUR=0;BYMINUTE=0;` `BYSECOND=0'`
The last day of each month at 9:30 p.m.	`FREQ=MONTHLY;BYMONTHDAY=-1;` `BYHOUR=21;BYMINUTE=30;BYSECOND=0`
Every Tuesday and Friday at 9:00 p.m.	`FREQ=WEEKLY; BYDAY=TUE,FRI;` `BYHOUR=21; BYMINUTE=0; BYSECOND=0`
First Monday of each Quarter	`FREQ=MONTHLY; BYMONTH=1,4,7,10;` `BYDAY=1MON`
Last day of the Month	`FREQ=YEARLY; BYMONTHDAY=-1`

Programs

A program is a collection of metadata detailing what the Scheduler will run. A schedule specifies when the program will be executed. You can create a job using existing programs and schedules.

If a program is to be scheduled by a single Job, then the program can be defined within the job definition, but if the same program is to be scheduled under different circumstances and more than once, then the use of programs should be considered.

There are different kinds of programs:

- **PL/SQL Blocks**: These are anonymous PL/SQL blocks written at program creation time.
- **Stored Procedures**: This is a regular stored procedure PL/SQL unit.
- **Operating System Executables**: This is a shell script or any other OS executable. Scheduling programs inside the database is a more convenient way to schedule OS tasks, this allows more integration and more control over the task execution cycle. If the regular OS Scheduler is used (crontab in Unix like systems and Task Manager on Windows platforms) then there is no way to monitor, control or regulate the task behavior. The user depends only on the OS scheduling mechanism to launch the job. Even though the Windows Task Manager has a good degree of complexity to schedule a task, it definitely doesn't have a point of comparison with the Oracle Scheduler. On the other hand, the crontab mechanism is too far primitive if we make the same comparison. So if the program requires a complex schedule, it will be much easier to define and manage it using the Oracle scheduling infrastructure.

When launching a program you must be aware of the permissions at the Operating System level, otherwise you may receive the **ORA-27369: job of type EXECUTABLE failed with exit code: Permission denied** error message. This may happen even though you may have the proper privileges when you execute the task directly at the operating system. In Unix like system this error has to do with the privileges of the extjob program located in the $ORACLE_HOME/bin directory, by default this runs with a SUID, making an external job run as the nobody user belonging to the nobody group.

Creating programs manually

A program is defined using the CREATE_PROGRAM procedure from the
DBMS_SCHEDULER package. It requires us to specify the program name, owner, type
of program, and argument definition. The program can be created in an enabled
status from the beginning, but in this case the program is enabled once the complete
configuration task is finished.

To create a program based on an already existing program unit:

```
BEGIN
DBMS_SCHEDULER.CREATE_PROGRAM(
   program_name        =>'OSCHEDULER.LOG_INFO_PROG',
   program_action      =>'OSCHEDULER.INS_JOB_LOG_ENTRY',
   program_type        =>'STORED_PROCEDURE',
   number_of_arguments=>1,
   comments            =>'Log Info Stored Procedure Program',
   enabled             =>FALSE);
END;
```

Once the program is created, the next step is to define the required arguments:

```
BEGIN
DBMS_SCHEDULER.DEFINE_PROGRAM_ARGUMENT(
   program_name        =>'OSCHEDULER.LOG_INFO_PROG',
   argument_name       =>'LOG_INFO',
   argument_position=>1,
   argument_type       =>'VARCHAR2',
   default_value       =>'',
   out_argument        =>FALSE);
END;
```

And finally the program is enabled.

```
BEGIN
DBMS_SCHEDULER.ENABLE(
   name=>'OSCHEDULER.LOG_INFO_PROG');
END;
```

The following piece of code shows the way to create an OS program using
DBMS_SCHEDULER.

In this piece of code a simple shell script is scheduled. The script executes an echo
and redirects the output to an OS file:

```
echo 'date' Log Entry Generated from the OS > /tmp/OracleJob.log
```

This script is saved to /home/oracle/bin/record_os_log_entry.sh. Once the shell script is ready the next step is to create a dbms_scheduler program named OSCHEDULER.OS_LOG_RECORD_PROG:

```
BEGIN
DBMS_SCHEDULER.CREATE_PROGRAM(
   program_name        =>'OSCHEDULER.OS_LOG_RECORD_PROG',
   program_action      =>'/home/oracle/bin/record_os_log_entry.sh',
   program_type        =>'EXECUTABLE',
   number_of_arguments=>1,
   comments            =>'OS level log entry record',
   enabled             =>FALSE);
END;

BEGIN
DBMS_SCHEDULER.DEFINE_PROGRAM_ARGUMENT(
   program_name        =>'OSCHEDULER.OS_LOG_RECORD_PROG',
   argument_name       =>'LogEntryText',
   argument_position   =>1,
   argument_type       =>'CHAR',
   default_value       =>'Default log entry',
   out_argument        =>FALSE);
END;

BEGIN
DBMS_SCHEDULER.ENABLE(
   name                =>'OSCHEDULER.OS_LOG_RECORD_PROG');
END;
```

Defining a program using Enterprise Manager

Using **Enterprise Manager** to define a program is a convenient and pretty straightforward way to perform this task, it allows the user to view a list of all existing Scheduler programs, create new programs or clone a program from an existing template, edit a program and provide different maintenance levels to existing programs.

This screenshot shows how a program is defined using Enterprise Manager:

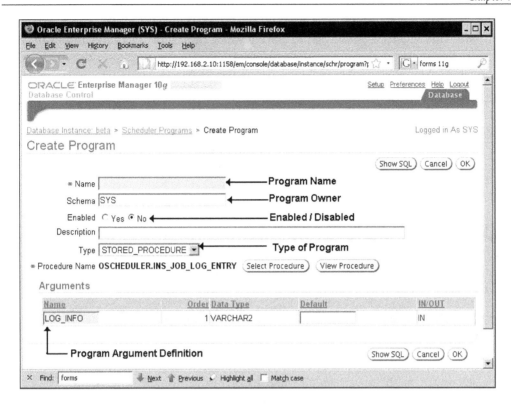

Schedules

Schedules are named, reusable calendar objects. They may be used for multiple jobs. Instead of declaring the same schedule for different jobs, just define it once and use it as a named schedule for different job definitions.

The schedule is created using DBMS_SCHEDULER.CREATE_SCHEDULE

```
PROCEDURE CREATE_SCHEDULE(
 SCHEDULE_NAME
 START_DATE
 REPEAT_INTERVAL
 END_DATE
 COMMENTS
 )
```

In this example a new schedule is created, it is defined to run hourly at an interval of six hours. This schedule is defined to start at invocation time and runs indefinitely.

```
BEGIN
DBMS_SCHEDULER.CREATE_SCHEDULE(
   schedule_name    => 'demo_schedule',
   start_date       => SYSTIMESTAMP,
   end_date         => null,
   repeat_interval  => 'FREQ=HOURLY;INTERVAL=6',
   comments         => 'Hourly schedule at an interval of six hours');
END;
```

Jobs and Job Classes

The **Job** is the programmed execution of a task at a given time and during a given period of time. Once the schedule and the program objects have been defined, they can be used in a job definition making it simpler and more readable.

```
BEGIN
sys.dbms_scheduler.create_job(
   job_name         => '"OSCHEDULER"."OS_LOG_RECORDS_JOB"',
   program_name     => 'OSCHEDULER.OS_LOG_RECORD_PROG',
   schedule_name    => 'OSCHEDULER.MINUTELY_SCHEDULE',
   job_class        => 'DEFAULT_JOB_CLASS',
   auto_drop        => FALSE,
   enabled          => TRUE);
END;
```

A **Job Class** is a way of grouping jobs and linking them to a resource consumer group, so that you can define common properties among different jobs in a single operation. This enables the same behavior and same properties among homogeneous jobs. You can specify attributes at the class level; you can also define the order in which a job is started. Linking to resource manager is important as this is a way you can emphasize the resources allocated to all the jobs that run under a given Job Class.

A **Job Class** is created using the CREATE_JOB_CLASS procedure. In this example it is defined as a resource consumer group, and this is assigned to a job class. All the jobs belonging to this job class will have the same resource allocation policies defined for the class.

In the demonstration database there are several consumers groups currently defined:

```
SQL> select CONSUMER_GROUP
  2  from    DBA_RSRC_CONSUMER_GROUPS;

CONSUMER_GROUP

------------------------------

OTHER_GROUPS
DEFAULT_CONSUMER_GROUP
SYS_GROUP
LOW_GROUP
AUTO_TASK_CONSUMER_GROUP
OLTP
DSS
```

When creating a Job Class this can be defined to run under the LOW_GROUP:

```
SQL> BEGIN
  2      dbms_scheduler.create_job_class (
  3         job_class_name          =>  'LOW_GROUP_JOB_CLASS',
  4         resource_consumer_group =>  'LOW_GROUP');
  5  END;
  6  /
```

We verify the Job Class by querying the DBA_SCHEDULER_JOB_CLASSES view:

```
SQL> select JOB_CLASS_NAME,
  2          RESOURCE_CONSUMER_GROUP
  3  from    DBA_SCHEDULER_JOB_CLASSES;

JOB_CLASS_NAME                    RESOURCE_CONSUMER_GROUP

------------------------------    ------------------------------

DEFAULT_JOB_CLASS
AUTO_TASKS_JOB_CLASS              AUTO_TASK_CONSUMER_GROUP
LOW_GROUP_JOB_CLASS              LOW_GROUP
```

Now a Job can belong to this class, automatically being enforced to comply with the resource allocation policy that governs the Job Class.

```
BEGIN
sys.dbms_scheduler.set_attribute(
  name      => '"OSCHEDULER"."TEST_MINUTELY"',
  attribute => 'job_class',
  value     => 'LOW_GROUP_JOB_CLASS');
END;
/
```

And finally we can see the job belongs to the LOW_GROUP_JOB_CLASS:

```
SQL> select OWNER,
  2          JOB_NAME,
  3          JOB_CLASS
  4   from   DBA_SCHEDULER_JOBS
  5   where  OWNER = 'OSCHEDULER';

OWNER       JOB_NAME              JOB_CLASS
----------  --------------------  ----------------------
OSCHEDULER  TEST_SCHEDULER        DEFAULT_JOB_CLASS
OSCHEDULER  TEST_MINUTELY         LOW_GROUP_JOB_CLASS
OSCHEDULER  MONTHLYTEST           DEFAULT_JOB_CLASS
OSCHEDULER  OS_LOG_RECORDS_JOB    DEFAULT_JOB_CLASS
```

Managing the Scheduler

While defining a schedule it is not required to launch the schedule immediately afterwards. A scheduled task can be created in a disabled status so that the user can schedule it at a later time.

All tasks leave a log that can be used to validate that the task was successful or to find out if a scheduled task failed and why. The user should know how and when to purge it so it doesn't grow too big.

Enable or disable components

The DBMS_SCHEDULER.ENABLE enables a Scheduler component, such as a program, job, window or window group, and DBMS_SCHEDULER.DISABLE disables components.

This procedure enables a job belonging to the demo Scheduler. In the previous section the TEST_MINUTELY Scheduler job was defined.

```
EXEC sys.dbms_scheduler.enable( '"OSCHEDULER"."TEST_MINUTELY"' );
```

Managing job logs

There are two important tasks to perform with the logs; these tasks are to **monitor** them and **schedule a purge task** on them. All job related activity generated by means of the dbms_scheduler leaves a log behind for forensic purposes in case something goes wrong with the job or just to make sure the job ran successfully. Once the user has made sure everything went well and there is nothing else to debug, the log information becomes a ballast the user should get rid of, otherwise this can easily flood the database with useless information.

Monitor a Job Execution

The outcome from the job Scheduler can be monitored at the **[DBA | USER | ALL]_ SCHEDULER_JOB_LOG** views. The views are listed later in this chapter.

```
SQL> SELECT LOG_ID, LOG_DATE, JOB_NAME, STATUS
  2  FROM USER_SCHEDULER_JOB_LOG
  3  WHERE LOG_DATE > TRUNC(SYSDATE)
  4* ORDER BY LOG_ID
    LOG_ID LOG_DATE                             JOB_NAME          STATUS
---------- ------------------------------------ ------------- ----------
     17824 30-NOV-08 12.21.42.547453 AM -06:00  TEST_MINUTELY    SUCCEEDED
     17825 30-NOV-08 12.22.42.538071 AM -06:00  TEST_MINUTELY    SUCCEEDED
     17826 30-NOV-08 12.23.42.080787 AM -06:00  TEST_MINUTELY    SUCCEEDED
```

Several different queries can be issued against the database to monitor the job activity.

Requirement	Query
Details on Job runs	```select log_date, job_name, status, req_start_date, actual_start_date, run_duration from dba_scheduler_job_run_details;```
Running Jobs	```select job_name, session_id, running_instance, elapsed_time, cpu_used from dba_scheduler_running_jobs;```
Query Job History	```select log_date, job_name, status from dba_scheduler_job_log;```
Query all schedules	```select schedule_name, schedule_type, start_date, repeat_interval from dba_scheduler_schedules;```
Query all jobs and their attributes	```select * from dba_scheduler_jobs;```
Query all programs	```select * from dba_scheduler_programs;```
Query all program arguments	```select * from dba_scheduler_program_args;```

The job can also be monitored from **Oracle Enterprise Manager** in the **Operation Detail** section (**A**). This section can be accessed from **Main Page | Administration | Database Scheduler | Jobs | Job Name | Operation Detail** (**A**).

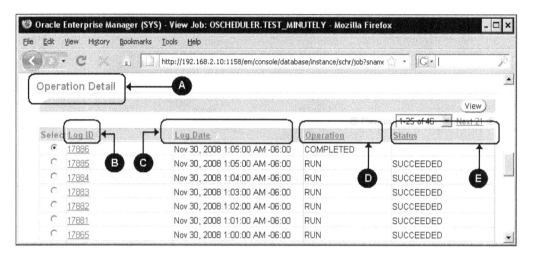

For each generated log entry a consecutive log ID value is generated, this ID is useful when manually referencing a log entry from the scheduled job log views (**B**). The table displays the time stamp when the log entry was generated (**C**), the **Operation** column (**D**) will display the current activity, in case the job ran at the specified time stamp the status will be RUN, if the task comes to an end, the most recently executed task will display the **COMPLETED** status. The **Status** (**E**) column shows how this job execution ended; each job will show either **SUCCEEDED** or **FAILED** as its status. The details of each job run can be seen by either clicking on the **Log ID** link or selecting the log ID with the select radio button and clicking on the **VIEW** button.

Purging the job log

Among the factory programmed jobs, Oracle provides a job named PURGE_LOG.

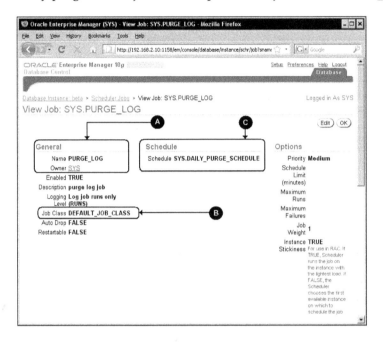

This job is in charge of purging the job log. PURGE_LOG (**A**) is a job owned by **SYS** which generates logs only when it runs, this job belongs to the DEFAULT_JOB_ CLASS (**B**) and is scheduled with the SYS.DAILY_PURGE_SCHEDULE (**C**), a schedule configured as a standard schedule to be launched daily at 03:00 a.m.

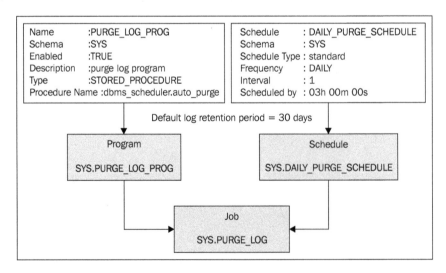

The PURGE_LOG job launches a **Program** named SYS.PURGE_LOG which is defined as a STORED_PROCEDURE and whose procedure name is DBMS_SCHEDULER.AUTO_PURGE. This stored program unit receives no arguments and it purges the logs based on its retention period. The DEFAULT_JOB_CLASS has no explicit retention period declared, so it takes the default value of 30 days. This should be enough to maintain a reasonable amount of log history for most practical situations, but as the purge log job has been defined using the standard DBMS_SCHEDULER infrastructure you can tailor it to fit your particular log retention needs.

Data dictionary related views

The Oracle Scheduler DBA related data dictionary views are:

View	Description
DBA_SCHEDULER_CHAINS	All Scheduler chains in the database.
DBA_SCHEDULER_CHAIN_RULES	All rules from Scheduler chains in the database.
DBA_SCHEDULER_CHAIN_STEPS	All steps of Scheduler chains in the database.
DBA_SCHEDULER_GLOBAL_ATTRIBUTE	All Scheduler global attributes.
DBA_SCHEDULER_JOBS	All Scheduler jobs in the database.
DBA_SCHEDULER_JOB_ARGS	All arguments with set values of all Scheduler jobs in the database.
DBA_SCHEDULER_JOB_CLASSES	All Scheduler classes in the database.
DBA_SCHEDULER_JOB_LOG	Logged information for all Scheduler jobs.
DBA_SCHEDULER_JOB_RUN_DETAILS	The details of a job run.
DBA_SCHEDULER_PROGRAMS	All Scheduler programs in the database.
DBA_SCHEDULER_PROGRAM_ARGS	All arguments of all Scheduler programs in the database.
DBA_SCHEDULER_RUNNING_CHAINS	All steps of all running chains in the database.
DBA_SCHEDULER_SCHEDULES	All schedules in the database.
DBA_SCHEDULER_WINDOWS	All Scheduler windows in the database.
DBA_SCHEDULER_WINDOW_DETAILS	The details of a window.
DBA_SCHEDULER_WINDOW_GROUPS	All Scheduler window groups in the database.
DBA_SCHEDULER_WINDOW_LOG	Logged information for all Scheduler windows.
DBA_SCHEDULER_WINGROUP_MEMBERS	Members of all Scheduler window groups in the database.
V$SCHEDULER_RUNNING_JOBS	Currently running jobs.
DBA_QUEUE_SCHEDULES	Describes the current schedules for propagating messages.

Summary

Starting with release 10g, the scheduling mechanism has considerably evolved from a simple task launcher to a powerful Scheduler. Oracle Scheduler allows complex scheduling that would be otherwise very difficult to program in previous releases. The OS Scheduler is very limited compared with the potential provided by the Oracle Scheduler.

Oracle provides an enriched set of scheduling time expressions that allow the user to define complex time expressions. Even though Oracle Scheduler has greatly simplified the way to schedule tasks, its concepts and syntax are not quite clear at first glance, Oracle is aware of the scheduling complexity, but Enterprise Manager frees the DBA from this complexity, displaying the Scheduler mechanism in a very simple an intuitive way, allowing the DBA to be more productive when defining the different required schedules.

In this chapter, we learned the basic Scheduler concepts, the time expression syntax, and the Scheduler management basics. In the next chapter, we will explore a tool that is the keystone of certified security. When a simple username and password is not enough to provide an authentication mechanism, when managing certificates becomes a must, then you must get acquainted with a tool that is the gateway to a higher security level, the Oracle Wallet Manager.

8
Oracle Wallet Manager

The **Oracle Wallet Manager** (**OWM**) is the tool used by Oracle to manage the authentication processes. It is a key tool for managing most of the authentication and security related tasks in an Oracle environment, this includes; authenticating users, providing SSL communication, and configuring the **Transparent Data Encryption** (**TDE**) feature, among others. There are two modes to work with the Oracle Wallet, the first one is by using the Java Oracle Wallet Manager console and the second one is by means of the `mkwallet` command line version, this method is suitable for batch processing. The Wallet is a very sensitive element; there are several ways to store it, not only in its file at the file system level, but also in the registry (for Windows platforms only). It can also be stored in an LDAP compliant directory.

The Oracle Wallet Manager

Oracle Wallet Manager is a password protected stand-alone Java application tool used to maintain security credentials and store SSL related information such as authentication and signing credentials, private keys, certificates, and trusted certificates.

OWM uses **Public Key Cryptographic Standards** (**PKCS**) #12 specification for the Wallet format and PKCS #10 for certificate requests.

Oracle Wallet Manager stores X.509 v3 certificates and private keys in industry-standard PKCS #12 formats, and generates certificate requests according to the PKCS #10 specification. This makes the Oracle Wallet structure interoperable with supported third party PKI applications, and provides Wallet portability across operating systems. Additionally, Oracle Wallet Manager Wallets can be enabled to store credentials on hardware security modules that use APIs compliant with the PKCS #11 specification.

The OWM creates Wallets, generates certificate requests, accesses Public Key interface-based services, saves credentials into cryptographic hardware such as smart cards, uploads and unloads Wallets to LDAP directories, and imports Wallets in PKCS #12 format.

In a Windows environment, Oracle Wallet Manager can be accessed from the start menu. The following screenshot shows the **Oracle Wallet Manager Properties**:

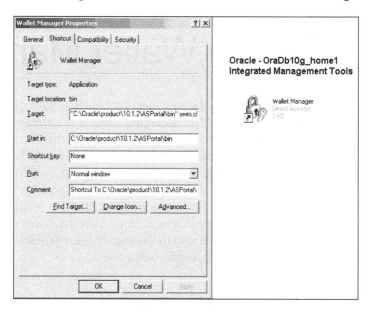

In a Unix like environment, OWM can be accessed directly from the command line with the `owm` shell script located at `$ORACLE_HOME/bin/owm`, it requires a graphical environment so it can be launched.

Creating the Oracle Wallet

If this is the first time the Wallet has been opened, then a Wallet file does not yet exist. A Wallet is physically created in a specified directory. The user can declare the path where the Oracle Wallet file should be created.

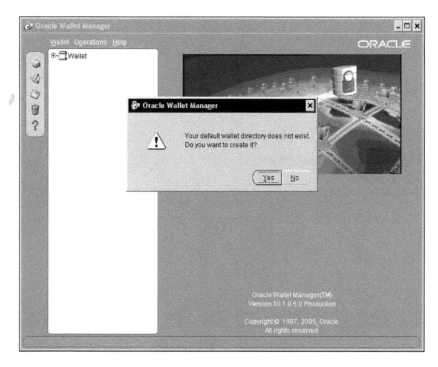

The user may either specify a default location or declare a particular directory. A file named `ewallet.p12` will be created in the specified location.

Enabling Auto Login

The Oracle Wallet Manager **Auto Login** feature creates an obfuscated copy of the Wallet and enables PKI-based access to the services without a password. When this feature is enabled, only the user who created the Wallet will have access to it.

By default, **Single Sign-On (SSO)** access to a different database is disabled. The auto login feature must be enabled in order for you to have access to multiple databases using SSO.

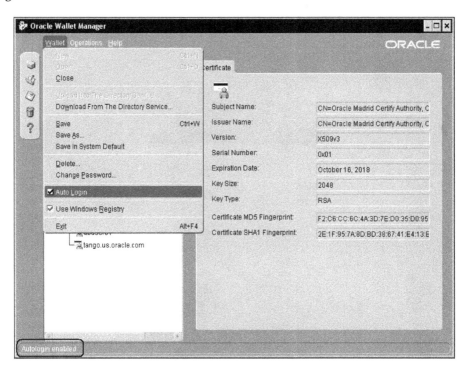

Checking and unchecking the **Auto Login** option will enable and disable this feature.

mkwallet, the CLI OWM version

Besides the Java client, there is a command line interface version of the Wallet, which can be accessed by means of the mkwallet utility. This can also be used to generate a Wallet and have it configured in **Auto Login** mode. This is a fully featured tool that allows you to create Wallets, and to view and modify their content.

The options provided by the mkwallet tool are shown in the following table:

Option	Meaning
`-R rootPwd rootWrl DN keySize expDate`	Create the root Wallet
`-e pwd wrl`	Create an empty Wallet
`-r pwd wrl DN keySize certReqLoc`	Create a certificate request, add it to Wallet and export it to `certReqLoc`
`-c rootPwd rootWrl certReqLoc certLoc`	Create a certificate for a certificate request
`-i pwd wrl certLoc NZDST_CERTIFICATE	NZDST_CLEAR_PTP`	Install a certificate | trusted point
`-d pwd wrl DN`	Delete a certificate with matching DN
`-s pwd wrl`	Store sso Wallet
`-p pwd wrl`	Dump the contents of Wallet
`-q certLoc`	Dump the contents of the certificate
`-Lg pwd wrl crlLoc nextUpdate`	Generate CRL
`-La pwd wrl crlLoc certtoRevoke`	Revoke certificate
`-Ld crlLoc`	Display CRL
`-Lv crlLoc cacert`	Verify CRL signature
`-Ls crlLoc cert`	Check certificate revocation status
`-Ll oidHostname oidPortNumber cacert`	Fetch CRL from LDAP directory
`-Lc cert`	Fetch CRL from CRLDP in cert
`-Lb b64CrlLoc derCrlLoc`	Convert CRL from B64 to DER format
`-Pw pwd wrl pkcs11Lib tokenPassphrase`	Create an empty Wallet. Store PKCS11 info in it
`-Pq pwd wrl DN keysize certreqLoc`	Create cert request. Generate key pair on pkcs11 device
`-Pl pwd wrl`	Test pkcs11 device login using Wallet containing PKCS11 information
`-Px pwd wrl pkcs11Lib tokenPassphrase`	Create a Wallet with pkcs11 info from a software Wallet

Managing Wallets with orapki

A CLI-based tool, **orapki**, is used to manage Public Key Infrastructure components such as Wallets and revocation lists. This tool eases the procedures related to PKI management and maintenance by allowing the user to include it in batch scripts.

This tool can be used to create and view signed certificates for testing purposes, create Oracle Wallets, add and remove certificate and certificate requests, and manage **Certification Revocation Lists (CRLs)** — renaming them and managing them against the Oracle Internet Directory.

The syntax for this tool is:

```
orapki module command -parameter <value>
```

`module` can have these values:

- `wallet`: Oracle Wallet
- `crl`: Certificate Revocation List
- `cert`: The PKI Certificate

To create a Wallet you can issue this command:

```
orapki wallet create -wallet <Path to Wallet>
```

To create a Wallet with the auto login feature enabled, you can issue the command:

```
orapki wallet create -wallet <Path to Wallet> -autologin
```

To add a certificate request to the Wallet you can use the command:

```
orapki wallet add -wallet <wallet_location> -dn <user_dn> -keySize
<512|1024|2048>
```

To add a user certificate to an Oracle Wallet:

```
orapki wallet add -wallet <wallet_location> -user_cert -cert
<certificate_location>
```

The options and values available for the `orapki` tool depend on the module to be configured:

orapki Action	Description and Syntax
orapki cert create	Creates a signed certificate for testing purposes.
	`orapki cert create [-wallet <wallet_location>] -request <certificate_request_location> -cert <certificate_location> -validity <number_of_days> [-summary]`
orapki cert display	Displays details of a specific certificate.
	`orapki cert display -cert <certificate_location> [-summary|-complete]`

orapki Action	Description and Syntax
orapki crl delete	Deletes CRLs from Oracle Internet Directory. `orapki crl delete -issuer <issuer_name> -ldap <hostname:ssl_port> -user <username> [-wallet <wallet_location>] [-summary]`
orapki crl diskplay	Displays specific CRLs that are stored in Oracle Internet Directory. `orapki crl display -crl <crl_location> [-wallet <wallet_location>] [-summary|-complete]`
orapki crl hash	Generates a hash value of the certificate revocation list (CRL) issuer to identify the location of the CRL in your file system for certificate validation. `orapki crl hash -crl <crl_filename|URL> [-wallet <wallet_location>] [-symlink|-copy] <crl_directory> [-summary]`
orapki crl list	Displays a list of CRLs stored in Oracle Internet Directory. `orapki crl list -ldap <hostname:ssl_port>`
orapki crl upload	Uploads CRLs to the CRL subtree in Oracle Internet Directory. `orapki crl upload -crl <crl_location> -ldap <hostname:ssl_port> -user <username> [-wallet <wallet_location>] [-summary]`
orapki wallet add	Add certificate requests and certificates to an Oracle Wallet. `orapki wallet add -wallet <wallet_location> -dn <user_dn> -keySize <512|1024|2048>`
orapki wallet create	Creates an Oracle Wallet or to set auto login on for an Oracle Wallet. `orapki wallet create -wallet <wallet_location> [-auto_login]`
orapki wallet display	Displays the certificate requests, user certificates, and trusted certificates in an Oracle Wallet. `orapki wallet display -wallet <wallet_location>`

orapki wallet export	Export certificate requests and certificates from an Oracle Wallet.
	
	`orapki wallet export -wallet <wallet_location> -dn <certificate_dn> -cert`
	
	`<certificate_filename>`

Oracle Wallet Manager CSR generation

Oracle Wallet Manager generates a certificate request in PKCS #10 format. This certificate request can be sent to a certificate authority of your choice. The procedure to generate this certificate request is as follows:

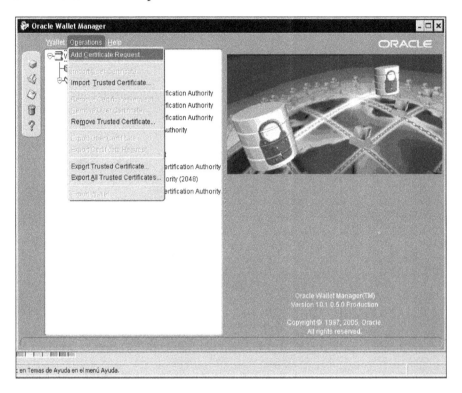

From the main menu choose the **Operations** menu and then select the **Add Certificate Request** submenu. As shown in the following screenshot, a form will be displayed where you can capture specific information.

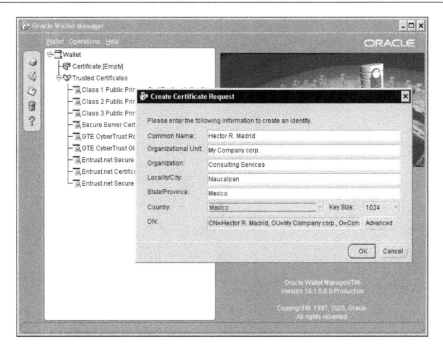

The parameters used to request a certificate are described next:

Common Name: This parameter is mandatory. This is the user's name or entity's name. If you are using a user's name, then enter it using the first name, last name format.

Organization Unit: This is the name of the identity's organization unit. It could be the name of the department where the entity belongs (optional parameter).

Organization: This is the company's name (optional).

Location/City: The location and the city where the entity resides (optional).

State/Province: This is the full name of the state where the entity resides. Do not use abbreviations (optional).

Country: This parameter is mandatory. It specifies the country where the entity is located.

Key Size: This parameter is mandatory. It defines the key size used when a public/private key pair is created. The key size can be as little as 512 bytes and up to 4096 bytes.

Advanced: When the parameters are introduced a **Distinguished Name** (**DN**) is assembled. If you want to customize this DN, then you can use the advanced DN configuration mode.

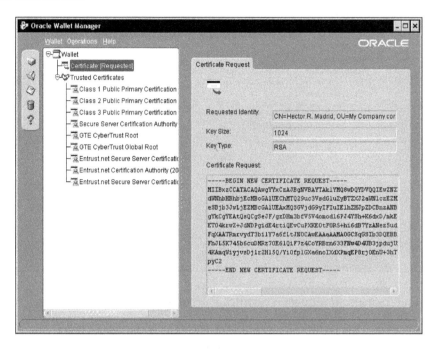

Once the **Certificate Request** form has been completed, a PKCS#10 format certificate request is generated. The information that appears between the BEGIN and END keywords must be used to request a certificate to a **Certificate Authority** (**CA**); there are several well known certificate authorities, and depending on the usage you plan for your certificate, you could address the request to a known CA (from the browser perspective) so when an end user accesses your site it doesn't get warned about the site's identity. If the certificate will be targeted at a local community who doesn't mind about the certificate warning, then you may generate your own certificate or ask a CA to issue a certificate for you. For demonstration purposes, we used the **Oracle Certificate Authority** (**OCA**) included with the Oracle Application Server. OCA will provide the Certificate Authority capabilities to your site and it can issue standard certificates, suitable for the intranet users. If you are planning to use OCA then you should review the license agreements to determine if you are allowed to use it.

Storing the Oracle Wallet in the Windows registry

On Windows operating systems the Wallet can either be stored in the file system or in the Windows registry. Storing the Wallet in the registry has several advantages. It creates an additional security layer, allowing transparency for all other users. When a user profile is removed, the Wallet in the profile is also removed. The Wallet is transparent to all other users and when the user logs out, access to the Wallet is automatically precluded.

The supported operations are:

- Save a Wallet to the registry
- Open a Wallet from the registry
- Save as to a different registry location
- Open Wallet from the file system, save it to the registry, and vice versa
- Delete a Wallet from the registry

Save Wallet to the registry

In order for you to save a Wallet to the Windows registry, make sure the **Use Windows Registry** check box is marked; when you command the Wallet to be saved, it will use the Windows registry.

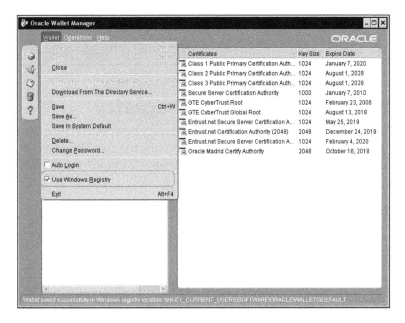

The Wallet will only be available to the user who saved it. At the time to save it, the Wallet will ask the user for a location at the registry to save the Wallet.

The user can either specify a location or let the Wallet define a default binary entry at **\\HKEY_CURRENT_USER\SOFTWARE\ORACLE\WALLETS**. The name of the Windows registry where the Wallet will be stored is **ewallet.p12**, as you can see in the following image:

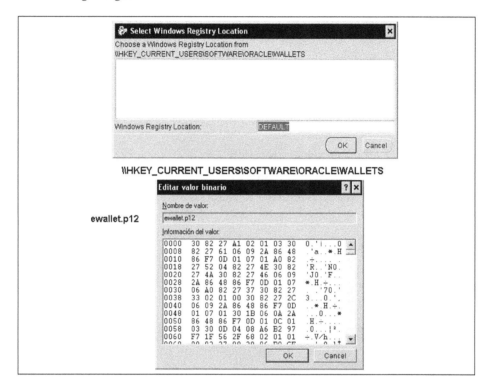

Open the Wallet from the registry

Once the Wallet has been saved to the registry, it can be opened from the registry. When asking Wallet manager to open a Wallet, mark the **Use Windows Registry** check box. This will ask for the registry path where it will look for the Wallet.

Save as to a different registry location

The Wallet can be stored in a different registry location. It is enough to use save as, providing a different registry path.

Open the Wallet from the registry, save it to the file system and vice versa

If the Wallet currently resides as a regular Wallet on the file system, it can be stored in the Windows registry, just use the **Save As** menu option and make sure the **Use Windows Registry** option is marked. If the database currently resides in the Windows registry and you want to save it to the file system, it is enough to use the **Save As** option with the **Use Windows Registry** option marked.

Delete the Wallet from the registry

You can get rid of a Wallet that currently resides in the registry by selecting the option **Delete** from the **File** menu. This will remove the entry from the registry and will permanently delete the Wallet. You must absolutely make sure this is what you want to do, as this option cannot be rolled back. Deleting a Wallet would mean all the certificates contained in the Wallet will be lost.

Configuring the Wallet location

The client side networking profile file (`sqlnet.ora`) must be configured to let Oracle know where the Wallet is located, so PKI-based applications know where to look for the Wallet.

Assuming the Wallet was stored in the default location `\\HKEY_CURRENT_USER\SOFTWARE\ORACLE\WALLETS\DEFAULT`, the `sqlnet.ora` declaration would be:

```
WALLET_LOCATION =
    (SOURCE =
            (METHOD=REG)
            (METHOD_DATA =
                    (KEY=DEFAULT)
            )
    )
```

`WALLET_LOCATION` supports the following sub parameters:

- `SOURCE`: Specify the type of storage for Wallets and storage location
- `METHOD`: Specify the type of storage
- `METHOD_DATA`: Specify the storage location
- `DIRECTORY`: Specify the location of Oracle Wallets on file system
- `KEY`: Specify the Wallet type and location in the Windows NT registry

This will store the encrypted Wallet in `\\HKEY_CURRENT_USER\SOFTWARE\ORACLE\WALLETS\DEFAULT\ewallet.p12` and the obfuscated wallet in `\\HKEY_CURRENT_USER\SOFTWARE\ORACLE\WALLETS\DEFAULT\cwallet.sso`.

The previously declared value is the default location, and it is the first path that Oracle will use to look for the obfuscated Wallet if a path has not been explicitly declared.

If no obfuscated Wallet is found there, Oracle PKI applications look for it in the file system of the local computer at: `%USERPROFILE%\ORACLE\WALLETS`.

Storing the Wallet in an LDAP server

An LDAP compliant directory can also be used to store and retrieve a Wallet, providing a single point of access. It is more secure than storing it at the client side, as it provides a way to let the manager provide more secure procedures to access the Wallet.

Uploading the Wallet to an LDAP server

Oracle Wallet Manager can store and retrieve certificates to and from a centralized LDAP compliant server. In order for you to be able to store a Wallet, the Wallet must already have a user certificate installed.

The LDAP directory must have been previously configured so the Wallet can be stored there. If the Wallet doesn't have an SSL certificate installed, then password-based authentication will be used to access the Wallet.

You should be aware that there are two passwords to be used in an LDAP/OWM environment, one password is used to access the LDAP server, and a second password is used to access the Oracle Wallet. These passwords are independent and the user should adequately handle them.

In order for you to perform the Wallet upload process, choose **Wallet | Upload into the directory service...**. Then the dialog box appears asking you first to save the Wallet prior to uploading it.

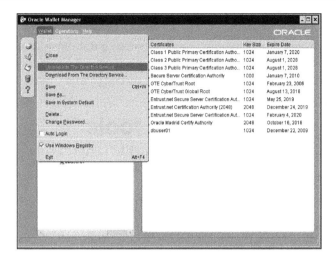

If at least one certificate has SSL key usage then the Oracle Wallet tries to connect using SSL, otherwise the user will be prompted for a password. It is assumed the Wallet password is the same as that of the directory password.

Downloading the Wallet from LDAP

When asking Oracle Wallet Manager to download a Wallet from the LDAP server, a dialog appears, asking the user for the User DN, directory password, and the connection information to the LDAP server.

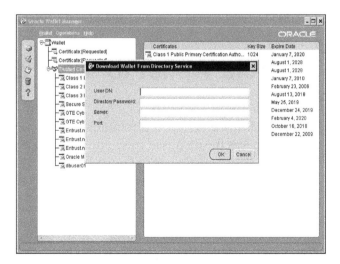

Once the Wallet has been downloaded it resides in the OWM's memory, and it needs to be explicitly saved to the file system.

Using certificates for authentication

Using a simple password as a means to authenticate a database user is a weak authentication method. A stronger authentication method can be achieved with certificates, this requires the advanced security to be installed and configured.

Public Key Infrastructure tools

The Oracle database **Public Key Infrastructure (PKI)** implementation requires:

- Oracle Advanced Security
- Oracle Identity Management Infrastructure
- Oracle Wallet Manager
- Enterprise Security Manager

The procedure to configure authentication is as follows:

1. Install the PKI Tools.
2. Configure SSL on the server side. Store a certificate in the Wallet at the server side.
3. Configure the network configuration files `listener.ora` and `sqlnet.ora` on the server side so it supports SSL
4. Configure the client network files, `sqlnet.ora` and `tnsnames.ora` so it supports SSL.
5. Create a user whose authentication is performed with a certificate.

Using the Oracle Wallet to store database credentials

Storing your users' credentials in OS scripts is a common practice when performing batch tasks, but doing so exposes the database users and creates a security breach. The Oracle Wallet can be used to store the user's credentials, so instead of exposing passwords in clear text format in a batch script, those can be safely stored in the client's Wallet without compromising them.

This procedure stores a database user's credentials inside the Wallet. This features uses the auto login feature, so it is not required to provide the Wallet password to access to the user's credentials, the OS file permissions regulate access to the Wallet.

Once the Oracle Wallet has been configured and the database credentials have been stored the user can access the Oracle database from any tool requiring the user to provide access to the database. The access granted to the user will be just like as though the user has provided the password at connect time.

As the database credentials are stored in an area different from the area where the PKI certificates are stored, you cannot use the graphical interface to manage the database user credentials, you must use the `mkstore` command line utility instead.

There are different options available for the `mkstore` utility:

- Listing External Password Store Contents.

  ```
  mkstore -wrl <wallet_location> -listCredential
  ```

- Adding Credentials to an External Password Store.

  ```
  mkstore -wrl <wallet_location> -createCredential <db_alias> <user-name> <password>
  ```

- Modifying Credentials in an External Password Store.

  ```
  mkstore -wrl <wallet_location> -modifyCredential <dbase_alias> <username> <password>
  ```

- Deleting Credentials from an External Password Store.

  ```
  mkstore -wrl <wallet_location> -deleteCredential <db_alias>
  ```

Using the `mkstore` utility a Wallet is created at the client side (**A**).

```
mkstore -wrl /home/user1/wallet -create
```

The password being requested is the Wallet's password.

Once the Wallet has been created, using the same `mkstore` utility, the user's credential is stored inside the Wallet (**B**).

```
mkstore -wrl /home/user1/wallet -createCredential scott_secure
scott tiger
```

The `createCredential` option requires three parameters:

- The `tnsnames` entry (`SCOTT_SECURE`)
- The database user name (`SCOTT`)
- Its database password (`TIGER`)

The `tnsnames` entry doesn't need to exist right now.

Next the existence of the credential is confirmed. Using the `listCredentail` (**C**) option of the `mkstore` utility:

```
mkstore -wrl /home/user1/wallet -listCredential
```

It shows the existence of one stored credential inside the Wallet that corresponds to the `SCOTT` user at the database pointed by the `SCOTT_SECURE` tnsnames entry.

Now there are two files that must be modified at the client side, `sqlnet.ora` (**D**) and `tnsnames.ora` (**E**), the first one defines where the Wallet resides and the last one defines where the `SCOTT_SECURE` tnsnames entry is pointing.

```
WALLET_LOCATION =
        (SOURCE =
                (METHOD=FILE)
                (METHOD_DATA=
                        (DIRECTORY=/home/user1/wallet)
                )
        )
SQLNET.WALLET_OVERRIDE = TRUE
```

The `WALLET_LOCATION` parameter defines the physical location of the Wallet, meanwhile the `SQLNET.WALLET_OVERRIDE` parameter defines if the values stored inside the Wallet will be used to authenticate the user (`TRUE`), if the value is set to `FALSE` then it means that the SSL certificate will be used instead.

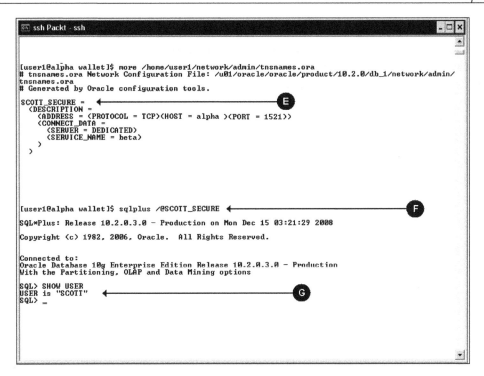

The `tnsentry` found in the `tnsnames.ora` file (**E**) is just a regular `tnsentry`, the name defined here must match the parameter used with the `createCredential` option of the `mkstore` command.

```
SCOTT_SECURE =
  (DESCRIPTION =
    (ADDRESS = (PROTOCOL = TCP)(HOST = alpha)(PORT = 1521))
    (CONNECT_DATA =
      (SERVER = DEDICATED)
      (SERVICE_NAME = beta)
    )
  )
```

And finally, the most interesting part of the procedure, using the credentials stored for the particular `tnsentry`, a new connection is opened against the database without exposing the database user name and its password (**F**).

```
sqlplus /@SCOTT_SECURE
```

It is then confirmed that the user has successfully opened a database session (**G**).

```
SQL> SHOW USER
USER is "SCOTT"
```

Summary

When security requirements go beyond a simple username and password authentication, then more sophisticated authentication mechanisms are required. This is when certificated authentication comes up. Oracle Wallet Manager and all other CLI related tools are the key elements to maintain and manage authentication information to protect passwords, provide single sign on, enable secure socket layer, store data, and provide encryption mechanisms to cipher communications.

Oracle Wallet Manager is the key element used to provide secure access to the certificates used to authenticate users and enable all other advanced security related features.

9
Security Management

Oracle provides several tools to protect your data against unauthorized access. Encrypted backups, encrypted data pump exports, certified security, and user authentication are just some of the useful tools and techniques that can be used to enhance security management. The keystone tool used to manage security is the Oracle Wallet Manager, a tool which was explained earlier in this book.

Backups are a must do task wherever an information system exists. Backing up information is a task that should be routinely performed. The point here doesn't actually have to do with backups by themselves, but how to manage those backups once they are taken. A backup holds the information required to restore the system. It allows you to restore it somewhere else, but to the original system where it was taken from. If this is not an authorized location, or if the user is not supposed to be authorized to restore the data, then the data's security could be compromised. Oracle provides mechanisms based on the Oracle Wallet to protect sensitive data, not only data stored inside the database, but also data stored on backup media.

Using the Oracle Wallet to encrypt backups

Backups are a mandatory condition for all enterprises. They are required to ensure data recovery is possible in case of systems failure. However, it is important not only to have a valid backup, but also to manage the backup correctly. A backup, once taken, is stored at some place. What would happen if a user has access to the physical backup media, and this user performs an unauthorized backup test? The good news is that the backup is being tested; the bad news is that we will never know the result, not to mention that the enterprise data confidentiality will be compromised.

Considering these circumstances, the use of encryption techniques to protect the backups should be considered, both for Recovery Manager and Data Pump.

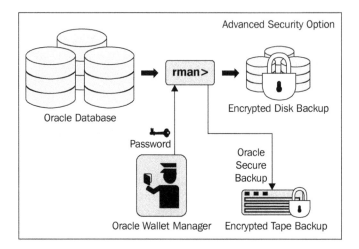

Recovery Manager encryption

Recovery Manager provides three encryption modes, the **transparent mode**, the **password mode**, and the **dual mode**. You must consider that Recovery Manager encrypts only backup sets, not image copies. These encryption techniques are available on Enterprise Edition using the **Advanced Security Option** and the COMPATIBLE instance parameter must be set to at least 10.2.0.

- **Transparent mode**: This mode requires you to have the Oracle Wallet Manager properly configured. It uses the Oracle key management infrastructure. Transparent mode is best used for regular backups that are meant to be restored on the same system where they were taken from.

- **Password mode**: This mode requires you to declare the password in the rman scripts by means of the SET ENCRYPTION ON IDENTIFIED BY password ONLY clause.

- **Dual mode**: This mode is flexible, it uses both the transparent mode and the password mode. This kind of backup is useful when the data is to be recovered on environments where the wallet is not available. This provides an alternative means to restore the backup.

Using the transparent mode

This mode requires the user to configure the Wallet location and set the Master Encryption Key. The user must have Recovery Manager configured in encryption mode and declare the encryption algorithm to use.

Configure the wallet location at the `sqlnet.ora` file:

```
NAMES.DIRECTORY_PATH= (TNSNAMES, EZCONNECT)
WALLET_LOCATION =
        (SOURCE =
                (METHOD = FILE)
                (METHOD_LOCATION =
                        (DIRECTORY = /u01/oracle/product/11.2.0/
                                                dbhome_1/wallet)
                )
        )
SQLNET.WALLET_OVERRIDE = TRUE
```

Create the Master Encryption Key:

```
SQL> ALTER SYSTEM SET ENCRYPTION KEY
IDENTIFIED BY "welcome1";
```

 If the Master Encryption Key is not set, then these error messages will appear:

ORA-19914: unable to encrypt backup

ORA-28361: master key not yet set

Configure the encryption mode in Recovery Manager. This is a one-time operation. From a RMAN prompt issue the command to configure it, as shown next.

```
[oracle@alpha ~]$ rman target /

Recovery Manager: Release 11.2.0.1 - Beta on Sun Jan 25 00:42:28 2009

Copyright (c) 1982, 2007, Oracle.  All rights reserved.

connected to target database: GAMMA (DBID=2978335724)

RMAN> SHOW ALL;

using target database control file instead of recovery catalog
RMAN configuration parameters for database with db_unique_name GAMMA are:
CONFIGURE RETENTION POLICY TO REDUNDANCY 1; # default
CONFIGURE BACKUP OPTIMIZATION OFF; # default
CONFIGURE DEFAULT DEVICE TYPE TO DISK; # default
CONFIGURE CONTROLFILE AUTOBACKUP OFF; # default
CONFIGURE CONTROLFILE AUTOBACKUP FORMAT FOR DEVICE TYPE DISK TO '%F'; # default
CONFIGURE DEVICE TYPE DISK PARALLELISM 1 BACKUP TYPE TO COMPRESSED BACKUPSET;
CONFIGURE DATAFILE BACKUP COPIES FOR DEVICE TYPE DISK TO 1; # default
CONFIGURE ARCHIVELOG BACKUP COPIES FOR DEVICE TYPE DISK TO 1; # default
CONFIGURE MAXSETSIZE TO UNLIMITED; # default
CONFIGURE ENCRYPTION FOR DATABASE OFF; # default                    <---- A
CONFIGURE ENCRYPTION ALGORITHM 'AES128'; # default
CONFIGURE COMPRESSION ALGORITHM 'BZIP2';
CONFIGURE ARCHIVELOG DELETION POLICY TO NONE; # default
CONFIGURE SNAPSHOT CONTROLFILE NAME TO '/u01/oracle/product/11.2.0/dbhome_1/dbs/snapcf_gamma.f';
 # default


RMAN> CONFIGURE ENCRYPTION FOR DATABASE ON;

new RMAN configuration parameters:                                   <---- B
CONFIGURE ENCRYPTION FOR DATABASE ON;
new RMAN configuration parameters are successfully stored

RMAN> _
```

Originally, the encryption mode is not enabled (**A**). You must enable the encryption for the database by setting the **ENCRYPTION FOR DATABASE** parameter to **ON** (**B**). Optionally, you can set an encryption algorithm, which by default uses AES128. A complete list of all supported encryption algorithms can be found in the V$RMAN_ENCRYPTION_ALGORITHMS dynamic view.

Algorithm Name	Algorithm Description
AES128	AES 128-bit key
AES192	AES 192-bit key
AES256	AES 256-bit key

Advanced Encryption Standard (**AES**) is an encryption standard adopted by the U.S. government. AES comprises three block ciphers, AES-128, AES-192 and AES-256. Each cipher has a 128-bit block size with key sizes of 128, 192 and 256 bits respectively. AES requires less memory than its predecessor DES and performs fast on both hardware and software.

The longer the key, the more time it takes to process data, and the harder it is to attack it. The encryption algorithm you choose depends on your company's security requirements.

Prior to starting the encrypted backup, you must open the wallet with the wallet password (**C**). To do this from the RMAN prompt, issue the command to open the wallet.

```
SQL 'ALTER SYSTEM SET ENCRYPTION WALLET OPEN
IDENTIFIED  BY "WalletPassword" ';
```

Opening the wallet can be done once the Oracle instance has opened the database. This operation is required for **Transparent Data Encryption** (**TDE**) to work. It is not recommended to write this command to a script as this would expose the wallet password. Once set, just issue a regular backup command, this procedure will create a transparent mode encrypted backup (**D**).

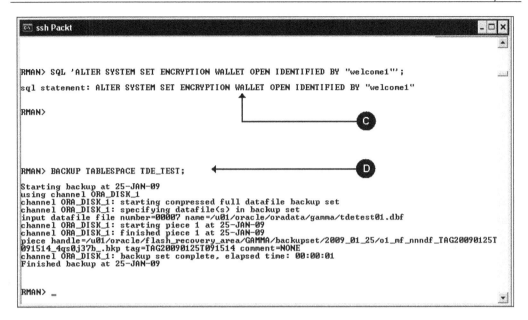

```
RMAN> SQL 'ALTER SYSTEM SET ENCRYPTION WALLET OPEN IDENTIFIED BY "welcome1"';

sql statement: ALTER SYSTEM SET ENCRYPTION WALLET OPEN IDENTIFIED BY "welcome1"

RMAN>                                                              C


RMAN> BACKUP TABLESPACE TDE_TEST;    ←                             D
Starting backup at 25-JAN-09
using channel ORA_DISK_1
channel ORA_DISK_1: starting compressed full datafile backup set
channel ORA_DISK_1: specifying datafile(s) in backup set
input datafile file number=00007 name=/u01/oracle/oradata/gamma/tdetest01.dbf
channel ORA_DISK_1: starting piece 1 at 25-JAN-09
channel ORA_DISK_1: finished piece 1 at 25-JAN-09
piece handle=/u01/oracle/flash_recovery_area/GAMMA/backupset/2009_01_25/o1_mf_nnndf_TAG20090125T
091514_4qs0j37b_.bkp tag=TAG20090125T091514 comment=NONE
channel ORA_DISK_1: backup set complete, elapsed time: 00:00:01
Finished backup at 25-JAN-09

RMAN> _
```

Watch out
You must maintain a backup policy for the Wallet. The Oracle Wallet is the only way to access the backup when a restore operation is required. If you lose the Wallet and the backup is totally useless!

The DBA may change the master key at any time, but this operation doesn't affect access to previously taken backups as Oracle keeps the old master keys stored in the Wallet. The DBA must make sure the backup policy includes the Oracle Wallet.

Using the password mode

The password mode encrypted backup process is used when the backup is meant to be restored at a location different from the one where it was originally taken from.

When using a password mode encrypted backup, you must supply the same password used to generate the encrypted backup. If you loose your password, you loose your backup.

This encryption mode is suitable for environments where you must not move the Wallet and you need to perform the restore operation somewhere else.

In order for you to enable password mode, you must issue this command in your RMAN session:

```
SET ENCRYPTION ON IDENTIFIED BY "yourPassword" ONLY;
```

The password defined in the previous command is enclosed in double quotes; this is because it is a literal string. All characters are *case-sensitive* and are not converted to uppercase.

In the next sequence a backup in password only mode is performed. First, a regular tablespace is created (**A**), this will be used for testing purposes.

In a RMAN session, it is declared that a password only backup will be performed (**B**), this clause must be issued prior to the backup instruction.

```
SET ENCRYPTION ON IDENTIFIED BY "password" ONLY;
```

Afterwards a regular backup clause is issued (**C**). In this example, a simple tablespace backup is performed.

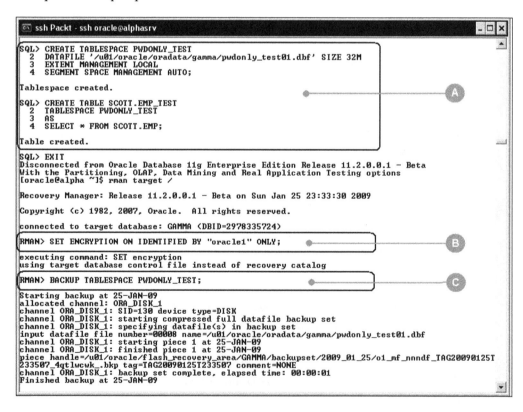

In this demonstration, the test datafile is physically removed from the file system (**D**), and if someone tries to perform any operation against the tablespace, it will result in an error. So it is time for the DBA to perform a recover operation. The DBA must use the same password during the restore operation.

First, the password must be set prior to restoring the datafile (**E**). Failing to provide the password will result in the ORA-19870 and ORA-19913 error codes.

```
SET DECRYPTION IDENTIFIED BY "password 1" {, "password 2", ... "password
n"} ;
```

In this example, we only had to deal with a single backup piece, so a single password is required, in the event that there are more backup sets involved, there may be different passwords involved too. Oracle will read the entire password list and if the password is able to open the backup set, it is automatically matched. If none of the provided passwords are able to decrypt the backup set, an error is immediately raised.

From this point on, a regular restore or recover operation takes place.

The datafile is set offline (**F**), a restore operation is performed (**G**), followed by a recover operation (**H**).

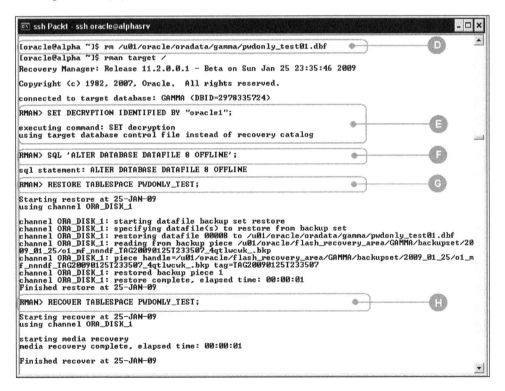

The DBA just needs to make sure that the tablespace is accessible, then it can be put back online.

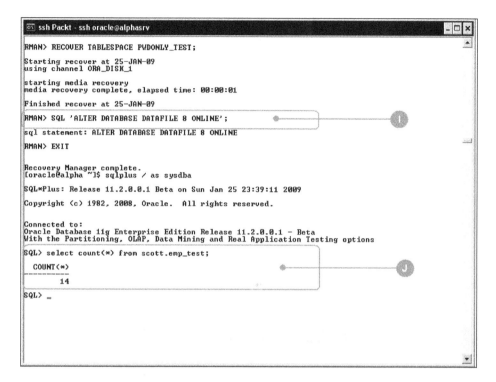

```
RMAN> RECOVER TABLESPACE PWDONLY_TEST;

Starting recover at 25-JAN-09
using channel ORA_DISK_1

starting media recovery
media recovery complete, elapsed time: 00:00:01

Finished recover at 25-JAN-09

RMAN> SQL 'ALTER DATABASE DATAFILE 8 ONLINE';

sql statement: ALTER DATABASE DATAFILE 8 ONLINE

RMAN> EXIT


Recovery Manager complete.
[oracle@alpha ~]$ sqlplus / as sysdba

SQL*Plus: Release 11.2.0.0.1 Beta on Sun Jan 25 23:39:11 2009

Copyright (c) 1982, 2008, Oracle.  All rights reserved.


Connected to:
Oracle Database 11g Enterprise Edition Release 11.2.0.0.1 - Beta
With the Partitioning, OLAP, Data Mining and Real Application Testing options

SQL> select count(*) from scott.emp_test;

  COUNT(*)
----------
        14

SQL> _
```

Using the dual mode

The dual mode provides two modes of access to the backup, by means of the Oracle Wallet (**transparent backup**) and by means of a **password set at encryption time**. The command used to declare a dual mode backup is similar to the one used for the password only mode.

```
SET ENCRYPTION ON IDENTIFIED BY "password";
```

The procedure to perform the backup task is the same. First, the password is set prior to the backup operation and when the restore operation takes place, it can either be specified, or the DBA can rely on the Wallet. RMAN will know which mode to use when the restore operation takes place; if the SET DECRYPTION command is issued then a password based restore operation will take place. If the ALTER SYSTEM SET ENCRYPTION WALLET OPEN command is issued, it will open the Wallet and it will use a transparent data encryption-based restore operation.

RMAN backup shredding (11g only)

The encryption key is the only means of restoring an encrypted backup. If the key is lost, the backup is automatically lost. In 11g you can *shred* a backup if you intentionally remove the master key from the Wallet. Once the key is removed, the backup set is rendered inaccessible.

In order for you to shred a backup set, you don't need physical access to the backup set as this operation takes place at the Wallet level.

1. Configure transparent encrypted backups:

   ```
   RMAN> CONFIGURE ENCRYPTION FOR DATABASE ON;
   ```

2. Shred the backup:

   ```
   RMAN> DELETE FORCE;
   ```

The backup shredding command applies only to backups performed in transparent mode, not for dual mode or password only mode.

You must think twice before using the backup shredding command as this operation is not reversible.

Data pump encryption

Data pump encryption relates to the already encrypted columns using TDE techniques. When a data pump export is performed against tables that contain TDE columns, information will be dumped in clear text in the dump file, compromising the confidentiality of the dumped data.

Data pump includes a parameter to re-encrypt the columns, ENCRYPTION_PASSWORD. This parameter is set at dumping time and it encrypts the information in the TDE based columns. This password is not related to the **Master Key**. If you want to restore the data, you must provide the same password that was used at export time.

```
expdp username/password TABLES=t1,t2... DIRECTORY=dp_dest_directory
DUMPFILE=dp_file.dmp ENCRYPTION_PASSWORD=password
```

A parameter file should be specified instead of the command line when the ENCRYPTION_PASSWORD parameter is used.

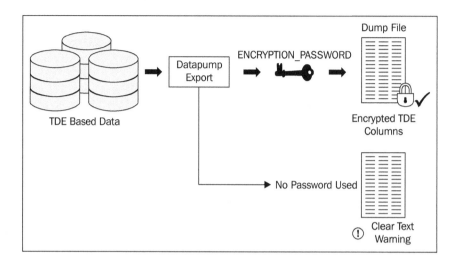

When using this option, you should consider the following:

- When you perform a data pump export against TDE data, the export will be performed, but a warning will be displayed letting know the user that TDE data will be written in clear text format

- ENCRYPTION_PASSWORD applies only to TDE data, not to the entire dump file

- The ENCRYPTION_PASSWORD parameter is neither supported with external tables nor in network mode

The enterprise user

Managing users means the administrator will have to enrol the real user to the systems the user is authorized to access. From the user's perspective we have a single physical user who is required to log in to the different systems this user has been granted to, and who is not willing to be authenticated against each system. If the user was authenticated against each single system, sooner or later the system administrator would have a hard time trying to manage the community with a non scalable solution as either the number of users, or systems or both number of users and systems, increases.

The user is authenticated once against a centralized SSO server, and the tool to manage the user's enrolment and provisioning is the Enterprise Security Manager. This scenario assumes the existence of an Oracle Identity Management infrastructure which is available through the application server infrastructure installation.

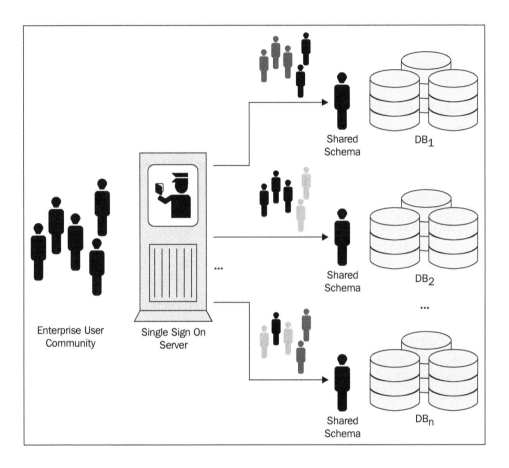

Configuring the environment

In this example, it is assumed that the Oracle Application Server infrastructure has been properly installed and configured. This provides the required components to run the SSO service. A 10g Rel. 1 or Rel. 2 is assumed. The Enterprise Security Manager in 10g can be accessed through the Enterprise Manager Java Console. In 10g this tool is still available as an EM Java Console component; in 11g the Java Console has been deprecated and the functionality provided by this tool can be accessed through the Enterprise Manager DB Control Console.

How Oracle SSO works

Oracle **Single Sign-On (SSO)** is a service provided as part of the Oracle Application Server Infrastructure installation. This service is meant to manage the identity of the user centrally through the use of an **Oracle Internet Directory (OID)**. In the next image you will see how SSO works to identify a user and log it in to the application server.

1. The user requests access to the server.

2. The **Oracle HTTP Server (OHS)** looks for a mod_osso cookie for the client. If the cookie exists then the server gathers the client's identity and logs the user in to the requested application.

3. If the cookie does not exist, the Web server redirects the user to the Single Sign-On server.

4. The SSO looks for the authentication cookie, if there is no cookie then the SSO redirects the user to an authentication screen. If authentication is successful, then the SSO Server creates a cookie signaling the user was already authenticated.

5. The Single Sign-On server returns the user's encrypted identity and credentials to the Web server.

6. The Web server creates its own cookie for the user in the browser and redirects the user to the requested URL.

From this moment on and as long as the user's session remains valid, the user will be no longer prompted to provide authentication information.

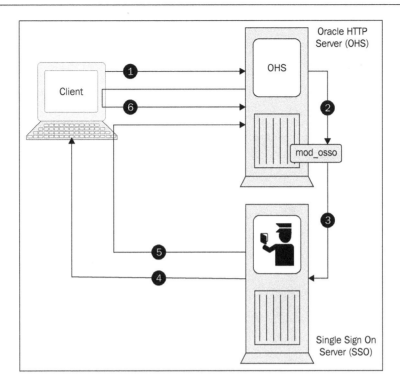

Configure access to the LDAP directory

The Oracle SSO service is based on OID, an LDAP v3 compliant directory service. The administrator can configure access to this component by means of the Oracle **Network Configuration Assistant (netca)**.

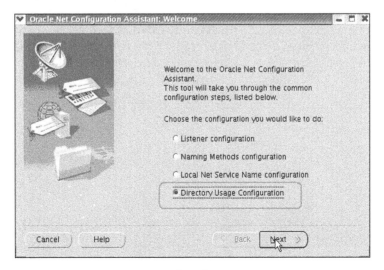

The Net Configuration Assistant is used to declare how to access the OID server. It declares the directory type as Oracle Internet Directory and defines the access parameters (hostname, LDAP port and LDAP SSL port). Usually port 389 is used for non SSL OID and port 636 is used for SSL OID port, you should first verify which ports were actually assigned by taking a look at the `<Oracle Home>/install/portlist.ini` or from the Enterprise Manager Application Server Control Ports tab.

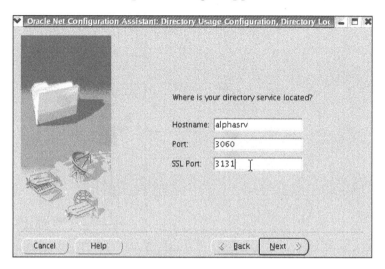

Registering the database against the OID

The Database must be registered against the OID. The Database Configuration Assistant is the tool used for this purpose. When asked if the database is to be registered against the OID, the answer should be **Yes** (**A**). Next there are two credentials that must be provided, one for the `orcladmin` user (OID Manager) the distinguished name `cn=orcladmin` must be provided as well as its password; the second requested credential is the Oracle Wallet password. It is confirmed and the configuration is accepted. After a while the database is registered against the OID. This operation should not take a long time as this is done by querying the LDAP server

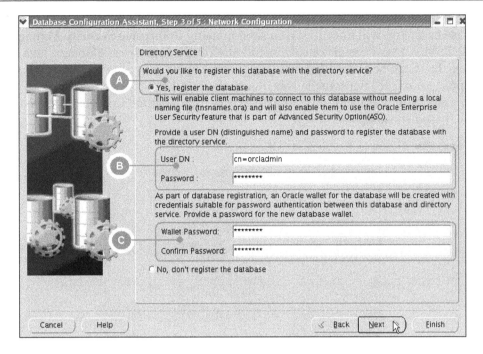

Shared schema

Once the database has been registered, you can create a schema that can be shared among the Enterprise Users.

Connected as SYSDBA a user named GUEST is created. This user is different from a regular user, as this user is not authenticated at the database level but at the SSO level. When a user is created using the IDENTIFIED GLOBALLY clause, the user is authenticated in the LDAP.

Once the user has been created it is granted privileges, just like any regular user, with the GRANT command.

```
$ sqlplus / as sysdba
SQL> create user GUEST identified globally;
SQL> grant CREATE SESSION to GUEST;
```

Next, an Enterprise user is created, and this Enterprise user is mapped to the database user. You will have to start a session using **Enterprise Security Manager** (**ESM**). ESM is a Java based console included with the Enterprise Manager Java Console. ESM can be started from the OS prompt by issuing `oemapp esm`. In 11g Enterprise Manager Java console was deprecated, so it is no longer available as a Java Console, it was included in the Enterprise Manager DB Control Console (HTML based console).

`$ oemapp esm`

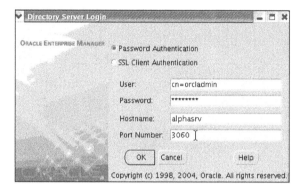

Expand the tree under the host name until you reach the **OracleDefaultDomain** (**D**) entry. When this is selected in the right hand panel, you will see a tabbed screen, by selecting the **Database Schema Mapping** (**E**) you can access the panel where new Enterprise Users are added (**F**).

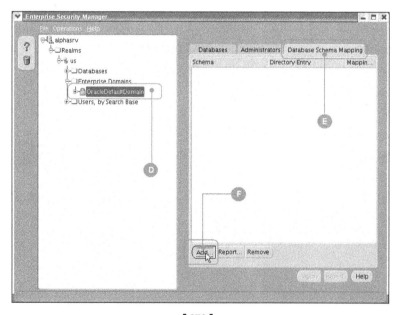

You can either type in or point to the entry corresponding to the User Distinguished Name (**G**), and on the **Schema** field declare the name of the Shared Database Schema.

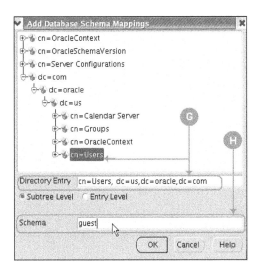

The **Users** node is expanded, and at the **Operations** menu (**I**) a request for a new user is made. After filling in the **Create User** form (**J**), you have a new Enterprise User.

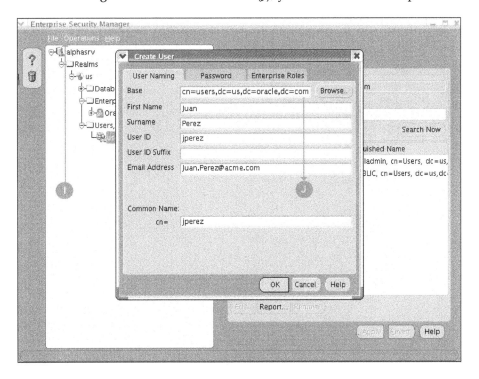

In the last step a connection with the recently created user is performed. At the OS prompt a new session with the newly created Enterprise User is made:

```
$ sqlplus jperez/welcome1@orcl
SQL> SHOW USER
USER IS "GUEST"
SQL> SELECT USER FROM DUAL;
USER
----------------
GUEST
SQL> SELECT SYS_CONTEXT ('userenv', 'external_name') from dual;

SYS_CONTEXT('USERENV','EXTERNAL_NAME')
------------------------------------------------------------
cn=Juan Perez,cn=users,dc=us,dc=oracle,dc=com
```

The code snippet shows that the Enterprise User works as expected. We have a general schema named GUEST, and an identified particular Enterprise User named **jperez**. This user was able to connect to the database after being mapped to the GUEST user.

The user **jperez** can open a session at the database level and individual grants can be made for this user.

Using the same Enterprise Security Manager tool, you can create global roles. These roles work just the same as the regular database roles, and you can assign privileges to them and grant those roles to the users.

Summary

In this chapter we have explored some practical usages of the Oracle Wallet Manager as a keystone to provide encryption services for RMAN backups. This allows the DBA to protect data confidentiality in case a backup is taken.

On the other side, working in an environment where users are centrally authenticated once against a Single Sign On security server means the database must be properly configured. There are several tools involved in this process; **Network Configuration Assistant (NETCA)** which assists the DBA in configuring the files to find the LDAP server, **Enterprise Security Manager (ESM)** to create and manage enterprise users and roles and **Database Configuration Assistant (DBCA)** which was used to register the database against the LDAP server.

Once the environment has been properly configured and the user has been globally provisioned, they do not need to be locally authenticated for each database, providing a scalable solution for user management. In the demonstration, you saw how to orchestrate a complete security solution to centrally manage and authenticate users, and how each tool takes part in this security strategy.

In the next chapter, we will further discuss the DBCA, a key tool which has several uses, including enabling you to manage the initial database configuration more efficiently.

10
Database Configuration Assistant

The **Database Configuration Assistant** (**DBCA**) is much more than just an interactive tool to easily create a database, it is also a tool that can be used to manage **Automatic Storage Management** (**ASM**). It can create and manage database templates, it can be used to manage database services and it is useful when a database massive batch deployment is required. In this chapter, we will explore the different options available in the DBCA that make it a versatile and productive database management tool.

The DBCA can not only create a database, it can also configure an existing database, it is an easy means to add options to a database and configure the enterprise manager. It can manage database creation through templates, and it can configure the ASM feature.

DBCA

The DBCA is a Java based tool used to create a database, either from a template or from scratch. This tool is useful to perform ASM configuration and manage RAC services.

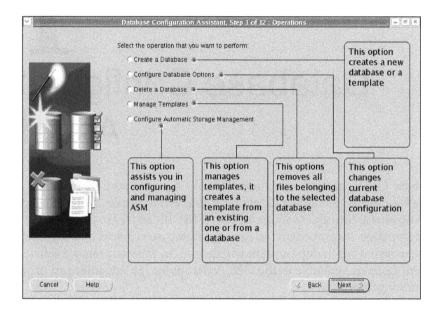

The available options are as follows:

Create a Database: This option guides you through the steps of database creation. A database can be created from an existing template, which may or may not include the database files. This option allows you to not only create the database, it also allows you to save the database configuration as a new template. It can save the database creation and configuration as scripts which can be used for future reference, or to manually create the database.

Configure Database Options: This option is used to configure additional options after database creation. This option is disabled if there are currently no databases. The options you can configure here are Data Mining, Text, OLAP, Spatial, Ultra Search, and Label Security. If you have not already configured Enterprise Manager, you can also do it from this option, and you can also configure the Sample Schemas. Other options available are the Standard Database Components, the JVM, XML DB, and Intermedia.

Delete a Database: This option removes the physical database files. You must only use this if you are certain you want to delete the database, as this operation cannot be undone. Make sure you have a backup prior to deleting anything of even small value.

Manage Templates: This option allows you to manage database templates. A DBCA template consists of the configuration file and optionally the physical seed database files. You can create a template from an existing template, an existing database, or, at database creation.

Instance Management: This option is available only with RAC configurations. DBCA is a cluster aware tool, and it automatically displays this option in RAC environments. This option allows you to add or remove an instance to an existing RAC database.

Service Management: This option is also available only with RAC configurations. This allows you to distribute the availability of the different services among Oracle instances. Here you can configure the **Transparent Application Failover (TAF)** policies, and specify the preferred instance where a service will run.

Configure Automatic Storage Management: If you plan to use ASM as your database storage manager, then you must first configure the ASM instance. Here you can configure the disk groups and configure how redundancy will be managed. You can add disks to existing disk groups or create new disk groups.

Database creation

The DBCA is mostly known as the tool used to create a database. If the DBA performs a default installation with the database creation option, it can be seen how the DBCA creates the started database. This section is a walk-through of the DBCA creating DB screens.

Database templates

Creating a database can of course, be done using the command line CREATE DATABASE command, but most DBA's prefer using the DBCA because it is pretty easy and intuitive, and it allows DBA's to easily manage different database options. This section introduces us to the concepts of templates, and this topic will be developed in further detail later in this chapter.

The Database Creation option can create the database internally using the CREATE DATABASE command with the Custom Database option, or it can create the database an existing template (**A**) which may or may not include datafiles (**B**). If datafiles are included then the database is created by a cloning procedure. Optionally, you can click the **Show Details** button to display data from the existing template in HTML format.

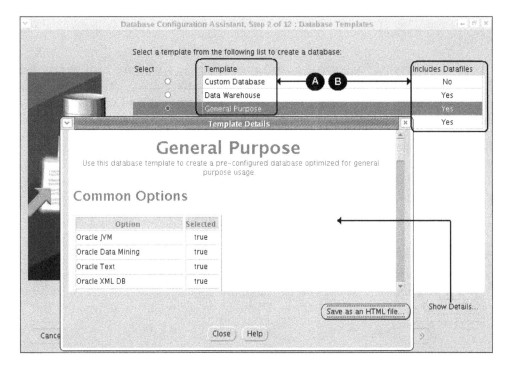

Database identification

You must specify a name for the database. In this section you can specify the global database and the SID name. The global database is used to uniquely identify the database in a network environment meanwhile the SID is the Oracle instance identifier. The name of the Oracle instance must be at most eight characters long and it must start with an alphabetic character.

Management options

In this section you can decide to configure which management graphical interface you will use for your database, you can decide among the Enterprise Manager database control or the Grid Control. The Grid Control option will be enabled only if a grid agent is found. If you decide to configure database control, the port assigned to it cannot be set here, so if you are looking for a specific port, you should use the **Enterprise Manager Configuration Assistant (EMCA)** tool to manually assign a port number. By default the EM port number is 1158 for the first configured EM port, the second EM configured port will be assigned the 5500 port number, and from this point on the port number will be monotonically increasing by one.

If you decide to configure **Enterprise Manager (C)**, then you can optionally configure email notifications and a default backup policy. If you decide not to choose these options now you can configure them later by going to the Enterprise Manager Configuration menu.

The email notifications require both, the **Outgoing** mail (SMTP) server (**D**) and the email address to be set. The default backup policy schedules a daily full database backup; this requires the OS credentials of a user allowed to execute `rman` (**E**).

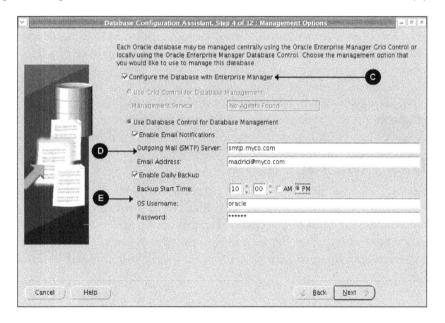

Database credentials

This option allows you to define the password for SYS and SYSTEM users, and if you have chosen to configure DB Control Console, then you can specify the password for SYSMAN and DBSNMP. You can choose to define the same password for all users or a different password for each one of them. It is advisable to take note of the password set at this stage; it may be required in the future if you want to reconfigure the Enterprise Manager DB Console. SYSMAN and DBSNMP users are particularly important to properly set up the Enterprise Manager repository, these users will be further explained in the EMCA chapter.

Storage options

When creating a database you can choose which storage method to use. They can be File System, **ASM**, or Raw Devices. ASM is a storage method that requires an ASM instance to already exist. ASM has been available since 10.1.0 and it is a simplified database storage method that optimizes I/O performance and simplifies datafile management. A database can use any storage option or it can combine the three of them. This screen only defines the initial storage method used by the database and the DBA can later change or combine it.

The File System is the most commonly used storage option, it requires a regular file system, and it utilizes the OS buffer cache and block mode devices. The Raw devices option doesn't use OS resources to access the database files, it lets Oracle directly manage the access to the unformatted device. ASM is the Oracle storage option that has been increasingly gaining popularity among DBA's, as it is simple and combines the best characteristics of raw devices and file system options.

Database file locations

The location of database files can be taken from the template (**F**), or you can choose to define a common file location for all your files (**G**); a third option is that you can choose the **Oracle-Managed Files** (OMF) (**H**), this configures the db_create_file_dest instance parameter, allowing Oracle to set the file names. The file location variables used during this procedure can be seen by clicking on the **File Location** button (**I**).

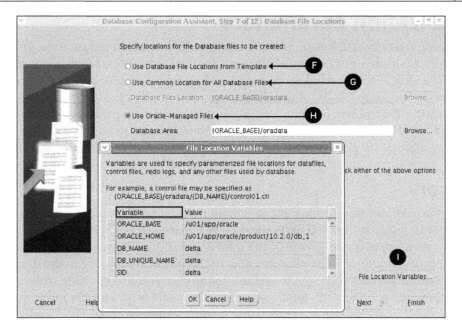

Database content

If you want to create Sample Schemas for this database then the Sample Schemas check box must be selected.

 For security reasons a production database should not have the Sample Schemas created. If you omitted them at creation time and you want to add them to a database you can still do it by installing the demo scripts from the companion disk.

If you want to execute your own custom scripts then you can declare them on the **Custom Scripts** tab. If you wish to always execute a set of SQL scripts of your own to customize the database, create additional schemas, or whatever you require; you can add a list of your scripts here and let the DBCA run them as soon as it finishes creating the database.

Initialization parameters

This window lets the DBA configure the instance initialization parameters. They are the maximum number of processes allowed, the character set, and the connection mode. The Oracle instance has more than two hundred and fifty instance parameters. You can see the complete list of the instance parameters by clicking on the **All Initialization Parameters** button. A brief description of each parameter can be obtained from the parameter window. You are encouraged to read the Oracle reference manuals to get a more detailed description of the initialization parameters.

Memory

The first tab defines the memory management method and the memory sizing. Memory can either be defined as **Typical (J)** or **Custom (K)**. A typical configuration allocates memory as a percentage of the total physical memory. It should be pointed out that by default the DBCA allocates 40% of the physical memory to the database. If the database is created using this default parameter you may quickly run out of physical memory if a second database is created. Oracle estimates the minimum value in typical configuration. If this value is underestimated then DBCA will automatically issue a warning specifying the minimum allowed value.

 By default, the DBCA allocates 40% of the physical memory in a typical configuration.

If you choose a custom configuration then you can choose between **Automatic Shared Memory Management (ASMM)** and **Manual Shared Memory Management (L)**; unless you have previously calculated adequate parameters for each individual SGA component parameter you should choose a typical configuration or a custom ASSM configuration. In the ASSM mode, Oracle dynamically calculates adequate values for each SGA component, and dynamically reassigns memory granules to components requiring them.

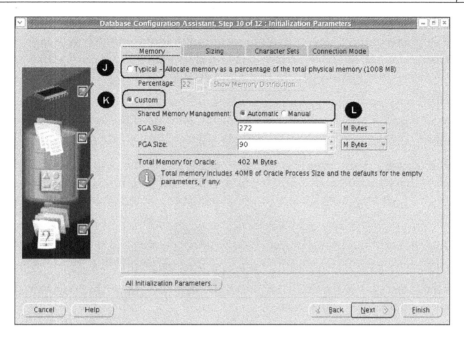

Character sets

This section specifies the **Database Character Set** (**M**), the **National Character Set** (**N**), the **Default Language** (**O**), and the **Default Date Format** (**P**).

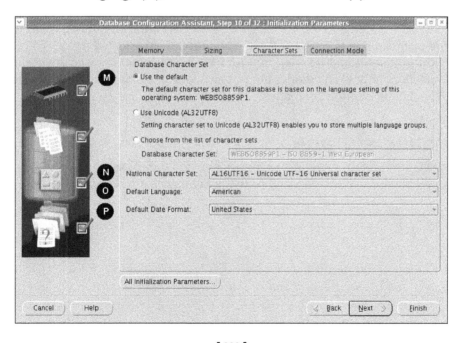

Database Character Set: This parameter determines the encoding schema used to display characters on the screen. The character set determines what languages can be represented in the database. This is used for data stored in CHAR, VARCHAR, CLOB and LONG datatypes, identifiers and PL/SQL variables, and SQL/PLSQL source code storage.

National Character Set: The National Character Set is used to store Unicode characters in a database that does not have a Unicode character set.

Default Language: This parameter determines the NLS_LANGUAGE instance parameter, this parameter specifies day and month abbreviations, symbols for A.M. and P.M., SQL Ordering, writing direction, and other locale parameters derived from the language.

Default Date Format: This specifies which regional convention will be used to display the date format. It specifies the NLS_DATE_FORMAT instance parameter value.

Even if these last two parameters have been defined here, they can be redefined later at instance, session or command level.

Connection mode

Here you can specify either a dedicated or a shared server connection mode. By default the dedicated server mode is chosen. In a dedicated server environment a single Oracle server process is dedicated for each user connected to the database. In a Shared Server connection mode a more complex architecture is defined. The Oracle server is shared among several processes, this connection mode is advised in OLTP environments as this allows more scalability; the dedicated mode is advised for DSS environments and it is required for SYS connections. You can always use both connection modes. The modes are not mutually exclusive, and this screen only defines the default connection mode.

Database storage

The final stage of database definition shows how the database structure will be built. It shows the datafile, controlfile, and redo log file names and locations.

Creation options

On this last screen, you can specify whether you will actually create the database (Q), or if you will **Save as a Database Template(R)**, or if you want to **Generate Database Creation Scripts (S)**; all of the options can be selected.

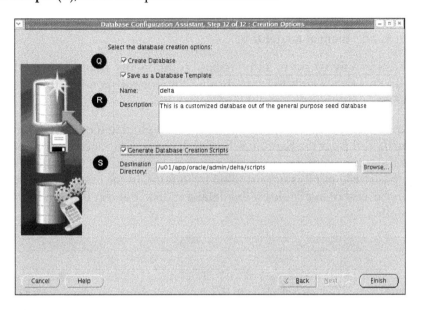

Once the database definition process has finished you will have, if you have specified the proper options, a fully working database. The DBCA will automatically start the database.

You should be aware that, in Windows environments the DBCA configures a Windows service that will automatically start the Oracle database at OS boot time. In Unix like systems you should have this manually configured and you should have your OS configured so it automatically starts databases at boot time; The DBCA will only modify the /etc/oratab file and it will specify the database not to be considered by dbstart/dbshut by default.

```
/etc/oratab
orcl:/u01/app/oracle/product/10.2.0/db_1:N
delta:/u01/app/oracle/product/10.2.0/db_1:N
+ASM:/u01/app/oracle/product/10.2.0/db_1:N
```

Database edition

Defining which options to install can be done at creation time as long as the database doesn't come from a seed database. If you created a database using the DBCA customized creation option then you may want to install other options later.

Don't install more options than required; either way you can go back to the DBCA edit Option to add them at a later time.

Database Edition only works to add database components, not to remove them, that is why if you come back later to try to disable components you will find that the already selected components are not eligible.

There are other components that may appear as not eligible too, such as **Oracle Label Security** (OLS) or the Sample Schemas. If these components are grayed out this means the component has not been installed. In the case of OLS this is included on the database disk, but it is not installed by default. In the case of the Sample Schemas, those are not available on the database disk, but can be found on the companion disk.

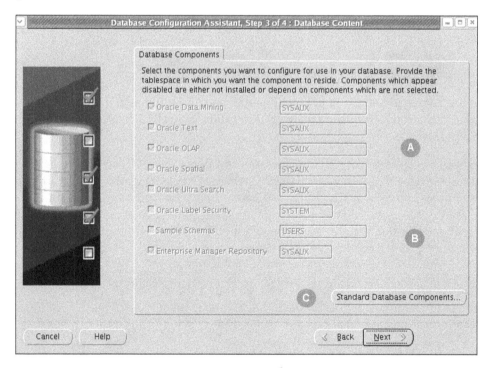

Database edition allows you to add these enterprise edition options (**A**):

- Oracle Data Mining
- Oracle Text
- Oracle OLAP
- Oracle Spatial
- Oracle Ultra Search
- Oracle Label Security

DBCA can also add these Standard Edition options (**C**):

- Oracle JVM
- Oracle XML Database
- Oracle Intermedia

 You should be aware that enabling options may require additional Oracle licenses.

Other options available are:

- Sample Schemas
- Enterprise Manager Repository

If Enterprise Manager was not originally configured for the database, you can come back here and have it configured in case you don't want to use EMCA and you don't want to further customize the Enterprise Manager DB Control Console.

On Windows, we have a Personal Edition which is designed to be used by Developers. It is equivalent to Enterprise Edition with nearly all options turned on. This is a very cost-effective alternate for developers, consultancies and small organizations where only one named user accesses the database.

Database template management

Creating several databases with the same parameters can be a time consuming task if the DBA has to define the same parameters each time. The DBA can save time when creating the database through templates. The templates can contain only a definition file, or they can contain both a definition file and the seed database files, which can be used to create a new database by means of a cloning procedure.

Template management operations

There are two kind of template management operations; create and delete a database template. When creating a new database template, there are three ways to create a new template, from an existing template, and from an existing database which may or may not include the seed database.

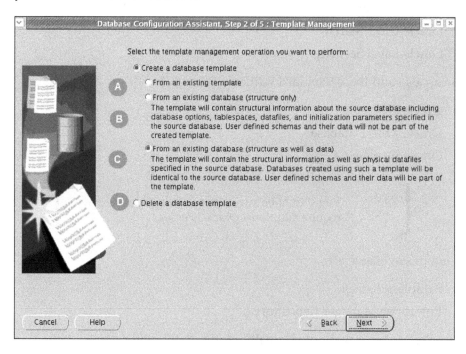

The options available to create templates are:

- Create a template **From an existing template** (**A**). This takes an existing definition which you can further modify and save with a different name.

- Create a template **From an existing database** (**structure only**) (**B**). This is useful to create a new database with the same components and configuration as those in an existing database. This kind of template is easily transported as it doesn't require the physical tablespaces.

- Create a template **From an existing database** (**structure plus data**) (**C**). This template is used to easily clone an existing database. This will allow the DBA to quickly and easily clone an existing database.

The Oracle templates are located at `$ORACLE_HOME/assistants/dbca/templates` and there you can find two different kind of files, the `*.dbt` (**Database Template Definition file**) and the `*.dfb` (rman backup files in compressed format). The database template management session creates or edits the `*.dbt` file, an XML structured text file that provides the template description details, and the `*.dfb`, the seed database.

Using templates is especially useful when creating testing or development environments, and when the company has to massively deploy the same configuration.

> If you create your templates remember that they require separate backup and recovery considerations.

Creating a seed database out of a current database

In the following image a database template is being created out from an existing database.

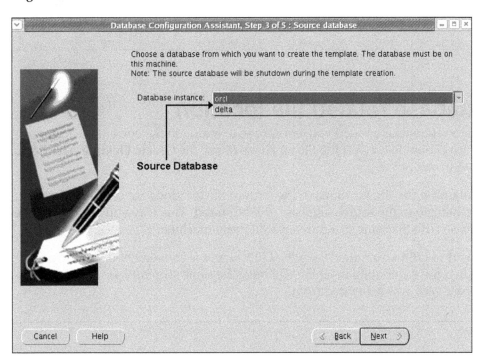

There are three parameters that must be defined, the **Name** of the template (**E**), the **Description** of the template (**F**) and the path where the compressed rman backup file will be stored (**G**).

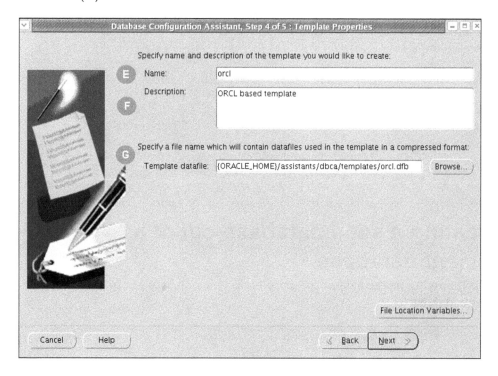

Database related file location

When a template is created you can choose to maintain the current file locations, or you can choose to convert the file locations to use the **Oracle Flexible Architecture (OFA)** structure.

Maintaining the file locations: If the current file locations are retained, then the paths defined in the source database will be stored. This way you can create a new database with the same structure on a different machine.

Convert to OFA structure: Using the OFA layout is convenient if you are not certain if the destination machine will have the same structure as the host where the database seed was generated from.

Processing the template: When the template is being processed, the DBCA will access the source database to gather information about it (**H**), afterwards, the DBCA will create the database backup file (**I**) and finally it will create the template file (**J**). All template information and database backup files will be stored in the default location of $ORACLE_HOME/assistants/dbca/templates with the name defined by the DBA.

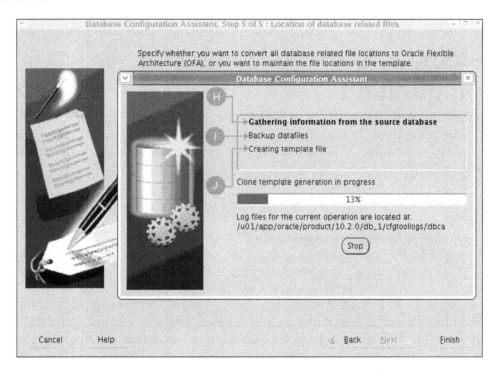

Once the process is finished you can copy the database files to another Oracle Home if you want.

If you are copying the template to another Oracle Home location you must make sure the target Oracle Home has the same version and patchset as that of the source database.

Migrating a single instance database to RAC

The template technique can be used to migrate a single instance database to an RAC environment. Just create a new template based on the target database, and make sure the template includes the datafiles. Once the template is created, make a new database using the previously created template and you'll have the database running in a RAC environment.

Automatic Storage Management configuration

Automatic Storage Management (ASM) can be configured from the DBCA in all versions starting from Oracle 10gR1. The 11gR2 has separated the ASM configuration into another tool named ASMCA. ASM is a convenient storage method for Oracle Databases starting with Oracle 10gR1.

ASM

ASM is a high performance storage method for Oracle Databases. This allows striping and mirroring, and a regular database can be completely or partially stored in ASM. ASM uses raw disks to store the data, and provides an Oracle-owned file-system structure (metadata) to identify where the data is stored. This provides a balance between Raw storage (high performance) and File systems (manageability) while addressing the unique concerns of a database. In RAC environments ASM is the preferred storage method used in case there is no cluster file system available.

ASM stripes files across the configured physical disks, it allows online disk reconfiguration and rebalancing, and it provides redundancy on a file basis. ASM doesn't override any currently installed volume manager; it can coexist with it and, if there is no volume manager ASM can assume its functions. As can be seen in the next image, database files are represented as both, regular files in a file system and Oracle database files in an ASM storage unit. ASM doesn't require any additional software, it can directly mange access to a raw device.

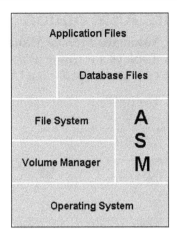

Oracle plans to deprecate raw devices for future major releases, so if you still use raw devices, it is advisable to get acquainted with ASM as an alternative method for storage.

How to setup ASM using DBCA

ASM requires a onetime Oracle **Cluster Synchronization Service (CSS)** setup. Assuming the OS has properly identified and configured raw disk devices, you can proceed with ASM setup as follows:

1. Select the Configure ASM option.
2. Run the `localconfig` shell script as root.
3. Set the password for SYSDBA or SYSASM (11g only) role access.
4. Optionally, define the ASM instance parameters.
5. Set up Disk Groups.

Select the Configure ASM option

When selecting the **Configure Automatic Storage Management** option and clicking on the **Next** button, the DBCA displays a warning asking the DBA to run the $ORACLE_HOME/bin/localconfig add script as root (**A**).

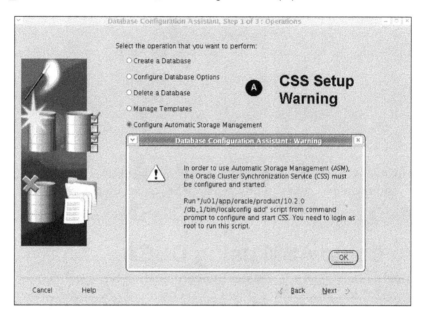

Run the localconfig shell script as root

The script is only run once and it will create a script named init.cssd which will be added to the startup configuration (**B**). This script is responsible for automatically starting the ocssd process at OS startup time. Once this is ready the script run by root will display the message letting the DBA know that the CSS service is up and running.

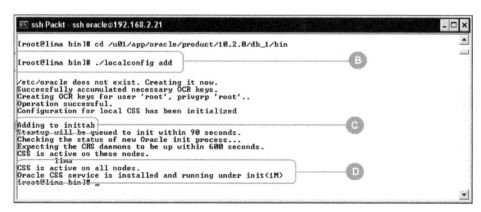

Set the SYS password and the ASM instance parameters

After the script has been run, the next step is to set up a password for the user SYS (**E**), which will be the ASM manager (11g has created a new role named SYSASM, so the SYSDBA role is no longer used starting this release, and will not be usable at all in future updates.). After setting the password for the SYSDBA (or SYSASM) role access you can optionally set the ASM instance initialization parameters **ASM_DISKGROUPS**, **ASM_DISKSTRING** and **ASM_POWER_LIMIT** (**F**).

- **ASM_DISKGROUPS** defines which groups ASM will automatically mount at startup time

- **ASM_DISKSTRING** specifies the paths where ASM can find candidate raw disk devices for new or existing ASM disk groups

- **ASM_POWER_LIMIT** defines the number of parallel servers used to perform the rebalancing disk group task

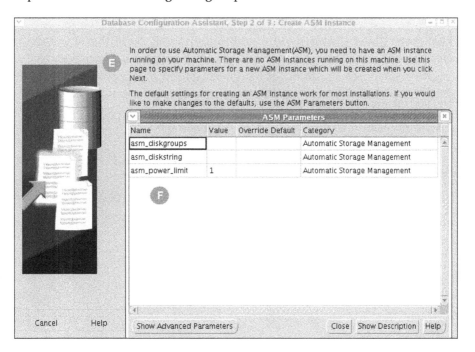

Setup disk groups

ASM organizes storage in Disk Groups, a concept similar to logical volumes, so you have to ask the DBCA to define a new disk group, then click on the **Create New** Button, this will display the **Create Disk Group** Window (**G**), where you can define the disk group name (**H**) and the raw disk devices (**I**) that will be part of this disk group; the DBCA will display all available candidate devices. If the expected raw devices don't appear you can click on the **Change Disk Discovery Path** (**J**) button to look for raw devices on another path. If the raw devices don't appear after changing the path, then validate the raw devices at the OS level and make sure the OS properly recognizes the physical devices. Most DBA's configure at least two disk groups, one for tablespaces and a second one for the flash recovery area, but you can configure as many disk groups as you require.

Candidate devices are automatically discovered by the DBCA. If the DBCA is not successful in finding candidate devices it could be because the device is already in use, or the discovery path is not properly set, or it is not started by the OS. You should refer to the specific OS documentation on how to setup and start raw devices. In the particular case of Linux, you must make sure that the raw device has been started using the Linux startup scripts, otherwise it won't be visible. The following script was used to set up raw devices in Linux. This is included here only for demonstration purposes, and it is not meant to be used in a production environment. It creates files that will later be 'seen' as raw devices; a feature available in Linux environments. Please take a look at the `losetup`, `raw` and `chown` commands. These are the commands used to define and reactivate `raw` devices in Linux.

```
echo Preparing ASM disks ...

WHOAMI='whoami'
if [ $WHOAMI != root ] ; then
  echo $0 must be run as root
  exit 1
fi

if [ ! -d /u01/asmdisks ] ; then
  mkdir -p /u01/asmdisks
fi
cd /u01/asmdisks

VDISK=0
DD=/bin/dd
LOSETUP=/sbin/losetup
RAW=/usr/bin/raw
LOGFILE=/tmp/asmsetup.log

date > $LOGFILE

while [ $VDISK -lt 5 ] ; do
```

```
VDISK='expr $VDISK + 1 '
echo -e Creating Virtual Disk $VDISK ... \\c
if [ ! -f /u01/asmdisks/asm_disk$VDISK ] ; then
  $DD if=/dev/zero of=asm_disk$VDISK bs=1024k count=400 2>&1>>
$LOGFILE
fi
$LOSETUP /dev/loop$VDISK asm_disk$VDISK 2>&1>> $LOGFILE
$RAW /dev/raw/raw$VDISK /dev/loop$VDISK 2>&1>> $LOGFILE
sleep 3
chown oracle:oinstall /dev/raw/raw$VDISK 2>&1>> $LOGFILE
chmod 777 /dev/raw/raw$VDISK
echo Done
done
echo -e \\n Please verify execution log $LOGFILE
```

When setting up the ASM environment you should select external redundancy, unless you have a Volume Manager that takes care of the stripping and mirroring tasks.

 Don't mix the High or Normal redundancy ASM configuration with an existing mirroring/stripping configuration.

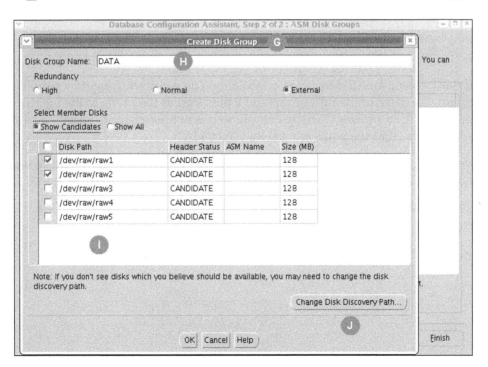

ASM disk group's validation

Once the process is finished you can see the disk groups in a **MOUNTED (K)** state. In the window shown below you can see the size of the disk group (**L**) and the space available (**M**).

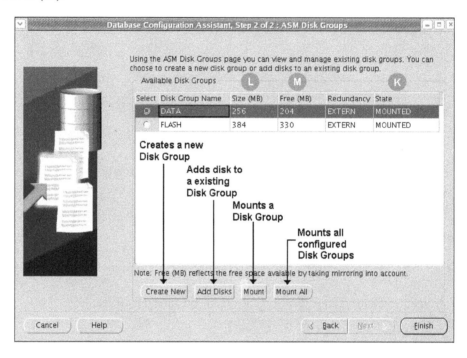

After this last step an ASM instance is available. You can start using it by simply specifying the name of the disk group and a plus sign as the prefix to the logical datafile path. ASM utilizes OMF by default, so it is not necessary to specify a path; actually, inside ASM the paths are just logical labels.

In the next example a new tablespace is created (**N**), the name of the datafile consists only of a plus sign followed by the name of the Disk Group.

```
create tablespace TablespaceName
datafile '+DiskGroupName';
```

If required, ASM creates the logical path and defines the database file name.

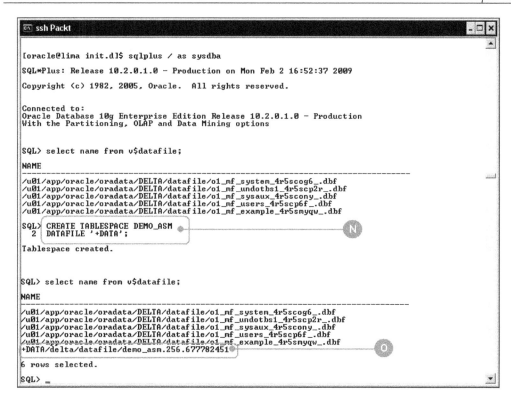

Setting up ASM in a Windows environment

This procedure refers to a **Unix** like OS. The procedure to setup ASM in Windows is quite different from the procedure in a Unix like environment. The reason is because of the partition concepts and the way Windows handles partitions.

ASM setup

There is a procedure to prepare raw disks to be used in a ASM environment on a Windows platform. The following procedure applies to a Windows 2003 environment.

Disk layout

At least one raw partition should available. The DISKPART utility should be used (Win2K3) or Disk Manager (Win2K & Win2k3).Windows does not automatically mount raw disks and make them visible. You must enable automounting. Using Diskpart, at the Diskpart prompt, type:

DISKPART> automount enable

At the Command Prompt, type:

diskmgmt.msc

This will start the Disk Management Windows utility. If the disk is in dynamic mode, change it to Basic mode. Create a new partition on the empty disk and select an extended partition. Select the partition size to fill the disk. Once the wizard is ready it will create the extended partition.

Logical partitions

Once the extended partition is created, the next step is to create the logical partitions. In the disk management utility, you should be able to see the extended partition created. Right click on the extended partition and create as many logical partitions as required. Make sure you don't assign a drive letter to the partition. Also, do not format the logical partitions; the assistant displays the option, and ensure no format is performed on the raw disk. At this point you should be able to see the logical partition created. Repeat these steps for as many logical partitions as required.

Setup ASM

Once you are ready with the logical partitions, the next phase is to set up the ASM environment. Once in the Configure ASM assistant, define the Disk Group Name (DATA for example) by clicking on the Stamp Disks. As there are currently no disks labeled, the asmtool performs the disk labeling. Using the asmtool you should be able to see the partitions, and the disk status, and if the **Candidate device** flag is set then it can be selected and labeled. The disk name format is something like \Device\ Harddisk1\Partition_N. Once they are labeled they will appear as candidate disks, you should be able to see them as a candidate disk back in the ASM assistant, they will be listed in a format similar to this:

    \\.\ORCLDISKDATA_N

In the final step you should be able to see the candidate disks, just compose the ASM disk groups as required and you are done with the ASM setup procedure.

DBCA, Batch mode

The DBCA is a friendly and very intuitive tool. Creating a database or performing any other activity is a straightforward task. However, assuming a massive deployment scenario, creating databases in the DBCA's interactive mode would be an inefficient, time consuming task, not to mention a human error prone task.

The DBCA has considered this scenario, and it can be launched in batch mode using either the command line or a response file.

This example shows how DBCA executes silently with no graphical interface displayed to the user.

```
dbca -silent -responseFile <response file>
```

The response file referred to in the previous example must be created by the user, as unlike the **Oracle Universal Installer**, the DBCA does not have a 'record' mode.

The next example starts DBCA in batch mode, showing the progress bar, if you want to run in character mode only use the previous example, as presenting the progress bar requires a graphical environment, you must have the DISPLAY environment variable properly set.

```
dbca -progress_only -responseFile <response file>
```

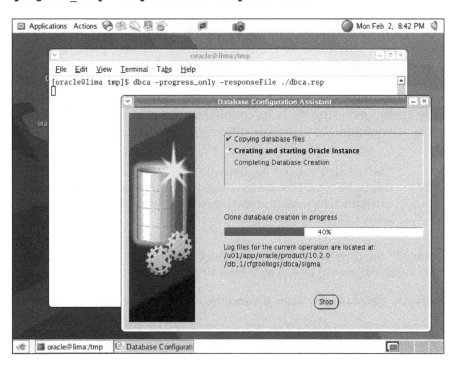

This case shows how the DBCA creates a database in silent mode with clone template.

```
dbca -silent -createDatabase -cloneTemplate -responseFile <response file>
```

A database can also be removed using the batch mode:

```
dbca -silent -deleteDatabase -responseFile <response file>
```

DBCA response file example

In this example a minimum response file was edited to have a database created.

```
[GENERAL]
RESPONSEFILE_VERSION = "10.0.0"
OPERATION_TYPE = "createDatabase"
[CREATEDATABASE]
GDBNAME = "sigma"
SID = "sigma"
TEMPLATENAME = "General_Purpose.dbc"
SYSPASSWORD = "oracle"
SYSTEMPASSWORD = "oracle"
CHARACTERSET = "WE8ISO8859P1"
NATIONALCHARACTERSET= "UTF8"
MEMORYPERCENTAGE = "12"
```

This example creates a database named sigma whose global name and instance name are the same. This database is based on a predefined template used to create a General Purpose database. In this example only the SYSPASSWORD and SYSTEMPASSWORD parameters have been defined as no Enterprise Manager DB Control Console configuration has been requested. This can either be configured here or it can be configured using the emca command (The emca command offers a more flexible way to configure the Enterprise Manager interface).

 The Template name is the name of the *.dbc file, not the name displayed in the DBCA template list. If this parameter is not properly configured, then an error message will be displayed letting the user know that the template doesn't exist.

A percentage of the physical memory is defined for this instance, it is important to define this value; otherwise DBCA will take 40% by default.

And finally, the database character set and the national character set are defined.

These parameters are just enough to create a database based on the "General Purpose" existing template and customizing a minimum number of parameters to fit a particular environment.

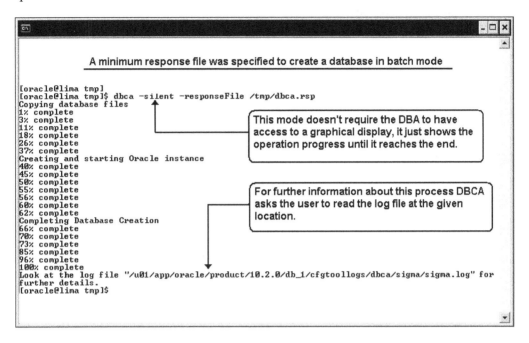

Where can you get a DBCA response file

A response file is available on the database installation disk, take a look under the response directory which is located at `MountPoint/database/response/dbca.rsp`. This file is divided into 10 sections. You don't have to configure all of them, just set the parameters according to the operation you are planning to do and remove all other unused sections except the GENERAL section.

- **General Section** [GENERAL]: This section is required for any operation you plan to perform in batch mode. Here the version of the response file and the operation type are defined.

- **Create Database Section** [CREATEDATABASE]: This section specifies that a new database will be created. Here both the global name and the instance name are defined. If an RAC database is to be created in batch, the node list is defined. When the database is created using an existing template, the template name is defined, the name of the template, as previously stated, refers to the compressed `rman` file name, not the displayed file name in the template catalog. SYS and SYSTEM passwords are defined here too among other database parameters.

- **Create template from existing database section** [createTemplateFromDB]: This section is useful if you are planning to create a DBCA template out from an existing database. This template doesn't include the rman compressed database file backup.

- **Create clone template section** [createCloneTemplate]: This is the same as the previous one, but this one includes the database files.

- **Delete database section** [DELETEDATABASE]: This section specifies the required parameters to remove an existing database.

- **Configure database section** [CONFIGUREDATABASE]: This section is used to configure different database options. There the database can be registered against an LDAP server, and the enterprise manager can be configured. If a grid control agent is found, it can be configured here so the database can be accessed through the DB Grid Control Console.

- **Generate scripts section** [GENERATESCRIPTS]: This section specifies where the generated scripts will be saved.

- **Add instance section** [ADDINSTANCE]: This section is used in RAC environments only, and is used to add an instance to an existing RAC configuration environment.

- **Delete instance section** [DELETEINSTANCE]: This section is also used in RAC environments only, and it is used to remove an instance from an existing RAC configuration.

- **ASM configuration section** [CONFIGUREASM]: This section configures an ASM environment.

Most of the parameters in the response file have default values, there are mandatory and optional parameters, in order for you to keep it simple, you may just want to declare the parameter you really need.

`dbca`—help displays all available options you can use
if you are planning to use DBCA in batch mode.

Summary

The Database Configuration Assistant, as previously seen, is much more than just a graphical assistant you can to create a database. It is a powerful tool that can be very useful when you need to configure different database options, customize the database creation process, and manage templates to save time for future database creation.

This tool is the entry point to configuring Automatic Storage Management and it is very useful in assisting the DBA in massively deploying databases with the same configuration.

In the next chapter we will explore the Oracle Universal Installer and we will discover how this tool is much more than just a graphical interface used to perform **next** → **next** kinds of installation.

11
Oracle Universal Installer

Oracle Universal Installer (**OUI**) is a Java-based tool used to perform the Oracle product installation. Most people know that this is the tool to perform the installation, however, once the software is installed, most people forget about the tool until the next time they need to perform a software maintenance task.

OUI makes the Oracle installation process look very easy, there are people who underestimate OUI and they think installing Oracle is just a **Next** button clicking task. If this task was that easy, then why does the OUI present several windows to the user who performs the installation? May be it would be easier if the same OUI could just be programmed to press the **Next** button by itself and report the outcome to the user.

OUI is more than just the installation tool. If the user requires the software to be installed more than once on a massive deployment scenario, he/she should take the time to get acquainted with the OUI batch mode. If the user wants to centrally manage installation stage areas, then the web install mode could be used. Getting to know the OUI in advance allows the user not only to perform more efficient software installation tasks, but also it allows the user to better protect and maintain existing Oracle installations.

OUI basics

OUI first appeared in Oracle 8i (8.1.5). Prior to this release, the installation tool was developed in C Language, and available in character mode. This installation tool was not very flexible, and it required an installer developed for each certified platform. Installing under a Unix like OS was a task with a look and feel different from the Windows based installer. OUI takes advantage of the Java principle of "compile once run everywhere", and provides the same look and feel, no matter which OS platform you are using.

OUI components

The next figure shows the main OUI components — the **Oracle Inventory**, the **Install log**, the **oraparam.ini** file and the **products.xml** file, as well as other optional files such as the **staticports.ini** and the **response.rsp** files.

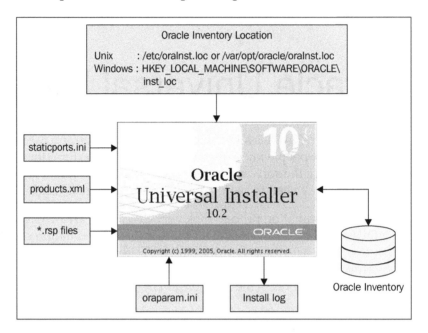

A brief description of each component is as follows:

Oracle Inventory: OUI manages a repository named Oracle Inventory. This is where Oracle keeps track of what is installed on the target machine. There is a single Oracle inventory for each host. The Oracle Inventory consists of a set of files whose location is kept in the `oraInst.loc` file (Unix like OS) or in the `inst_loc` (Windows) registry entry. The Oracle inventory has gone through an evolutionary process, and back in version 9.2.0.4.0 a major format change took place. The format used on releases prior to 9.2.0.4.0 is not compatible with the format that came thereafter, so mixing the inventory with old versions is not possible.

Oracle Inventory location:

On Unix like OSes: `/etc/oraInst.loc`, or `/var/opt/oracle/oraInst.loc`

On Windows: `HKEY_LOCAL_MACHINE\SOFTWARE\ORACLE\inst_loc`

oraparam.ini: This file configures the OUI session. It defines the JRE environment to be used, the location of the `products.xml` file, the OUI version, the certified OS version list, and any special requirements, if applicable for the different supported platforms. This file should be edited only under specific circumstances, or under the direction of Oracle Support.

Installation log: This file records the OUI output. You can use this to validate the installation process in case something goes wrong. The OUI log can be found at `<OUI Directory>/Inventory/logs/installActionsYYYY-MM-DD_HH-MM-SS[AM|PM].log`.

products.xml: This is an XML file that lists all the products contained in the installation media. This file is not editable and is read by OUI at install time to gather product information and validate it against the information it gathers from the Oracle Inventory, if it exists.

staticports.ini: This file includes a list of ports that the user wants to be considered by OUI at installation time. This file is particularly useful in Application Server environments where the user wants to have the ports predefined.

response.rsp: The response file is a file that provides instructions to OUI on how to perform an installation. This file is used when a silent mode installation is being performed. There is no particular naming convention for this file, you can name it with whatever name you want. The default extension for this kind of files is RSP.

Setting up a stage area

When the product installation files come on several different disks (database 9i rel. 1 and rel. 2, Application Server 10g and Oracle applications), instead of mounting and dismounting each CD, you can create an installation stage area. Each disk contents is copied under a directory named Disk1, Disk2, ... Diskn. The number must match with the number entry found at the `disk.label` file found on each physical disk at the stage directory.

```
[General]
Label=Oracle9i
Number=1
Size=600.0
ReservedSize=0.0
```

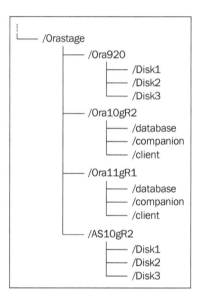

DVD distribution

Starting with Oracle RDBMS 10gR1, Oracle decided to organize the installation files in three different main sections. They are the **database** disk, **companion** disk and **client** disk. If you have the CD media, you'll find each one of these disks on a separate CD; if you have the DVD media then you'll find the related directories together, but not mixed. The disk most frequently used is the database disk, this contains the RDBMS files.

Troubleshooting an installation session

The most frequently-reported reasons why an installation procedure may fail are:

- The user responsible for the installation didn't thoroughly read the installation instructions.

- The OS doesn't meet all requirements as stated in the installation guide. That is all required patches, packages, and OS parameters.

- The user who performs the installation lacks administrative privileges on the target OS platform.

- Installation was attempted on a non supported OS Platform.

- A graphical environment was not properly set.

Even though installing Oracle on all certified platforms may look the same, and the process may appear easy at first glance, you must always read the installation instructions as well as any other available installation notes prior to actually performing the installation procedure. This will save you later headaches and installation rollbacks.

When an installation process fails, you must take a look at the installation log. This records all the steps taken during the process. There are a number of reasons why an installation process may fail. But as previously stated, most of them have to do with install requirements not being met. Oracle is aware of this issue, in previous releases (Oracle 9i Rel. 2) Oracle trusted the DBA had read the installation guide and the user had made sure the OS met all the requirements, but most of the *bugs* reported to Oracle support happened to be down to a lack of packages, patches or kernel parameters that were configured wrongly. So, Oracle decided to make a change starting with Oracle 9.2.0.7.0. In order for the DBA to be able to install this patchset, they had to go through the OUI validation process. The OUI used to install this patchset was the OUI 10g Release 1 version, which validates the OS requirements and makes sure the DBA has applied all installation requirements.

Oracle applies two validation levels. The first one is a generic validation, which is performed by the first character mode screen. Here the display characteristics (display capabilities and number of colors) and the OS version (certified OS) are validated. The installation process goes through a second validation, this second one has to do with product specific requirements, and it is performed after the **Select Installation Method** window.

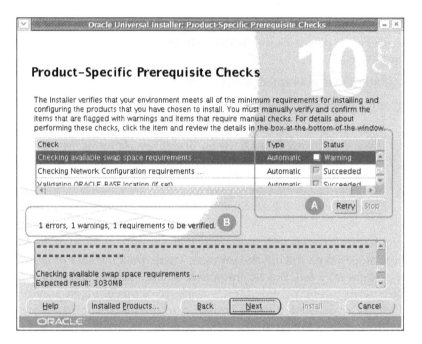

This window validates specific requirements. In this image, one of the requirements is not met. The user has the option to either correct it or skip it and proceed after user validates these checks (**A**). The user must be careful when marking the checkbox and, and he or she should only tick it if he or she is absolutely sure any side effects during the installation process or at production time, or that this is a requirement that can be deferred. In this particular example the swap space was left low on purpose just to display the warning (**B**).

Oracle Universal Installer JRE

OUI includes a JRE used to launch the OUI application; different versions have been released along with the different Oracle RDBMS installers.

OUI version	JRE Version	Related DB Version
2.2.x	1.3.1, 1.8.1	Oracle 9i Rel. 2
10.1.x	1.4.1.2	Oracle 9i Rel 2 (9.2.0.7.0) and 10.1.0
10.2.x	1.4.2	10.2.0
11.1.x	1.5.0	11.1.0

 OUI includes its own JRE environment. When performing an installation, don't mix any existing JRE with the JRE on the installation media, otherwise the installation will fail.

OUI system requirements

For each Oracle product, Oracle states the minimum system requirements you must meet. In the case of OUI, the minimum requirements for this application to run are:

Memory: A minimum of 32MB is required to launch OUI, but the specific memory requirements depend on the components OUI is to install. You should check the specific requirements for your chosen platform in the installation guide.

Disk space: OUI requires 60MB on Windows platforms and 50MB on Unix like platforms. OUI may need up to 1MB to store the inventory files.

Display: A graphical display with at least 256 colors and a resolution of 800x600 is required unless a character mode silent install is performed.

OUI basic and advanced installation modes

A rookie DBA may say "It is great that Oracle defines most of the parameters with default values" meanwhile a veteran DBA may declare "It is great that Oracle allows you to define most of its parameters", and the rest of the DBA's will be in the middle of those points of view. This position starts with the installation process. You may either let OUI make most of the decisions, assuming default values for most of the parameters and letting the user to define a minimum set of required parameters, or, on the other hand, you can take full control of the installation process.

OUI Basic Installation

OUI installation can be as easy as a **Next** → **Next** kind of installation. Starting from 10g Rel.1 Oracle decided to simplify the installation process as much as possible by gathering as few parameters as possible from the user. This installation mode is advantageous to a certain extent for the people who want to get started with Oracle as soon as they have the installation media available, but it is not best practice for production environments, as you could be installing more than required and the default installation may have inconvenient parameters that will have to be corrected sooner or later.

> Install what you really need to install. Do not perform a default installation just because this is the most simple and easy way to have your environment up and running. You may have an Oracle installation that does not comply with your license agreement and you may leave unused ports and services open.

The **Basic Installation** mode (**A**) is really simple. It only asks for the **Oracle Home Location** where Oracle RDBMS will be installed, the installation type (**Standard Edition** or **Enterprise Edition**) and the **Unix DBA Group** (**B**). If the user decides to create the starter database, it will ask for the **Global Database Name** (out of which Oracle can determine the instance name), and the password for the administrative users (**C**). Oracle will ask for the password twice just to make sure the password typed in the first password field matches the one written on the second password field.

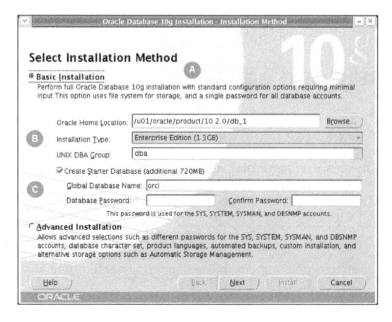

This installation mode optionally creates a default database named the **Starter Database.** This database is created using a standard file system and the same password for all users. The database will have the Enterprise Manager DB Control Console configured using either the default 1158 (first port assigned for Enterprise Manager) or the first available port starting with 5500.

This easy installation mode installs an Enterprise Edition RDBMS by default (this can be changed at the first screen shown), and other options that may require additional licenses.

Licensed installed options

When performing an Oracle installation, the reader is encouraged to verify the options installed. The user must make sure the installed software matches the licensed software listed in the license agreement. If a default installation is performed , it is very likely that there will be more options installed than those that the user is authorized to install. Oracle publishes the product options that are available for each different Oracle Edition at `http://www.oracle.com/database/ product_editions.html`. In case of doubt, contact your Oracle representative.

OUI Advanced Installation

The **Advanced Installation** option is a more comprehensive installation method. It allows the user to select different passwords for the administrative accounts, define the file storage method, specify custom initialization parameters, and specify the products and languages to install, among other features.

In the **Advanced Installation** option, you can customize what to install and what not to install. You can use the Advanced Installation system by choosing the **Custom** option in the **Select Installation Type** window. A customized installation should be used in cases when you want to install specific components. You can also perform installations for ASM, which requires no database, or install the Advanced Security Options. Here you can also choose which language your **Oracle Home** will support by clicking on the **Product Language** button.

This mode is useful if you are performing a **Software only** installation, which occurs with a basic install without the starter database, or if you are willing to configure and customize a starter database too.

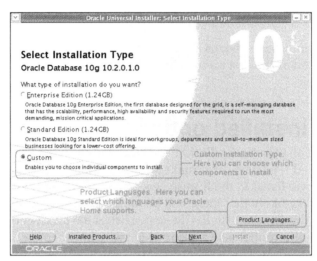

You can maintain the components currently installed in your Oracle Home. By default options such as **Oracle Label Security** (**OLS**), Connection Manager, or Data Mining Scoring Engine are not installed. You can launch OUI at a later time to perform product maintenance and have these individual components installed (**D**).

By marking the **Show all components, including required dependencies** checkbox (**E**), you can display a dependencies tree and determine whether the dependent components have already been installed or not.

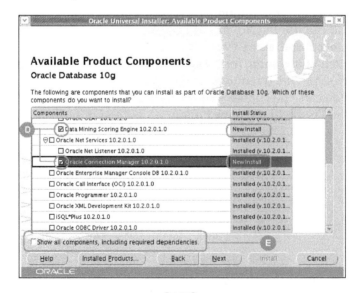

Modes of installation

When performing an installation, OUI can do it in any of these modes:

- **Interactive Mode**: This is the most widely used installation mode. To use this mode, you must have a graphical display available. This mode shows a number of screens which are used to gather configuration information from the user.

- **Suppressed-Interactive Mode**: This mode combines interactive mode with silent mode. This mode is useful when most of the installation process can be performed by a set of response files and specific tasks are to be performed by asking for specific parameters from the user.

- **Silent Mode**: This mode requires the user to set up a response file, this allows the user to perform a batch install without user intervention.

- **Cluster Install Mode**: OUI is a cluster aware tool, i.e. it can detect it is being used in an environment where Clusterware is enabled. This mode is used to maintain Oracle Homes in a cluster topology, adding or removing nodes from the cluster, or extending the Oracle Home of a product installation.

OUI command line parameters

OUI has several options available from the command line. These options are used to launch a silent install with a response file, or to build a response file after an actual installation. Other options are available to perform deinstall action, cloning, inventory rebuilds, and cluster-related, or RAC specific tasks.

```
runInstaller [-options] [(<CommandLineVariable=Value>)*]
```

Parameter	Meaning	10g Rel 2	11g Rel 1
clusterware oracle.crs,<crs version>	Version of Cluster ready services installed.	YES	YES
crsLocation <Path>	Used only for cluster installs. Specifies the path to the crs home location. Specifying this overrides CRS information obtained from central inventory.	YES	YES

Parameter	Meaning	10g Rel 2	11g Rel 1
`invPtrLoc <full path of oraInst.loc>`	Unix only. To point to a different inventory location. The orainst.loc file contains: `inventory_loc=<location of central inventory>` `inst_group=<>`	YES	YES
`jreLoc <location>`	Path where Java Runtime Environment is installed. OUI cannot be run without it.	YES	YES
`LogLevel <level>`	To filter log messages that have a lesser priority level than `<level>`. Valid options are: severe, warning, info, config, fine, finer, finest, basic, general, detailed, trace. The use of basic, general, detailed, trace is deprecated.	YES	YES
`paramFile <location of file>`	Specify location of `oraparam.ini` file to be used by OUI.	YES	YES
`responseFile <Path>`	Specifies the response file and path to use.	YES	YES
`sourceLoc <location of products.xml>`	To specify the `shiphome` location.	YES	YES
`addLangs`	To add new languages to an already installed product.	YES	NO
`addNode`	For adding node(s) to the installation.	YES	YES
`attachHome`	For attaching homes to the OUI inventory.	YES	YES
`cfs`	Indicates that the Oracle home specified is on cluster file system (shared). This is mandatory when `-local` is specified so that Oracle Universal Installer can register the home appropriately into the inventory.	YES	YES
`clone`	For making an Oracle Home copy match its current environment.	YES	YES

Parameter	Meaning	10g Rel 2	11g Rel 1
debug	For getting the debug information from OUI.	YES	YES
deinstall	For deinstall operations.	YES	YES
detachHome	For detaching homes from the OUI inventory without deleting inventory directory inside Oracle home.	YES	YES
enableRollingUpgrade	Used in cluster environment, to enable upgrade of a product on a subset of nodes (on which the product was installed).	YES	YES
executeSysPrereqs	Execute system pre-requisite checks and exit.	YES	YES
force	Allows silent mode installation into a non-empty directory.	YES	YES
help	Displays above usage help.	YES	YES
ignorePatchConflicts	Ignore all conflicts with existing interim patches during an upgrade. The conflicting interim patches are removed from the home.	YES	YES
ignoreSysPrereqs	For ignoring the results of the system pre-requisite checks.	YES	YES
local	Performs the operation on the local node irrespective of the cluster nodes specified.	YES	YES
printdiskusage	Log debug information for disk usage.	YES	YES
printmemory	Log debug information for memory usage.	YES	YES
printtime	Log debug information for time usage.	YES	YES
record -destinationFile <Path>	For record mode operation, information is recorded in the destination file path.	YES	YES

Parameter	Meaning	10g Rel 2	11g Rel 1
relink	For performing relinking actions on the Oracle home	NO	YES
	Usage: -relink -maketargetsxml <location of maketargetsxml> [-makedepsxml <location of makedepsxml>] [name=value]		
removeallfiles	For removing the home directory after deinstallation of all the components.	YES	YES
removeAllPatches	Remove all interim patches from the home.	YES	YES
silent	For silent mode operations, the inputs can be a response file or a list of command line variable value pairs.	YES	YES
updateNodeList	For updating the node list for this home in the OUI inventory.	YES	YES
waitforcompletion	For Windows, setup.exe will wait for completion instead of spawning the java engine and exiting.	YES	YES
suppressPreCopyScript	Suppress the execution of precopy script.	NO	YES
acceptUntrustedCertificates	Accept certificates that are not trusted from a secure site.	NO	YES
nobackground	Do not show background image.	YES	YES
noclusterEnabled	No cluster nodes specified.	YES	YES
noconsole	For suppressing display of messages to console. Console is not allocated.	YES	YES
nowarningonremovefiles	To disable the warning message before removal of home directory.	YES	YES

Parameter	Meaning	10g Rel 2	11g Rel 1
nowait	For Windows. Do not wait for user to hit Enter on the console after the task (install etc.) is complete.	YES	YES
formCluster	To install the Oracle Clusterware in order to form the cluster.	YES	YES
remotecp <Path>	Unix specific option. Used only for cluster installs, specifies the path to the remote copy program on the local cluster node.	YES	YES
remoteshell <Path>	Unix specific option. Used only for cluster installs, specifies the path to the remote shell program on the local cluster node.	YES	YES

Command line variables usage

Command line variables are specified using `<name=value>`; for example:

```
[ session: | compName: | compName:version: ]variableName="
valueOfVariable"]
```

Session and Installer variables are specified using:

```
        [session:]varName=value
    Ex 1:  session:ORACLE_HOME_NAME="OraHome"
    Ex 2:  ORACLE_HOME_NAME="OraHome"
```

The lookup order is `session:varName` then just `varName`. The session prefix is used to avoid ambiguity.

Component variables are specified using:

```
        [compInternalName:[Version:]]varName
    Ex 1:  oracle.comp1:1.0.1:varName="VarValue"
    Ex 2:  oracle.comp1:varName="VarValue"
```

The lookup order is `compInternalName:Version:varName`, then `compInternalName:varName`, then just `varName`.

Variable	Meaning	10g Rel 2
updateNodeList	For updating node list for this home in the OUI inventory.	YES
waitforcompletion	For Windows, `setup.exe` will wait for completion instead of spawning the java engine and exiting.	YES
nobackground	Do not show background image.	YES
noclusterEnabled	No cluster nodes specified.	YES
noconsole	For suppressing display of messages to console. Console is not allocated.	YES
nowarningonremovefiles	To disable the warning message before removal of home directory.	YES
nowait	For Windows. Do not wait for user to hit *Enter* on the console after the task (install and so on) is complete.	YES
formCluster	To install the Oracle clusterware in order to form the cluster.	YES
remotecp <Path>	Unix specific option. Used only for cluster installs, specifies the path to the remote copy program on the local cluster node.	YES
remoteshell <Path>	Unix specific option. Used only for cluster installs, specifies the path to the remote shell program on the local cluster node.	YES

Silent installation mode

By default OUI performs an interactive installation. This is not a practical approach if the user is to repetitively perform the same installation over and over again. A batch approach is more suitable in this case. Installing in batch mode requires the user to create a response file, this file can either be created from the available response files in the installation media or it can be created out of an actual installation.

The response file structure and syntax

The response file is a plain text format file encoded in US7ASCII character set. It contains a set of variables defined in the form of `VariableName=value` format. The variables can be of `String`, `Boolean`, `Number` or `StringList` type.

In the case of variables that don't have a default value and are required for a silent install to be successful, they have a place holder value `<Value Required>`. For all other variables which don't have a default value but are considered as optional, the value is labelled as `<Value Unspecified>`.

Comments are specified with a pound sign (#) at the start of the line.

The response file provided by default (`enterprise.rsp`) has the following sections:

- **General Section**: In this section, both the Oracle Home path and the Oracle Home name are specified, along with the top level components to install, and if an deinstall takes place, it defines which components will be deinstalled. The deinstall options are read only if the deinstall option is specified on the command line. Other options are specified such as the language packages to be installed, the installation type, and other cluster (RAC) related parameters.

- **Privileged operating system groups**: It is required to specify the privileged SYSDBA and SYSOPER groups.

- **Configuration options**: After the general section has been configured the remaining parameters have to do with database, storage and upgrade options.

- **Database configuration**: This section includes the database configuration and management options, and the database storage options. Here there are options that specify which kind of database will be created, the password for the administrative schemas, the name of the Database (global and SID), the character set and the Enterprise Manager options.

- **Backup and recovery options**: This defines the backup options; if the user defines the database will have a default backup policy from the start. This is used as additional options for the EM and the settings can be further customized later.

- **Automatic Storage Management Options (ASM)**: If ASM has been selected as a storage option, this section is used to define how ASM disk groups will be configured, the redundancy, and whether or not the user will perform the batch upgrade of an existing ASM environment.

- **Upgrade an existing database section**: The response file not only defines that a new database will be created and how it will be created, it also specifies if an existing database will be upgraded.

- **Read only section**: This section can be seen at the end of the default `enterprise.rsp` file, this is not user modifiable.

Customizing a response file

You may get a response file from the files included in your installation media at
<mount point>/database/response. There you can find response files for OUI,
DBCA, EMCA, and NETCA, which are installation utilities that can be launched in
batch mode too.

It is important to point out that configuration assistants such as DBCA, EMCA and
NETCA are launched by OUI. If you want the assistants to be launched at install
time through a response file then you must edit the response file and parameterize it
so the assistants are launched as well. You should be aware that even if you record a
session using the assistants, the assistant related actions won't be recorded.

Depending on the license you wish to install, you can choose either the
standard.rsp (Standard Edition) or the enterprise.rsp (Enterprise Edition)
file to be customized. In the next example, a response file was created out of the
enterprise.rsp response file.

```
RESPONSEFILE_VERSION=2.2.1.0.0
UNIX_GROUP_NAME=dba
FROM_LOCATION="/stage/Ora10gR2/database/stage/products.xml"
ORACLE_HOME="/u01/app/oracle/product/10.2.0/db_1"
ORACLE_HOME_NAME="OraDb10g_home1"
TOPLEVEL_COMPONENT={"oracle.server","10.2.0.1.0"}
SHOW_SPLASH_SCREEN=false
SHOW_WELCOME_PAGE=false
SHOW_NODE_SELECTION_PAGE=false
SHOW_SUMMARY_PAGE=false
SHOW_INSTALL_PROGRESS_PAGE=false
SHOW_CONFIG_TOOL_PAGE=false
SHOW_XML_PREREQ_PAGE=false
SHOW_ROOTSH_CONFIRMATION=false
SHOW_END_SESSION_PAGE=false
SHOW_EXIT_CONFIRMATION=false
NEXT_SESSION=false
NEXT_SESSION_ON_FAIL=false
SHOW_DEINSTALL_CONFIRMATION=false
SHOW_DEINSTALL_PROGRESS=false
SHOW_END_OF_INSTALL_MSGS=false
COMPONENT_LANGUAGES={"en"}
INSTALL_TYPE="Enterprise Edition"
s_nameForDBAGrp="dba"
s_nameForOPERGrp="oper"
n_configurationOption=3
```

This response file performs the installation process reading the `products.xml` file from the `FROM_LOCATION` location. It installs the `ORACLE_HOME_NAME` at the `ORACLE_HOME` location. OUI installs the `INSTALL_TYPE` edition

Creating a response file out from an actual installation

If you are planning to reproduce the same installation a number of times then you can record the installation session in a response file you can edit later if you require further customization.

This code creates a response file from an actual installation:

```
./runInstaller -record -destinationFile <PathAndFileName>
```

This response file records the parameters used during the current installation, afterwards the user can use this file to repeat the installation process in batch mode.

```
./runInstaller -silent -responseFile <PathAndFileName>
```

The path and file name refers to the location of the generated response file name and location.

The Batch installation, step by step

Once the response file has been either created or customized, the user can perform the batch install. Depending on the product that will be installed, the screen will be different from the one shown in the next images.

Here a response file has been created to perform a 10g Rel. 2 RDBMS install.

```
RESPONSEFILE_VERSION=2.2.1.0.0
UNIX_GROUP_NAME=dba
FROM_LOCATION="/stage/Ora10gR2/database/stage/products.xml"
ORACLE_HOME="/u01/app/oracle/product/10.2.0/db_1"
ORACLE_HOME_NAME="OraDb10g_home1"
TOPLEVEL_COMPONENT={"oracle.server","10.2.0.1.0"}
SHOW_SPLASH_SCREEN=false
SHOW_WELCOME_PAGE=false
SHOW_NODE_SELECTION_PAGE=false
SHOW_SUMMARY_PAGE=false
SHOW_INSTALL_PROGRESS_PAGE=false
SHOW_CONFIG_TOOL_PAGE=false
SHOW_XML_PREREQ_PAGE=false
SHOW_ROOTSH_CONFIRMATION=false
```

```
SHOW_END_SESSION_PAGE=false
SHOW_EXIT_CONFIRMATION=false
NEXT_SESSION=false
NEXT_SESSION_ON_FAIL=false
SHOW_DEINSTALL_CONFIRMATION=false
SHOW_DEINSTALL_PROGRESS=false
SHOW_END_OF_INSTALL_MSGS=false
COMPONENT_LANGUAGES={"en"}
INSTALL_TYPE="Enterprise Edition"
s_nameForDBAGrp="dba"
s_nameForOPERGrp="oper"
n_configurationOption=3
```

The configuration option specifies a software install only installation type will be performed, the Oracle Home and the Oracle Home Name have been specified, and the Installation Type and the languages to be installed are defined too. In this response file, all the screens have been suppressed so it can completely run in character mode. It is useful to let the progress screens appear only when the batch install is going to be performed on a graphical screen to let the user know how the install is progressing.

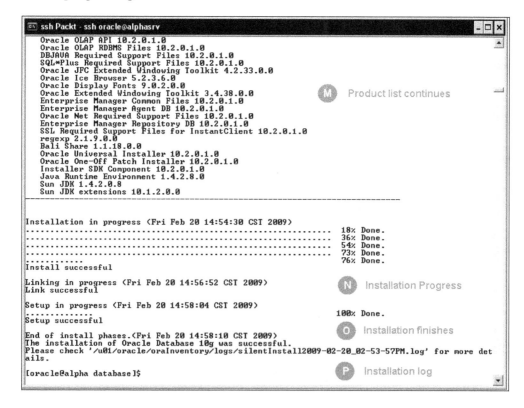

The silent mode installation is triggered with this command line (**A**):

```
runInstaller -silent -responseFile <responseFileNameAndPath>
-ignoreSysprereqs
```

In this particular case the `ignoreSysprereqs` line was required as the installation was a RDBMS 10gRel2 on an Oracle Enterprise Linux 4 platform. Even though it is a supported platform, by the time DB10gR2 was released OEL4 didn't exist, so it is incorrectly considered to be a non supported platform by OUI, and this is a workaround to avoid the non supported platform error.

The OUI parameter `ignoreSysprereqs` must be carefully used. It prevents the installation prerequisites from being validated, so it is the DBA's responsibility to make sure the prerequisites can be waived.

OUI shows the initial prerequisite checking output (**B**) where the supported platform is listed and it makes sure the initial prerequisites are met. OUI then reads the action to be performed (**C**), the dependency analysis is performed (**D**), and the OS platform is checked (**E**). Once it finishes the first analysis, it goes to the OS package checking.

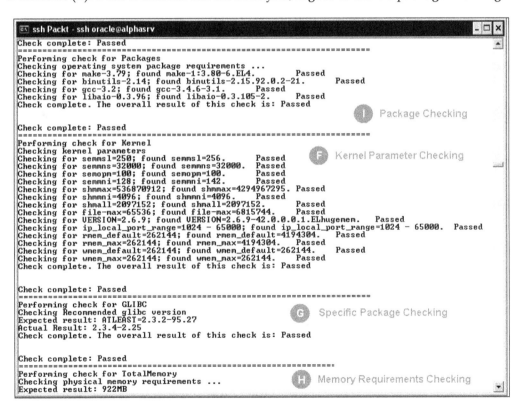

Further analysis is performed to make sure the user has properly configured the OS and the installation prerequisites have been met. In this example **Package Checking (I)**, **Kernel Parameter Checking (F)**, **Memory** Requirement **Checking (H)** and **Specific Packages Checking (G)** are performed. These steps depend on the particular OS and the options to be installed.

Other parameters are checked (**J**) until it reaches 100% (**K**). If all stages are successfully passed, then it goes to the next step. The list of products to install; in this case, it was specified to install all the Oracle Home products.

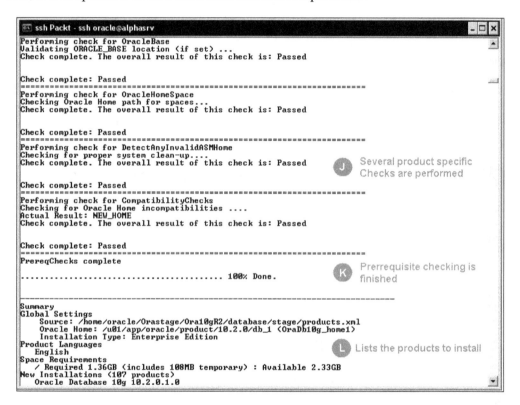

After the list is displayed (**M**), it shows the installation progress (**N**). Once the install process has completely finished (**O**) OUI reminds the user to read the Installation log for detailed information about the process (**F**).

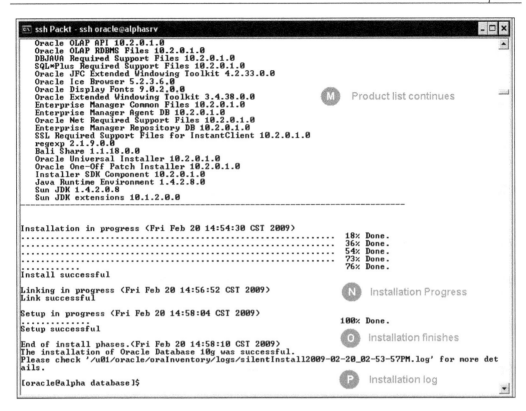

Creating a response file to perform a batch deinstallation

A deinstallation task can also be performed in batch mode. In the next example, a response file was created which specifies the Oracle Home is to be removed along with the installed software.

The following is the response file used to perform the deinstall task:

```
RESPONSEFILE_VERSION=2.2.1.0.0
UNIX_GROUP_NAME=dba
ORACLE_HOME="/u01/app/oracle/product/10.2.0/db_1"
ORACLE_HOME_NAME="OraDb10g_home1"
DEINSTALL_LIST={"oracle.server","10.2.0.1.0"}
SHOW_SPLASH_SCREEN=false
SHOW_WELCOME_PAGE=false
SHOW_SUMMARY_PAGE=false
SHOW_END_SESSION_PAGE=false
SHOW_EXIT_CONFIRMATION=false
```

```
NEXT_SESSION=false
NEXT_SESSION_ON_FAIL=false
SHOW_DEINSTALL_CONFIRMATION=true
SHOW_DEINSTALL_PROGRESS=true
REMOVE_HOMES="/u01/app/oracle/product/10.2.0/db_1"
SHOW_END_OF_INSTALL_MSGS=true
```

This response file configures a session to perform the deinstall task on the OraDb10g_
home1 Oracle Home. It removes all the available products in there starting with the
oracle.server root product.

When the user performs the deinstall task it uses the following command line (**A**):

runInstaller -silent -deinstall -responseFile <responseFileNameAndPath>

Oracle Universal Installer notifies the user that the OUI session has started (**B**), then
it shows the deinstall process progress by displaying dots on the screen until it
reaches 100% and the process finishes. The deinstall complete message (**C**) is shown
and the status is displayed on the screen (**D**). In this case the status was successful.
Finally OUI notifies the user that a log file has been generated (**E**). The log file can be
used to further analyze the session, if there were any errors.

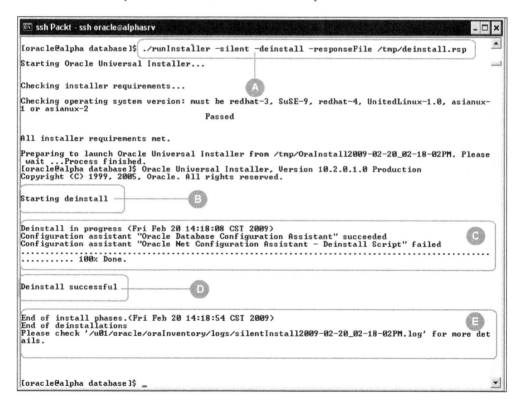

The oraparam.ini file

The `oraparam.ini` file can be found at `<MediaMountPoint>/install/oraparam.ini`. It includes definition of where the JRE environment will be taken from, which platforms are supported, and other basic validations. This file is not supposed to be modified by the user, unless explicitly requested by Oracle support. It has a general [Oracle] section where the basic OUI start-up environment is defined. There is another section named [Certified Versions] where the list of the Oracle supported platforms for the specific software distribution are supported, and other optional sections that define the particularities of each supported platform.

You can start OUI with a different `oraparam.ini` file. This started in Oracle 10g when Oracle Enterprise Linux first appeared as a valid platform. The Linux distro appeared when Oracle 10g R2 was already in the market. People who installed 10gR2 on this platform surprisingly found that this Oracle OS was not a supported platform. Oracle support then suggested creating a copy of the `oraparam.ini` file and adding Enterprise Linux as a supported platform in the [Certified Versions] section.

OUI determines the Linux distro using the information found in `/etc/redhat-release`.

 For production environments you must always perform the installation on an officially supported platform otherwise your installation won't be supported by Oracle and you will be on your own.

This trick is used by people who plan to install Oracle for personal training and testing on platforms such as Ubuntu or Fedora, to name just a few. Also, even if it works, people must be aware that this is not supported for production environments.

Installing Oracle 10gR2 on either RHEL5 or OEL5 was similar, this was a supported platform but it was not listed on the list of certified versions. In the next example the `oraparam.ini` file was modified to support the installation of Oracle 10gR2 on Red Hat 5

Original [Certified Versions] entry:

```
[Certified Versions]
Linux=redhat-3, SuSE-9, redhat-4, UnitedLinux-1.0, asianux-1, asianux-
2
```

Modified [Certified Versions] entry:

```
[Certified Versions]
Linux=redhat-3,SuSE-9,redhat-4,UnitedLinux-1.0,asianux-1, asianux-2,
redhat-5
```

OUI return codes

At the end of an install operation OUI can return one of three different return codes. They are 0, -1 or 1. The interpretation of these values is as described in the next table:

Return Code	Code Description
0	The installation process ended successfully.
1	The installation process was successful, but some configuration assistant failed.
-1	There was at least one failed installation.

The return codes are useful in batch processing to decide whether to continue or abort an installation process.

Installing Oracle from the Web

When OUI reads the source files at installation time, it can do so in a seamless way, it doesn't matter if the source files are located in a CD or DVD, hard disk, network shared file system or web, it is enough to declare the path to the products.xml file and OUI will take care of the file transfer process to proceed with the installation. You can take advantage of this fact and create a centrally managed software depot accessible from the intranet. This is particularly useful when you have an environment where remote massive deployments are to be performed.

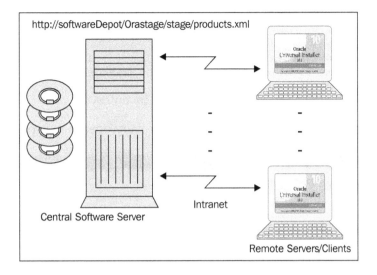

The procedure to set up a web install is as follows:

1. Copy the disk to a stage area.
2. Publish the root of the stage area on a web server.
3. Start the Oracle Universal Installer and point to the http URL for the `products.xml` file.
4. From this point on the installation will run as if the install media was on a local device, the only difference will be that all the required files will be dispatched from the web.

Recovering a lost Inventory

What should you do in case a central inventory gets lost? There are a couple of scenarios here; you could have a valid Oracle Home either intact or restored from a backup, but the central inventory is lost, if this is the case Oracle will work, but you will notice the missing inventory when you try to do an upgrade or apply a patch. In Oracle 10gR1 and earlier releases there is no other option but to restore the inventory from a backup, so you should include in your backup policies a periodic ORACLE_BASE backup which includes the different Oracle Homes and the central inventory. In Oracle 10gR2 and 11gR1, you can register it using the following procedure:

Change to the `oui/bin` directory inside the target Oracle Home:

```
cd $ORACLE_HOME/oui/bin
```

From this point, run the `runInstaller` (or `setup.exe` command in Windows) and use the `attachHome` and `invPtrLoc` modifiers:

```
./runInstaller -silent -attachHome -invPtrLoc ./oraInst.loc ORACLE_
HOME="<Oracle_Home_Location>" ORACLE_HOME_NAME="<Oracle_Home_Name>"
```

Your Oracle Home will be back again in the OUI Inventory.

In the following example an Oracle Inventory recovery operation is performed.

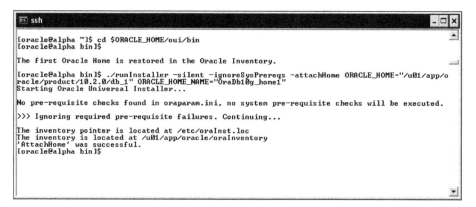

This procedure is repeated for each Oracle Home to be restored in the Oracle Inventory.

Once the procedure is finished for each Oracle Home the inventory is fully restored.

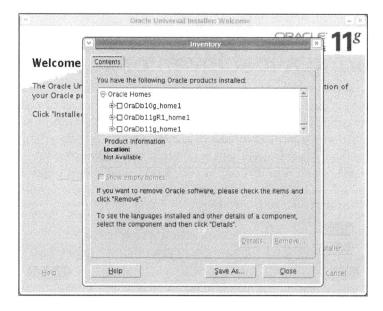

Cloning Oracle Home using OUI

You can clone an existing Oracle Home in the same host using this procedure:

1. Install **Oracle Home** in its source directory, include all necessary patchsets and patches.

2. Perform a recursive copy of the source **Oracle Home** to the target **Oracle Home** This step must be run as root to preserve the file permissions (use the `cp -Rp` command options).

3. Verify Oracle has the proper file and directory permissions in the target directory.

4. Run the following command to clone the installation with the OUI:

   ```
   cd $ORACLE_HOME/clone/bin

   perl clone.pl ORACLE_HOME="<target_home>" ORACLE_HOME_
   NAME="<unique_home_name>"
   ```

   ° An alternative method of cloning can be achieved using the following commands:

     ```
     cd $ORACLE_HOME/oui/bin

     ./runInstaller -clone -silent -ignorePreReq ORACLE_
         HOME="<target_home>" ORACLE_HOME_NAME="<unique_home_
         name>"
     ```

   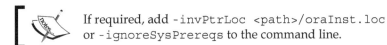 If required, add `-invPtrLoc <path>/oraInst.loc` or `-ignoreSysPrereqs` to the command line.

5. As root, run the `root.sh` file which is located at the target Oracle Home directory.

Summary

Oracle Universal Inventory is more than just the Oracle Installer. It allows you to more efficiently perform the installation tasks in an environment where batch installs are a very frequent requirement.

Creating a silent install allows you to create a character mode installer that requires no graphical interface. You can link several OUI sessions in batch mode and you can use the silent mode of other tools such as DBCA and NETCA to perform a full setup including the database and other configuration assistants.

It allows you to perform software deployments using a centralized Oracle software depot where you can install from anywhere in your intranet or even more by combining automatized batch scripts. You can have users with basic technical skills perform the tasks in batch mode from anywhere in your intranet.

There are post installation tasks that are to be performed such as configuring enterprise manager, this can be done in batch mode too, and it can be fully customized, this will be explored in more detail in the next chapter.

12
Enterprise Manager Configuration Assistant

The **Enterprise Manager Configuration Assistant** (**EMCA**) is a command line Java based configuration tool for the Enterprise Manager DB Control Console. Nowadays, when thinking about a 11g or 10g databases' day-to-day administration most DBA's think about Enterprise Manager. This reason is because **Enterprise Manager** (**EM**) is a friendly and very intuitive tool for performing daily interactive database management tasks. Issuing SQL commands from the **Command Line Interface** (**CLI**) is an option when thinking about batch commands, mostly because the syntax has impressively expanded and for most enterprises getting the work done is more important than considering how it is achieved. This has made the modern DBA depend more on the EM graphical interface. If the database doesn't have the console configured it makes the modern DBA feel like they have gone back more than fifteen years in Oracle administration history, to when there was no option but CLI. The CLI is not that bad, but it does require a good memory, a lot of practice and a very good cheat sheet to refer to. Changes in administrative passwords or network topology turn the EM lights off. EMCA is the key tool for bringing the EM back to business, and getting to know it makes the difference between using modern interactive database management and the traditional less productive CLI mode.

Enterprise Manager Components

The Enterprise Manager DB Control Console is a Java application that runs on an **Oracle Container for Java (OC4J)**, it requires a repository stored on the managed database whose owner is the SYSMAN user. In the DB Control Console mode you can configure only one console per database; Enterprise Manager Console can be shared only in the Grid Console.

The console can be accessed either in http or in https mode, depending on the version and on the access configuration the DBA has defined. It should be pointed out that starting with version 10.2.0.4.0 Oracle no longer allows the console to be in open mode, and after applying the patchset, the upgrade process secures the console. For each console a different port is assigned and a different set of configuration files is created. The Java application accesses the SYSMAN repository through JDBC.

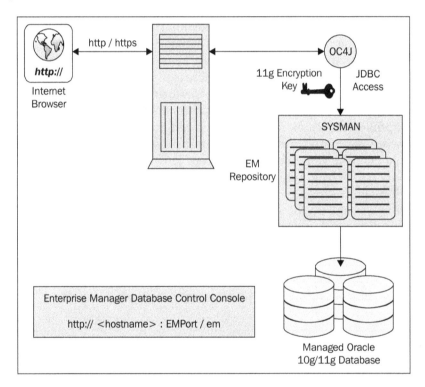

Differences between EM DB Control and EM Grid Control

Grid Control and DB Control are two different administrative environments. The scope of the DB Control is restricted to the database where it was originally configured. Meanwhile, Grid Control is a tool to manage data centers, which means that its scope ranges from the hardware to the application level. Grid control can manage databases ranging from 8.1.7.4.0 to 11gR2, operating systems, application servers, Oracle eBusiness Suite, Collaboration Suite as well as some certified third party databases, application servers, storage managers and networks. Grid Control is based on two basic principles, **Manage Many as One** and **Implement One from Many**.

The discussion about Grid Control goes far beyond the scope of this book, but it is important to inform the DBA that there is a robust environment which has remained obscure and unnoticed by many DBAs.

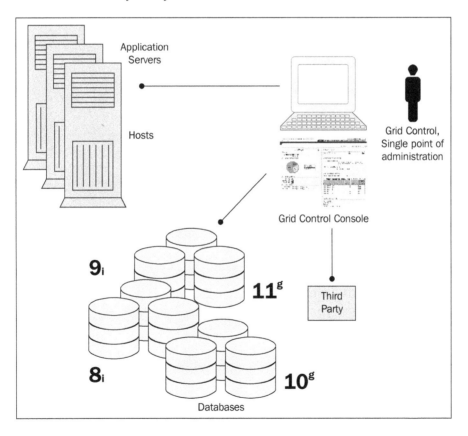

Enterprise Manager configuration

Most DBA's have the EM automatically configured by the time Oracle creates a database with the DBCA. The default port assigned is 1158, but if ever the DBA needs to create and configure an additional database on the same host the default assigned port will be 5500, then 5501 and so on. After the RDBMS installation you should read the `portlist.ini` file located at `<Oracle Home>/install/portlist.ini` for details on ports assigned by Oracle. The easiest way to configure EM is with the DBCA, but this is the least customizable way to do it. You can have EM configured in a fully customizable fashion using the EMCA command line.

How to find out if the console components are currently installed

You can easily find out if your current Oracle installation includes the Enterprise Manager DB control console components installed by querying the installation with the `opatch` tool. The command used to find out if the console components are installed is:

```
<Oracle Home>/opatch lsinventory -detail
```

Then look for the following entries:

```
Enterprise Manager Agent Core
Enterprise Manager Agent DB
Enterprise Manager Baseline
Enterprise Manager Common Files
Enterprise Manager Minimal Integration
Enterprise Manager plugin Common Files
Enterprise Manager plugin Common Files
Enterprise Manager Repository Core
Enterprise Manager Repository DB
Oracle Enterprise Manager Console DB
```

This output corresponds to an Oracle 10g Rel. 2 Oracle Home, meanwhile the following output corresponds to an Oracle 11g Rel. 1 Oracle Home.

```
Enterprise Manager Agent
Enterprise Manager Agent Core Files
Enterprise Manager Common Core Files
Enterprise Manager Common Files
Enterprise Manager Database Plugin -- Agent Support
Enterprise Manager Database Plugin -- Management Service Support
```

```
Enterprise Manager Database Plugin -- Repository Support
Enterprise Manager Grid Control Core Files
Enterprise Manager Minimal Integration
Enterprise Manager plugin Common Files
Enterprise Manager Repository Core Files
Oracle Enterprise Manager Console DB
```

This information can also be found in the Oracle Universal Installer's graphical interface.

Console setup prerequisites

The easiest and least customizable procedure to setup Enterprise Manager Console is by means of the DBCA at creation time. You just have to ask the DBCA to configure a console for you. However, you should be aware that even the DBCA cannot take care of basic setup prerequisites such as the host name. You must define the host name so it doesn't contain underscores as this does not comply with DNS standard naming conventions and you may face problems when trying to access the EM Console.

When configuring Enterprise Manager you must first properly configure the hosts file (`/etc/hosts` on Unix like OSes and `%WINDIR%\system32\drivers\etc\hosts` on Windows platforms), the host name can either be simple or fully qualified, but do not leave the default `localhost` address. This name will be read by EMCA and it will be used to create the console administrative directories.

 Oracle RDBMS should be installed on a host with fixed IP address, and even though it is supported to install on DHCP based servers, you must fix the IP address by means of a loopback adapter and have this loopback address declared as the main IP address in the hosts file. Otherwise the Console will stop working as soon as the IP address changes.

The reason why DHCP based server configuration is not encouraged is because if an Oracle product binds to a DHCP address or host name, it can take a lot of administration effort to convert the product to a newly assigned address or name.

Most of the times Enterprise Manager Console fails, it is because people mistakenly leave the IP address to be dynamically assigned. If you are using dynamic IP addresses then you must follow the above advice.

Configuring EM using DBCA

Assuming the database currently has no EM repository configured it can be easily configured by the DBCA. This configuration tool is aware of the existence of the EM repository and it can have both the Enterprise Manager repository and the console configured. When accessing the DBCA, choose the **Configure Database Options** option, then select the target database.

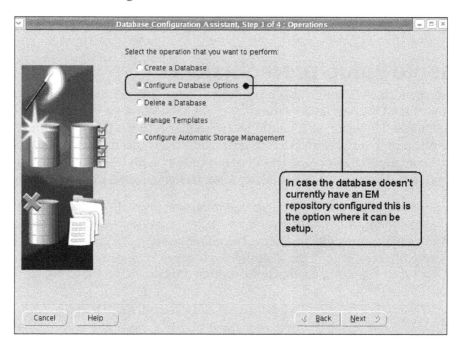

If the DBCA then realizes that there is no repository configured at the target database, it displays a screen asking the DBA if the EM access should be configured for the target database. This management option allows the DBA to decide whether an EM console will be configured for the target database or not (**A**), the options available are Database Control and Grid Control console. In case a grid control agent is found then it will enable the **Use Grid Control for Database Management** option, otherwise it will enable the **Configure the Database with Enterprise Manager** option only (**B**). This screen also prompts the DBA for email notifications and the daily backup default strategies. If the DBA wants to enable email, an SMTP server is required as well as an email address for notifications to go to (**C**). For the Backup strategy (**D**) the DBA should be aware that this is a full backup the user is supposed to schedule at a given time. This default strategy as well as the email notifications can be enabled at a later time or reconfigured if the DBA chooses to use them.

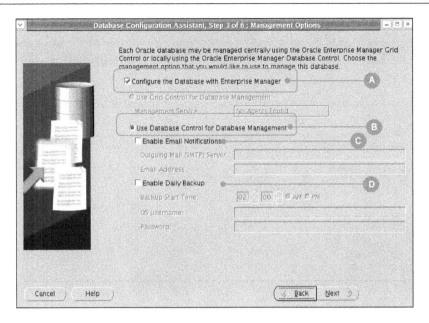

If the DBA decides to configure the management console then the repository is created. This option is automatically selected in the Database Content screen of the DBCA, and the option is grayed out so that it cannot be deselected. The EM Repository is configured at the SYSAUX tablespace, and this tablespace cannot be changed.

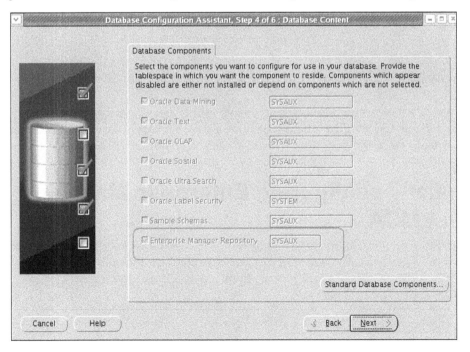

The next step in configuring the EM Console is defining the password for the administrative accounts DBSNMP and SYSMAN. You can choose to set the same password for both of these accounts or define a different password for each one.

 Take note of the passwords set for DBSNMP and SYSMAN database users and keep them in a safe place. These passwords are required if the user decides they need to change console options in the future.

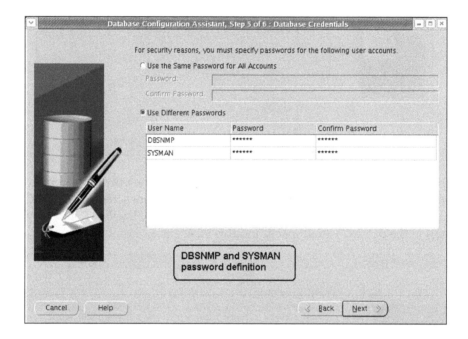

After a while the enterprise manager console will be configured and the repository will be created. On Windows based systems a new Windows service will be created; this service is by default configured to automatically start at OS boot time.

Manually configuring Enterprise Manager with EMCA

Enterprise Manager Configuration Assistant is the character mode configuration tool for the Enterprise Manager DB Control console. This tool can be found at <ORACLE_HOME>/bin/emca and if no options are specified then it displays the complete command line parameters.

The basic command line options used to create a console configuration on a database where it has not previously been configured is as follows:

```
emca -config dbcontrol db -repos create
```

If the database comes from a seed database, this one will already have the SYSMAN user created, if you proceed with using this database then the EMCA will fail and the log files will show an error letting you know about the problem. If this happens, you must drop the repository and configure a new one, using this command:

```
emca -deconfig dbcontrol db -repos drop
```

Prior to issuing the emca command to configure Enterprise Manager make sure the DBSNMP account is unlocked and you have the right password. Also, make sure there is no SYSMAN user currently on the database, as this may mean a repository already exists. You must also make sure there is no user nor a role named MGMT_VIE, MGMT_USER, otherwise the configuration will fail.

The main difference between the emca and the dbca is that it cannot customize the options of an already configured console.

In the next slide a basic EMCA session is started, this session creates a new repository and configures the console.

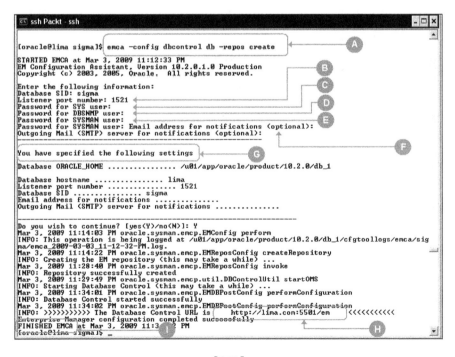

Here the image shows a basic command line is issued to create a new repository and configure the DB Control Console (**A**). As there are more parameters required to configure the console EMCA prompts for additional parameters; it asks the user to provide the listener port (**B**), which DBAs typically configure to be **1521**, which is the default TNS Listener port. Then it asks for three passwords; the **SYS** (**C**), **DBSNMP** (**D**), and **SYSMAN** (**E**) passwords. In the image it looks like the EMCA is asking twice for the SYSMAN password, this is actually a harmless display bug that can be safely ignored.

 Make sure the DBSNMP account is unlocked and it has a non expired valid password.

The EMCA feeds back the provided values (excluding the passwords) to the user and waits for the user to confirm them (**G**). If everything is correct then the EMCA proceeds with the configuration. The user should pay attention to the process progress and confirm that it successfully reaches the end. The output is logged to the directory shown on the screen, and the user must be aware of it, as if there is an error a summary and a detail log file will be generated.

The path where the EMCA logs the executed actions as well as their outcome is located at `<Oracle Home>/cfgtools/emca/<Oracle SID>/emca_YYYY-MM-DD_HH-MI-SS-PM.log` this file will record the progress and main information; it will also provide the name of a secondary file where further progress details are provided.

The EMCA provides progress information until it reaches the end of the configuration process, the time it takes to finish the process depends on the I/O speed as well as the hardware performance in general.

The final step of the setup process shows the URL to access the console (**H**). Take note of this URL. This shows the EM Port to access the console, and finally (**I**) the message **FINISHED EMCA** is displayed; this is the end of the basic setup session.

The next image shows a basic setup session using 11.2.0 (11gR2), basically, the same command is issued (**A**):

```
emca -config dbcontrol db -repos create
```

The same issues must be considered prior to setting up the console. As the administrative passwords are required in this case, the EMCA will prompt the user for the passwords and the same information as in the 10g version (**B**). EMCA shows the input feedback (**C**) and then the process continues; at first glance it can be seen that there are more internal steps involved. When the process finishes it also displays the **URL** (**C**) to access the console. However, in the 11g version a difference can be seen if we compare the URL in this release with the provide URL for the 10g release, and it has to do with security, 11g included several security enhancements and securing the console and the Enterprise Manager repository is among them.

When the setup finishes it displays a warning that informs the user about the security features and how to deal with them. Both Oracle 11g Release 1 and 11g Release 2 encrypt repository information, and they require an encryption key. The outcome shows the location of the key Enterprise Manager Encryption key file, take note on this, it is very important.

 You must provide backup procedures for the Encryption key file generated to encrypt repository information. If you fail to do so, in the event your installation faces a disaster scenario your repository information will become permanently inaccessible.

The previously exposed cases show a basic command line used to configure the console; however there are plenty of commands you can use to further customize the process and make it more comprehensive and batch oriented.

Manually assigning EM managing ports

In the previous examples the EMCA was used to configure the console with basic parameters. The HTTP port number is not required; the EMCA will automatically assign a default port number using a monotonically increasing value, which starts at 5500. If you want to manually assign a port number you can do it, just be careful to use a unique port number otherwise you may collide with another previously assigned port.

In this scenario the user assigns a port number to the console. Two prerequisites must be met prior to this operation. They are as follows:

- Check the port number is free
- Make sure the target Oracle instance is up and running

Checking the port means ensuring that the port is currently not in use nor taken by another application, even if the application is currently down. A good practice is to plan your installations, this way you can always control the assigned ports and you will always know which ports are already assigned. You can issue the netstat command from the command line to find out if the port is currently in use as shown in the next image.

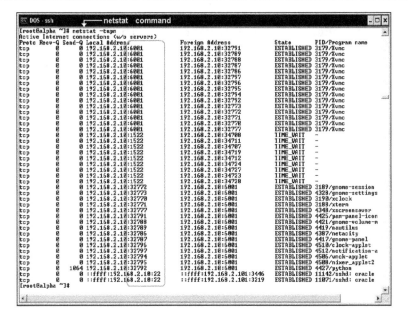

Another command that can be used to determine currently taken port numbers is the `lsof` command as shown in the next image. The outlined columns show the ports currently in use.

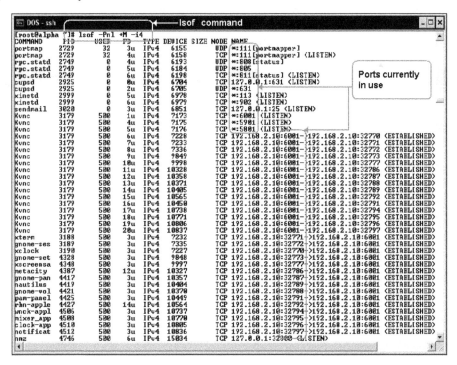

You can check the EM Console configuration files to find out if the selected port has already been configured for another EM console. The configuration files are located at `<ORACLE_HOME>/<hostname>_<OracleSID>/sysman/config/emoms.properties`, there you will find an entry named `oracle.sysman.emSDK.svlt.ConsoleServerPort`, which declares the port used by the console.

 The `emoms.properties` file cannot be directly modified by the user, the EMCA command must be used to set the EM http Port.

If the instance is not running then the EMCA will return an error and won't perform the configuration task.

Once you are ready, just issue the command below with the `DBCONTROL_HTTP_PORT` parameter set.

```
emca -reconfig ports -DBCONTROL_HTTP_PORT 1158
```

In the following image, the command has been issued (**A**), all actions were logged at the given path (**B**). If something doesn't work as expected, this is the first place you should go to get feedback.

In this particular scenario a duplicate port was selected. The EMCA notices the problem and shows the user a warning (**C**) alerting the user to the fact that the port is already in use. The operation will finish, as this is not a fatal error, but if ignored it will allow only a single EM Console to work.

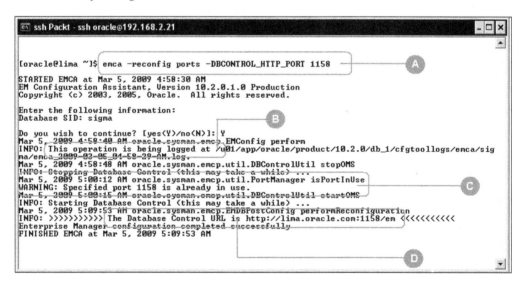

Once the process is finished the Database URL is displayed for the user to verify the new URL has the correct http port.

EMCA Command Line Interface

The EMCA has several command line parameters that allow you to fully configure your Enterprise Manager environment. The **EMCA's Syntax** takes up to four kinds of parameters, the **Operation** to be performed, the **Mode** of the command, the **Flags**, where required, and a list of optional **Parameters**. This line requires more or less parameters depending on the command to be issued.

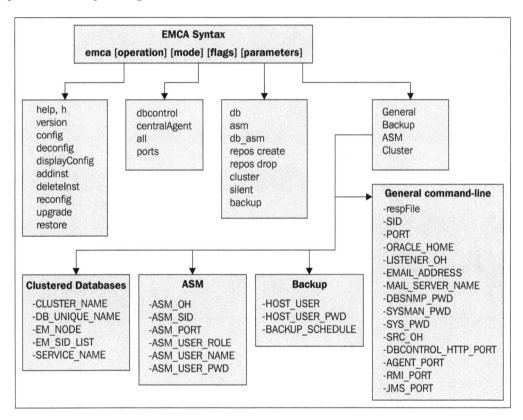

EMCA commands

The EMCA command has several options that allow the DBA to configure the EM DB Control Console by defining the http port the console will use, altering the Enterprise Manager configuration, and rebuilding a repository, amongst many other tasks. Knowing these options allows the DBA to customize the EM configuration process. The DBCA allows the DBA to configure an EM Console, but this assistant does not allow customization, and it assumes there is currently no EM repository configured at the target database.

Command	Description
emca -h	This command shows the online help available for the emca command; if the user types no arguments, or the user doesn't properly specify the parameters, then this command will be executed. Some other variants of the command are: emca --h emca -help emca --help
emca -version	Displays the EMCA version
emca -config dbcontrol db [-repos (create | recreate)] [-cluster] [-silent] [-backup] [parameters]	This command configures the EM control console and optionally it can either create or recreate the EM repository; you can also use this command to enable the automatic backup policy and perform the operation against a RAC configuration.
emca -config centralAgent (db | asm) [-cluster] [-silent] [parameters]	The agent can work as a standalone agent or it can work centrally if you have a grid control environment setup. The centralized management can be performed on a database or on an ASM configuration.
emca -config all db [-repos (create | recreate)] [-cluster] [-silent] [-backup] [parameters]	This command configures both the database files and the centrally managed agent. The arguments are similar to those used to configure the standalone console.
emca -deconfig dbcontrol db [-repos drop] [-cluster] [-silent] [parameters]	This command is used to deconfigure the Console and optionally drop the EM repository. This command can apply on a regular database or on a RAC configuration.
emca -deconfig centralAgent (db | asm) [-cluster] [-silent] [parameters]	The centrally managed agent is deconfigured with this command, either from the database or from the ASM level.

Command	Description
`emca -deconfig all db` `[-repos drop]` `[-cluster]` `[-silent]` `[parameters]`	This variant deconfigures both the centrally managed agent and the database.
`emca -addInst (db | asm)` `[-silent]` `[parameters]`	In an RAC environment this variant is used to add a new node to the RAC configuration, it can be related to a database or ASM.
`emca -deleteInst` `(db | asm)` `[-silent]` `[parameters]`	This option removes an instance from the RAC configuration. It can either be a database or an ASM instance.
`emca -reconfig ports` `[-cluster]` `[parameters]`	This option was previously used to reconfigure the HTTP port number assigned by default at Console definition time.
`emca -reconfig` `dbcontrol -cluster` `[-silent]` `[parameters]`	This command deconfigures DB Control deployment for a cluster database, in this case the `-cluster` modifier is mandatory.
`emca -displayConfig` `dbcontrol -cluster` `[-silent]` `[parameters]`	You can display the deployment configuration in a RAC environment. The `displayConfig` modifier can only be used in RAC environments.
`emca -upgrade (db | asm` `| db_asm)` `[-cluster]` `[-silent]` `[parameters]`	The upgrade option performs an upgrade from a previous DB control version to the current version. The upgrade process has to do with the configuration files. This is not a database or software upgrade, these tasks are supposed to be performed separately. The command will attempt to modify all `dbcontrol` instances available across the different Oracle Homes.
`emca -restore (db | asm` `| db_asm)` `[-cluster]` `[-silent]` `[parameters]`	If something doesn't work as expected after the upgrade process, this command can revert the changes made by an upgrade EMCA command.

EMCA flags

Parameter	Description
`db`	This flag instructs the EMCA to execute the action against a database.
`asm`	The operation will be performed against an ASM instance, either single or RAC.
`db_asm`	This option is used when performing upgrade actions, this instructs the EMCA to apply the action against both the ASM and the Database instance.
`-repos create`	A new repository will be created. It is assumed that there is currently no repository.

Parameter	Description
-repos drop	This option drops an EM repository
-repos recreate	Assuming there is currently a repository; this option drops and creates a repository.
-cluster	This option indicates that the requested action should take place on a clustered database or ASM instance
-silent	This option is used in batch mode, it tells the EMCA not to prompt for further information from the user or read any user input. When specifying this option you must also specify the -respFile to point to a properly configured response file.
-backup	This option tells the EMCA to configure the default backup policy. If this flag is present then the EMCA will require the db_recovery_file_dest instance parameter to be properly set at the target Oracle instance, otherwise the EMCA will return in an error state.

EMCA general Command-Line Parameters

Parameter	Description
-respFile	This option declares the location of the response file to be used when the -silent flag is declared
-SID	This is the target Oracle Instance where the actions will take place
-PORT	This parameter refers to the listener parameter
-ORACLE_HOME	This specifies the absolute path of the Oracle Home where the Oracle Instance resides. No symbolic links are allowed.
-LISTENER_OH	If the listener lives in a different Oracle Home from the one where the Oracle Instance is defined, then you must specify the Listener Oracle Home using absolute path
-EMAIL_ADDRESS	If you enable email notifications this parameter is used to declare the email address where the notifications will be sent to
-MAIL_SERVER_NAME	Using mail notifications requires you to define the outgoing mail (SMTP) server
-DBSNMP_PWD	This refers to the database level DBSNMP password
-SYSMAN_PWD	This is the database level SYSMAN password
-SYS_PWD	This is the SYS password
-SRC_OH	This specifies the absolute path to the Oracle Home of the database that will be upgraded or restored
-DBCONTROL_HTTP_PORT	This specifies the EM http port, if not specified the EMCA will automatically assign one. Make sure this port is not already taken.

Parameter	Description
-AGENT_PORT	This is the standalone management Agent port for DB Control. If this port is not specified, the EMCA will automatically assign one.
-RMI_PORT	This sets the **RMI (Remote Method Invocation)** port.
-JMS_PORT	This declares the **JMS (Java Messaging Service)** port to be used.

EMCA backup parameters

Parameter	Description
-HOST_USER	This parameter specifies the OS username
-HOST_USER_PWD	This specifies the password of the previously specified user
-BACKUP_SCHEDULE	This parameter specifies the time at which the daily backup will be scheduled in 'HH:MM' format

EMCA ASM parameters

Parameter	Description
-ASM_OH	This parameter declares the ASM Oracle Home full path
-ASM_SID	This specifies the ASM Instance name
-ASM_PORT	This specifies the ASM TNS listener port
-ASM_USER_ROLE	This parameter declares the role used to connect to the ASM instance
-ASM_USER_NAME	This parameter declares the ASM administrator's user name
-ASM_USER_PWD	This parameter specifies the password of the previously declared user

EMCA Cluster (RAC) parameters

Parameter	Description
-CLUSTER_NAME	This parameter declares the cluster name
-DB_UNIQUE_NAME	This parameter specifies the database unique name
-EM_NODE	This is the target node name where the command will be applied
-EMD_SID_LIST	This parameter is a list, in a comma separated format, declaring the names of the Oracle Instances for agent only configurations
-SERVICE_NAME	This parameter declares the service name in a clustered environment

EMCA 10g Release 1

The EMCA command parameters have changed from Ora10gR1 to Ora10gR2; if you still have Release 1 installed you must be aware that the EMCA parameters used in that release were completely different to the parameters in 10gR2. I would go so far as to say that one of the very few things these releases have in common is the tool name.

EMCA 10gR1 syntax

```
emca [options] [list of parameters][options] = -[a|b|c|e <node>|
f <node>|h|m|n <ndoe>|r|s|x <db>|RMI_PORT <port>|JMS_PORT <port>|
AGENT_PORT <port>|DBCONSOLE_HTTP <port>]

[list of parameters] = [HOST | SID | PORT | ORALCE_HOME | LISTENER |
HOST_USER | HOST_USER_PWD | BACKUP_HOUR | BACKUP_MINUTE |
ARCHIVE_LOG | EMAIL_ADDRESS | MAIL_SERVER | MAIL_SERVER_NAME |
ASM_OH | ASM_SID | ASM_PORT | ASM_USER_ROLE | AMS_USER_NAME |
ASM_USER_PWD | EM_HOME | DBSNMP_PWD | SYSMAN_PWD | SYS_PWD |
CLUSTER_NAME | DB_NAME | SERVICE_NAME | ]
```

EMCA 10gR1 options

Parameter	Description
-a	This option configures for an ASM database
-b	This configures for automatic backup
-c	Configures a cluster database
-e <node>	Removes a node from the cluster
-f <file>	Specifies the file name that contains parameter values
-h	Displays help
-m	Configures EM for a central agent
-n <node>	Adds a new node to the cluster
-r	This option skips the creation of the repository schema
-s	This option enables silent mode so the user is not prompted for information
-x <db>	This option removes a SID or DB configuration
-RMI_PORT <port>	This stands for the **Remote Method Invocation** (**RMI**) port
-JMS_PORT <port>	This is the **Java Messaging Service** (**JMS**) port to be used
-AGENT_PORT <port>	This is the standalone management Agent port for DB Control. If this port is not specified the EMCA will automatically assign one.
-DBCONSOLE_HTTP_PORT <port>	This specifies the EM http port, if not specified the EMCA will automatically assign one. Make sure this port is not already taken.

EMCA 10gR1 parameters

Parameter	Description
HOST	Database host name
SID	Database Instance name
PORT	TNS Listener port
ORACLE_HOME	Database Oracle Home
LISTENER	TNS Listener Name
HOST_USER	Host user name used for automatic backup
HOST_USER_PWD	Password for the previously declared user
BACKUP_HOUR	Scheduled backup hour [00-24] in number for the default backup policy
BACKUP_MINUTE	Scheduled backup minute [00-60] in number for the default backup policy
ARCHIVE_LOG	Archive log configuration
EMAIL_ADDRESS	Email address for the generated alerts
MAIL_SERVER	Outgoing mail (SMTP) server for the generated alerts
ASM_OH	ASM Oracle Home
ASM_SID	ASM Oracle SID name
ASM_USER_ROLE	This parameter declares the role used to connect to the ASM instance
ASM_USER_NAME	This parameter declares the ASM administrator's user name
ASM_USER_PWD	This parameter specifies the password of the previously declared user
EM_HOME	Enterprise Manager Oracle Home
DBSNMP_PWD	Password for the DBSNMP user
SYSMAN_PWD	Password for the repository SYSMAN user
SYS_PWD	Password for the SYS user

EMCA 10gR1 RAC parameters

Parameter	Description
CLUSTER_NAME	This parameter declares the cluster name
DB_NAME	This parameter specifies the database unique name
SERVICE_NAME	This is the target node name where the command will be applied

EMCA silent mode

EMCA is by default an interactive tool; if required it asks the user for information input. If needed, the EMCA can run in silent mode, thus allowing the user to include the EMCA in a batch script for massive deployments.

EMCA Silent mode requires a plain text format response file where the parameters are specified.

In the next example EMCA is launched in silent mode to have it reconfigured.

EMCA demo response file contents (drop):

```
#
# EMCA parameters for silent mode setup
#
SID=sigma
PORT=1521
ORACLE_HOME=/u01/app/oracle/product/10.2.0/db_1
DBSNMP_PWD=oracle
SYSMAN_PWD=oracle
SYS_PWD=oracle
```

Command to deconfigure console and drop EM repository:

```
emca -deconfig dbcontrol db -repos drop -silent -respFile /tmp/emca_
sigma_drop.rsp
```

EMCA demo response file contents (create):

```
#
# EMCA parameters for silent mode setup
#
SID=sigma
PORT=1521
ORACLE_HOME=/u01/app/oracle/product/10.2.0/db_1
DBSNMP_PWD=oracle
SYSMAN_PWD=oracle
SYS_PWD=oracle
DBCONTROL_HTTP_PORT=1158
```

Command to configure console and create the repository:

```
emca -config dbcontrol db -repos create -silent -respFile /tmp/emca_
sigma_create.rsp
```

EM directory structure

When talking about the Enterprise Manager directory related structure, there are basically four relevant sections in the Oracle Home, the first one has to do with EMCA, the EMCA directory is where Oracle stores the log files related to EMCA executions, there you will find a directory where generic EMCA output is stored, meanwhile under this directory you will find directories named the same as each Oracle Instance that has been configured by EMCA.

The second section is related to the specific EM console; here there are two main directories, one stores the console configuration, most of these configuration files are not supposed to be manipulated by the DBA unless explicitly directed by Oracle support. There are configuration files that are modified by EMCA.

There is a fourth section located under the Oracle Home named sysman. When a new console is created EMCA reads template configuration files from here and executes the scripts to create or recreate the EM repository.

As EM is a Java Enterprise Edition based application, it requires a JEE environment so it can be executed. Oracle provides an OC4J for each configured console. The directory can be located at the `oc4j` directory right at the Oracle Home level.

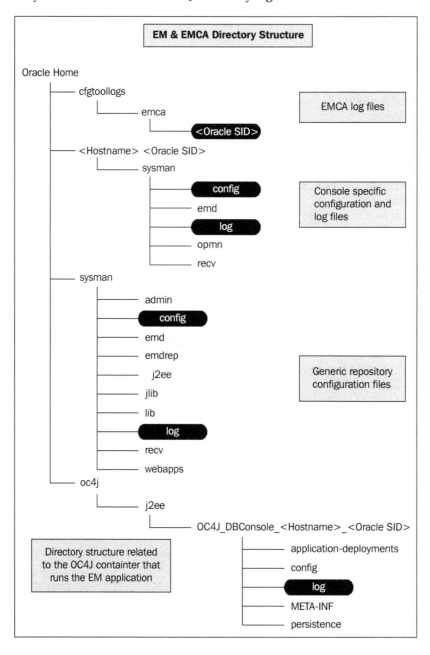

EMCA log files

When EMCA is used it records the activity in log files located at `$ORACLE_HOME/cfgtoollogs/emca/<ORACLE_SID>` you may just want to optionally backup and purge these files when they are no longer required.

The SYSMAN configuration files

There are two main configuration files located in the `<Oracle Home>/<hostname>_<Oracle SID>/sysman/log` directory. One is named `emd.properties` and a second file named `emoms.properties`. The first file defines the URLs used by the Upload Manager, the agent, the agent version and the agent TZ region; these two files should not be managed manually except when explicitly directed by Oracle Support. The second file, `emoms.properties`, defines how is the SYSMAN user going to connect to the target database, it also contains the SYSMAN password (encrypted). There is a procedure to change the password of the SYSMAN user if required.

The SYSMAN log files

Log and trace files are the first source of information when you want to troubleshoot the console. If the console doesn't start or it happens to be inaccessible you should first inspect the files located at `<Oracle Home>/<hostname>_<Oracle SID>/sysman/log` directory, there you will find several log and trace files. The log files will be growing on demand as required by the involved processes, the DBA must be aware of this and regularly maintain the files. The DBA can manage the files' growth by configuring the maximum file size, the maximum number of files as well as the log file location. The procedure to manage log files is outlined next.

> As you are working with sensitive configuration files, you must backup these files prior to modifying their contents.

Log/Trace File	Configuration File	File Entry	Description
`emoms.trc`	`<Oracle Home>/<hostname>_ <Oracle SID>/ sysman/config/ emomslogging. properties`	`log4j.appender. emtrcAppender. MaxFileSize`	Maximum File Size
		`log4j.appender. emtrcAppender. MaxBackupIndex`	Maximum Number of Files (Rotation)
		`log4j.appender. emtrcAppender`	File Location
`emoms.log`	`<Oracle Home>/ <hostname> _<Oracle SID> /sysman/config/ emomslogging. properties`	`log4j.appender. emlogAppender. MaxFileSize`	Maximum File Size
		`log4j.appender. emlogAppender. MaxBackupIndex`	Maximum Number of Files (Rotation)
		`log4j.appender. emlogAppender. File`	File Location
`http-web-access. log`	`<Oracle Home>/oc4j/ j2ee/OC4J_DBConsole_ <host>_<Oracle SID>/ config/ http-web-site.xml`	`<access-log path="../ log/http-web- access.log" split="day"/>`	Modify the split value to any of these values: none, hour, day, week, and month.
`rmi.log`	`<Oracle Home>/ oc4j/j2ee/OC4J_ DBConsole_<host>_ <Oracle SID>/config/ rmi.xml`	`<file path="../ log/rmi.log"/>`	Define the new location, if required, of the `rmi.log` file.
`emdb.nohup`	There are no files nor parameters to configure the log rotation or maximum size, you have to stop the console and manually backup or purge the file located at `<Oracle Home>/<hostname>_<Oracle SID>/sysman/log/emdb. nohup`		

Log/Trace File	Configuration File	File Entry	Description

`server.log`	`<Oracle Home>`
	`/oc4j/j2ee/OC4J_`
	`DBConsole_<host>_`
	`<Oracle SID>/config/`
	`server.xml`
		`<file path="../`
		`log/server.log"`
		`/>`
			You can only change the location of the log file.

`global-`
`application.log`
	`<Oracle Home>/oc4j/`
	`j2ee/OC4J_`
	`DBConsole_<host>_`
	`<Oracle SID>/config/`
	`application.xml`
		`<log>`
		`  <file`
		`path="../`
		`log/global-`
		`application.`
		`log"/>`
		`  <!-- Uncomment`
		`this if you`
		`want to use`
		`ODL logging`
		`capabilities`
		`  <odl path="../`
		`log/global-`
		`application/"`
		`max-file-`
		`size="1000"`
		`max-directory-`
		`size="10000"/>`
		`  -->`
		`</log>`
			Uncomment the ODL entry, this will allow log file rotation, and set suitable values for the path, max-file-size and max-directory-size as required.

`em-application.log`	`<Oracle Home>/oc4j/`
	`j2ee/OC4J_DBConsole_`
	`<host>_<Oracle SID>/`
	`config/`
	`orion-application.xml`
		`<file`
		`path="../../`
		`log/em-`
		`application.`
		`log" />`
			You can only change the location of the log file.

Environment changes

Changing the network environment may happen as often as, say, the administrative passwords get change, but when it happens, then the environment change directly affects database and Enterprise Manager availability, which can adversely affect the smooth operation of the site. When the environment changes you must be aware of the consequences these changes will bring and how to restore the service as soon as possible.

Changing the IP address or host name

Changing the IP address means Enterprise Manager Console won't be available and it won't be possible to start it; all the Oracle connectivity configuration files are affected too.

As this is an administrative change, it is strongly suggested to backup the current environment by taking a full Oracle Home and database backup. This will back-up the current configuration files as well as the current EM repository.

The procedure used to get the environment working is as follows:

1. Shut down enterprise manager, the database and all Oracle related services.
2. Perform the IP and/or host name changes.
3. Edit the `<Oracle Home>/network/admin/listener.ora` and `<Oracle Home>/network/admin/tnsnames.ora` files and replicate the change to these files. This list is not at all exhaustive, depending on the network configurations you have set up you may have to modify other files or network connectivity configuration systems such as LDAP centralized entries, wallets, and so on.
4. Start up the listener and databases do not start enterprise manager at this time as its configuration won't work with the environment setup, and it will need to be modified.
5. Deconfigure the EM Console and drop the repository.
6. Reconfigure the EM Console and have the repository created.
7. At the end of this procedure your Enterprise Manager console will be brought back to business.

Oracle RDBMS should work on fixed IP address servers, if your server has a dynamically assigned IP then you will have to configure a loopback adapter so you can fix the IP references to this adapter and have the OS hosts file configured so the official hostname and optionally the domain are associated with the loopback adapter's IP address instead of the host's actual IP address. This information will be read at the time EMCA performs the configuration.

Changing administrative passwords

Changing the SYSMAN password requires more than just changing the password at the database level, if you just change the password at this level then Enterprise Manager won't be accessible any more. The Enterprise Manager DB Console requires two users, one of them is the Agent monitor user (DBSNMP), and the other one is the owner of the EM repository (SYSMAN), there is a procedure to change these administrative passwords.

Changing SYSMAN password

The procedure to change the password starts with properly setting the environment variables: `ORACLE_HOME`, `ORACLE_SID`, and `PATH`.

1. Shut down Enterprise Manager Console and make sure it is completely off.

   ```
   emctl stop dbconsole
   emctl status dbconsole
   ```

2. From a SQL*Plus prompt connected with a privileged account (SYS, SYSTEM or SYSMAN) modify the SYSMAN's password with a regular ALTER USER command

   ```
   SQL> alter user SYSMAN identified by <SysmanNewPassword> ;
   ```

3. Verify you can open a SQL*Plus session using the SYSMAN user identified with the recently set password.

   ```
   sqlplus SYSMAN/<SysmanNewPassword>
   ```

4. The next phase has to do with replicating the change on the EM configuration files.

5. From an OS prompt change the current directory to `<Oracle Home>/ <Hostname>_<Oracle SID>/sysman/config` directory.

6. Backup the `emoms.properties` configuration file.

7. Edit the `emoms.properties` file with a text editor, look for the `oracle. sysman.eml.mntr.emdRepPwd` entry and replace the text string with the new SYSMAN password written in clear text, then look for the `oracle.sysman. eml.mntr.emdRepPwdEncrypted` entry and change the value to `FALSE`. Enterprise Manager will automatically change the value to `TRUE` and it will rewrite the password with the encrypted version.

8. Once you are ready, start the console using the regular `emctl start dbconsole` command and when this step is finished verify the password written in the previously modified configuration file has changed to the encrypted version.

Your Enterprise Manager console should be up and running now with the new password. You can verify the access of the SYSMAN user sessions in the database with a simple query to the `V$SESSION` dynamic view.

Changing DBSNMP password

This is the second administrative user related to Enterprise Manager and when you need to change its password there is a procedure you must follow.

It is assumed that the ORACLE_HOME, ORACLE_SID, and PATH environment variables are properly set.

1. Stop the standalone console:

   ```
   emctl stop dbconsole
   ```

2. Verify both the console and the agents are down:

   ```
   emctl status dbconsole
   emctl status agent
   ```

3. Connect with a privileged user at SQL*Plus and change the DBSNMP password:

   ```
   SQL> alter user DBSNMP identified by <DBSMPNewPassword>;
   ```

4. Verify you can open a SQL*Plus session using DBSNMP and the recently assigned password:

   ```
   sqlplus DBSNMP/<DBSNMPNewPassword>
   ```

5. At the OS level change to the directory and use a text editor to modify the targets.xml file (you must backup this file prior to proceed with the modification).

   ```
   <Oracle Home>/oc4j/j2ee/OC4J_DBConsole_<host>_<Oracle SID>/emd
   ```

6. Look for the line:

   ```
   <Property NAME="password" VALUE="<encrypted_string>"
   ENCRYPTED="TRUE"/>
   ```

7. Replace the encrypted value with the new password value, and the ENCRYPTED entry value to TRUE, this will allow you to write the password in clear text format, later EM will change this value with the encrypted password version.

8. Finally, start the console and verify the entry you modified has been changed to encrypted and the encryption flag is set back to TRUE.

Securing Enterprise Manager

By default Oracle 10g configures the Enterprise Manager Console to be accessed in HTTP mode, this means everything that travels from and to the EM console is visible to any third party who monitors the network connection. When the 10g Rel. 2 RDBSM is upgraded to 10.2.0.4.0 and the databases are consequently upgraded, Oracle modifies the console to be accessed in secure mode. In Oracle 11g Rel. 1 and 11g Rel. 2 Oracle configures the console in HTTPS mode by default.

If you have not upgraded to 10.2.0.4.0 and you want to secure the access to the EM DB Console, then you must use the `secure` option of the `emctl` command.

```
emctl secure dbconsole <sysman password> <registration password>
[<hostname>]
```

The command takes some minutes to complete; afterwards the console can be accessed in HTTPS mode.

In the next example a console is configured using the previously defined syntax (**A**), Enterprise Manager will look for the encryption key in the repository (**B**), then it will configure the wallet and the wallet access (**C**), and finally the console will be secured and the access can be made from this moment on in https mode.

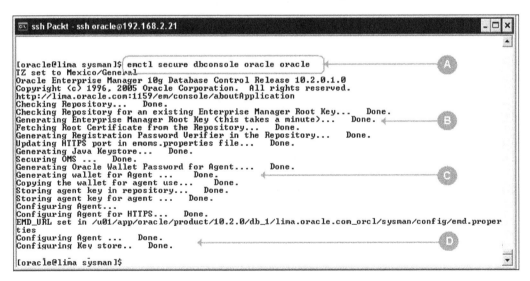

The configuration changes won't be considered until Enterprise Manager restarts, so you should stop and start the console at your earliest convenience.

```
emctl stop dbconsole db
emctl start dbconsole db
```

When accessing the console a warning will be displayed in the browser window, letting the user know that there are problems with the certificate, even though the certificate structure is valid, this is issued by a not known Certificate Authority. You can accept the certificate and proceed with your session.

You can verify the change in the agent configuration, this was also modified and the upload process will be performed in HTTPS mode too. Issue the `emctl status agent` to verify the change.

Summary

Today, efficient database interactive administration cannot easily be achieved without Enterprise Manager, this does not mean the command line interface is obsolete, it simply means that using commands to perform the daily database management tasks will take longer than using the graphical interface.

Considering this, keeping Enterprise Manager DB Control Console available will provide the DBA with a more efficient way to easily manage the complexities of Oracle databases. The tool to assist the DBA in making sure EM will be properly configured is the EMCA, and as we have seen, the EMCA is much more than just a tool to initially configure the console. It is a tool that allows the DBA to customize the nuts and bolts of the console.

On the other hand, keeping the software up to date is a good practice, it wipes off known bugs and it lets you prevent possible security breaches with a more robust and secure software version. **OPatch** is the tool that allows you to manage your software updates related to **Critical Patch Updates** (CPU) or individual patches. In the next chapter OPatch will be explored.

13
OPatch

Oracle Corporation provides dynamic software which is constantly improving. Oracle periodically releases software updates by means of **Critical Path Updates** (**CPUs**). Oracle also releases individual patches depending on the circumstances. These one-off patches can easily be applied using the OPatch tool. Oracle also releases major maintenance updates known as Patch Sets. A Patch Set is a group of one-off patches that have been tested and verified to work together. There may be additional functionality as well as bug fixes included in a Patch Set. When a Patch Set has been applied, the component-specific release number (`http://download. oracle.com/docs/cd/B19306_01/server.102/b14231/dba.htm#sthref94`) is incremented. Patch Sets are applied with the Oracle Universal Installer included within the same patchset, and the other kinds of patches are applied using OPatch.

It is strongly suggested to keep your Oracle software updated to the last available Patch Set level so that known bugs can be avoided and if the database faces an issue that requires Oracle Support Services it is easier for the analyst to eliminate the possibility of the issue being caused by a known bug from the beginning. In case of doubt you should contact Oracle Support Services.

OPatch

OPatch is a Java based utility that requires installation of the Oracle Universal Installer. Starting Oracle 10g Rel. 2, this tool is included in the Oracle Home. Prior to this release the DBA had to download a patch from Metalink to install OPatch (`p2617419_10102_GENERIC.zip`). OPatch in 10gRel2 is not compatible with previous Oracle releases.

Even though OPatch is an executable, it is not located in the `ORACLE_HOME/bin` directory. It has its own directory located at `ORACLE_HOME/OPatch`. The `opatch` executable is a shell script that launches the OPatch Java class, the actual OPatch executable.

What is the version of the OPatch currently used? This is one of the most frequently asked questions regarding OPatch. There is a command to find the version number, but taking a look at the OPatch execution with no parameters will also give you some basic useful information regarding the main commands as well as the OPatch version.

This image shows the output of a simple OPatch command execution.

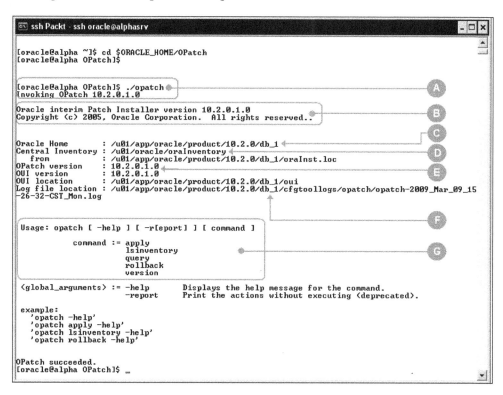

Issuing ./opatch (**A**) directly from <Oracle Home>/OPatch with no arguments, shows the OPatch version. In this case, it is the same as that of the Oracle Home (10.2.0.1.0) (**B**). It shows information about the **Oracle Home** (C) and the **Central Inventory** location (D), confirms the **OPatch version** (E), displays the log file location (F), and finally displays basic help messages of the main OPatch commands (G).

Downloading the latest OPatch version

You can get the latest OPatch version from metalink. Oracle distributes the OPatch tool by means of a patch; you can get it from: http://updates.oracle.com/download/6880880.html. Select the version and the platform that corresponds to your environment.

You must have a valid CSI and username to access the updates.oracle.com site.

OPatch requirements

In order for you to use OPatch, some requirements must be met:

1. Set the Oracle Home environment variable to point to a valid Oracle Home directory. This Oracle Home must match the one used during the installation.

2. Java SDK 1.4 or higher must be installed.

3. The environment variable that points to the shared library must be properly set (LD_LIBRARY_PATH or SHLIB_PATH, which depends on the OS platform).

4. OPatch creates a rollback script in case the patch installation has to be undone. It also performs a backup of the Inventory, so you must make sure you have enough free space for these operations.

5. Use a compatible version, 10gR2 requires OUI to be 10.2.0.1.0 or higher.

6. When working in RAC environments, make sure the user equivalence between hosts is correctly set.

7. Verify the Oracle Inventory is valid, you can check this by issuing the command `OPatch lsinventory -detail`. This command displays the software installed on the target Oracle Home. If this command returns no information or it shows an error message, it means that the Inventory within the Oracle Home is either missing or corrupt.

OPatch syntax

The `opatch` executable can be found at `<Oracle Home>/OPatch` directory and it has this syntax:

```
<Oracle Home>/OPatch/opatch option [-arguments]
```

You should be aware that the OPatch for 10g Release 1 was a Perl script and it had a different syntax. For more information, refer to the Metalink note 242993.1 OPatch FAQ.

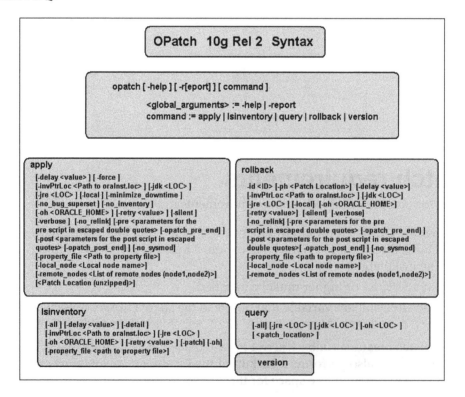

OPatch options

OPatch 10g Release 2 has five main options. The main options are used to list the contents of the inventory, apply the patch, and retrieve information about the patch and the system to be patched. These options are further detailed in the next section.

lsinventory: This option lists the inventory for a particular Oracle Home. This is used to list the installations that can be found. When launched with no options, this command shows the top level components found for the current Oracle Home.

apply: This option applies an interim patch to an Oracle Home from the current directory. The patch location can be specified using the parameter `patch_location`.

query: This option provides information about the patch and the system being patched.

rollback: This option is used to remove a specific interim patch from the current Oracle Home.

version: This option is used to display the version number of the OPatch utility being used.

Oracle maintenance using OPatch

There are several situations when an interim patch is required. The most common one is to apply patches that correct specific bugs which you have encountered. Another situation where software maintenance is required is when Oracle releases the quarterly Critical Patch Update bundle. The patch task can consist of applying a single patch or several patches at once. Specific detailed instructions are always available in the companion README file.

 Never skip the README file and never take a patch for granted; you may face particular circumstances that, if neglected, may leave your software in an unstable condition.

In case something goes wrong or you want to uninstall the patch OPatch, always performs a backup of the affected files so you can apply a rollback procedure to return things to how they were when OPatch session has started.

It is strongly suggested to have an Oracle Home, Oracle Inventory, and a backup of the database handy just in case something doesn't work as expected.

Applying a single patch using OPatch

In order for you to be able to apply a patch, a generic procedure can be defined:

Thoroughly read the companion README file. Instructions stated there supersede any procedure. This outline is merely a suggestion that can be overridden by any specific patch instructions.

1. Make sure the Oracle environment variables are properly set.

2. Include the `<Oracle Home>/OPatch` directory in the PATH environment variable.

3. Each patch requires the execution of OS commands, the PATH variable must be able to see them.

4. Unzip the file patch file to a stage area, if you don't already have a predefined location, the `<Oracle Home>/OPatch` directory is suggested as a stage area.

5. Once you are ready, at the OS prompt, change the current working directory to the patch directory `<Oracle Home>/OPatch /<PatchNumber>`. Now issue the `opatch apply` command, or whatever options were defined in the README file.

6. Once the OPatch task is finished, read the contents of the log files to verify if the patch apply task ended successfully. If a problem shows up, the log files are the starting point for a troubleshooting session.

In the next image, a simple OPatch session is started to apply a patch against a given Oracle Home.

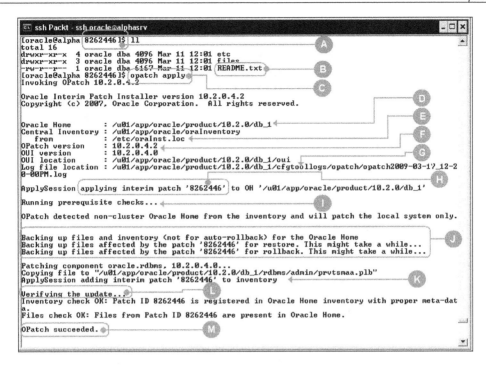

In this session, a patch was downloaded from Metalink and it was unzipped to a stage area (**A**). Listing the files included in the patch, you can see the README.txt file at the patch root level (**B**). This file could be in plain text or HTML format, there are patches that include both formats.

Once all of the prerequisites have been met and the environment has been properly configured, the opatch apply command is issued (**C**). This starts the OPatch session. OPatch displays the Oracle Home that will receive the patch (**D**), the **OPatch version** (**E**), the **OUI version** (**F**), the **OUI location**, and the **Log File location** (**G**).

OPatch notifies the user that the specific patch-apply session has started (**H**). It starts by performing some prerequisite checks (**I**). In case you are required to perform a rollback session, OPatch performs a backup of the directly affected files (**J**). Then it proceeds with the actual patch apply (**K**) and finally it verifies the update process (**L**). If everything went as expected, it will notify the user that the OPatch session ended successfully (**M**).

Querying the Oracle inventory

The simplest way to verify if a given patch has been applied is by listing the Oracle Inventory contents. This is achieved by issuing the `opatch lsinventory` [-detail] command.

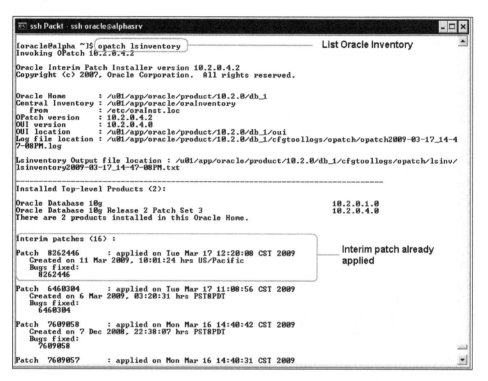

Rolling back a failed OPatch session

During the patch apply session, Oracle creates a directory under the Oracle Home named `.patch_storage`. Oracle creates a structure to store the procedures and backup files to undo a patch apply session.

A basic rollback session can be started using `opatch rollback -id PatchNumber`. You may require a rollback session if a patch-apply session fails:

- if you find a conflicting patch
- if the patch doesn't meet the user expectations
- if the patch does not fix the problem

Considerations after applying a patch

After a patch has been applied, there will be things that will change. It is a good idea to perform a backup after the patch has been applied and keep it in a safe place in case the Oracle Home or the Oracle Inventory get compromised due to a media failure or accidental deletion in future.

Oracle databases can still be created using DBCA, but if the patch modified the structure or contents of the database dictionary, then you must be aware that these changes are not replicated against the seed databases. So if you are using DBCA to create a new database using the current seeds, the scripts or other post apply procedures must be manually applied against the new database. If you create a new database using the CREATE DATABASE command, there is no need to apply the scripts that modify the database dictionary. These are already considered when the catproc.sql or catalog.sql scripts are run.

You should have a test plan so that after applying a patch you ensure the system works as expected. A good set of regression tests is important to verify that the patch has not accidently broken application functionality.

OPatch in Oracle 11g

You should be aware that OPatch is tool sensitive to the version. You cannot use the OPatch tool from one release to patch another release. Oracle 11g introduced several new options. The next three images show the OPatch syntax in 11g, how it changed from the 10g release, and which options were added in this release.

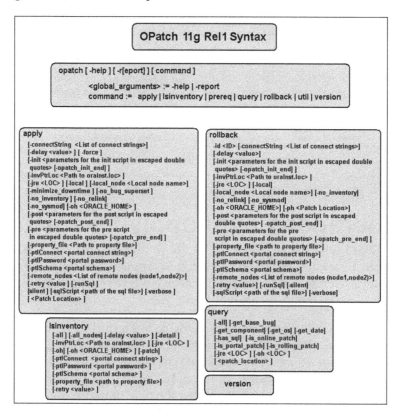

Here you can see from the syntax summary that there were many more options added, and in the next two images, the syntax of the new options is shown. The util commands are depicted in the next image. The commands available are used to apply SQL commands, clean up the backup, perform file copies, restore an Oracle Home, or perform other remove or rollback actions.

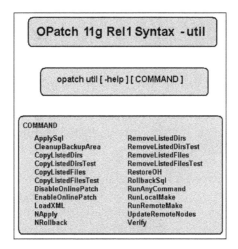

In the next image the detailed options of the `prereq` command are shown. The `prereq` command listed is used to check the central inventory, look for conflicting patches, verify the Oracle home, OUI, and Oracle installer locations, among other checking operations. These options are particularly useful to validate the actions before applying the patch. Checking the environment, resolving patch conflicts, and validating the target platform are shown among many checks it carries out. This `prereq` options provides reduces your chances of ending with a failed OPatch session.

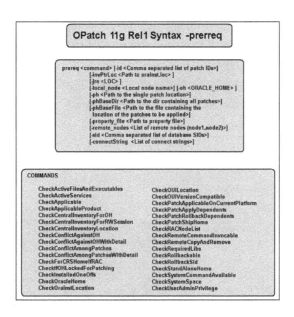

Oracle Configuration Manager Registration

Starting with the Oracle 10.2.0.4.0 release, Oracle added the Oracle Configuration Manager Registration form as a part of the patchset setup. This tool allows you to associate your configuration information with your Metalink account. This tool lets you link your service requests with the pre-collected configuration data gathered from the current Oracle Home.

If you are planning to use this tool, you must have available the Oracle Support account information, which comprises of the **Customer Support Id (CSI)**, your **Metalink Account Username** and password, and the country where this CSI is valid. When checking the box in the registration form, a window with the "Terms of Use" is displayed. Make sure you read and understand it. Once you are ready, accept the "Terms of Use" and fill in the required form information.

 You should be aware that this functionality is available as long as your CSI remains valid. You should contact your Oracle representative if your CSI doesn't allow you to use this functionality.

If you require a Proxy server to access internet, fill in the required connection information, which can be accessed by means of the **Connection Settings** button.

If you don't complete the registration form at this time, you can do it later, but in the mean time if you need to apply an interim patch, a warning will be displayed letting you know that you have already installed the Oracle Configuration Manager tool but you have not configured it yet.

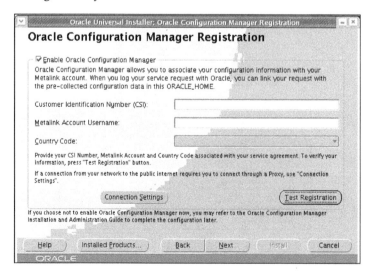

Critical Patch Updates

Oracle releases a patch bundle on a quarterly basis known as a **Critical Patch Updates (CPU)**. It is strongly advised to install this patch as this provides security fixes on a regular basis. The CPUs are released every January, April, July, and October. For further information about CPU releases, you can refer to the information provided on the **Critical Patch Updates and Security Alerts** page located at `http://www.oracle.com/technology/deploy/security/alerts.htm`.

The procedure to install the CPU is detailed in the companion `README.txt` or `README.html` file which describes the steps required to install the CPU in detail. You must read this file prior to starting the apply session. The key tool to perform the CPU install is OPatch and the specific options required to perform this task may vary from CPU to CPU, so you must read the instructions included in the CPU.

CPUs are cumulative, so you don't have to apply all the CPUs for a given release. If you apply the latest CPU available, you will automatically be applying all available CPU patches released so far for the given RDBMS version. At the above URL you will find CPU availability. When a CPU is made public, it doesn't mean it will be available to all platforms and it won't be available to all patchset levels, you must first verify if your platform qualifies for the released CPU. The patch number related to the CPU is not the same for all the platforms or for all the patchset levels. You must first find out which specific patch number corresponds to your platform and patchset level.

Find out the installed patches

As OPatch uses the same Oracle inventory used by OUI, you can use it to get information about the patches applied in the first instance. The information is displayed in the form of interim patches. The following command line lists all the applied patches so far:

```
opatch lsinventory -all
```

However, this does not differentiate between the regular interim patches and those applied by means of the CPU.

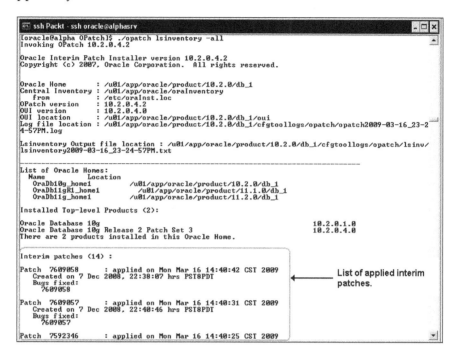

```
ssh Packt - ssh oracle@alphasrv
[oracle@alpha OPatch]$ ./opatch lsinventory -all
Invoking OPatch 10.2.0.4.2

Oracle Interim Patch Installer version 10.2.0.4.2
Copyright (c) 2007, Oracle Corporation. All rights reserved.


Oracle Home       : /u01/app/oracle/product/10.2.0/db_1
Central Inventory : /u01/app/oracle/oraInventory
   from           : /etc/oraInst.loc
OPatch version    : 10.2.0.4.2
OUI version       : 10.2.0.4.0
OUI location      : /u01/app/oracle/product/10.2.0/db_1/oui
Log file location : /u01/app/oracle/product/10.2.0/db_1/cfgtoollogs/opatch/opatch2009-03-16_23-2
4-57PM.log

Lsinventory Output file location : /u01/app/oracle/product/10.2.0/db_1/cfgtoollogs/opatch/lsinv/
lsinventory2009-03-16_23-24-57PM.txt
--------------------------------------------------------------------------------
List of Oracle Homes:
  Name          Location
    OraDb10g_home1          /u01/app/oracle/product/10.2.0/db_1
    OraDb11gR1_home1        /u01/app/oracle/product/11.1.0/db_1
    OraDb11g_home1          /u01/app/oracle/product/11.2.0/db_1

Installed Top-level Products (2):

Oracle Database 10g                                          10.2.0.1.0
Oracle Database 10g Release 2 Patch Set 3                    10.2.0.4.0
There are 2 products installed in this Oracle Home.


Interim patches (14) :

Patch  7609058     : applied on Mon Mar 16 14:40:42 CST 2009
   Created on 7 Dec 2008, 22:38:07 hrs PST8PDT
   Bugs fixed:
      7609058

Patch  7609057     : applied on Mon Mar 16 14:40:31 CST 2009
   Created on 7 Dec 2008, 22:40:46 hrs PST8PDT
   Bugs fixed:
      7609057

Patch  7592346     : applied on Mon Mar 16 14:40:25 CST 2009
```

List of applied interim patches.

When the CPU patches are applied they modify the contents of a set of registry tracking tables. The table SYS.REGISTRY$HISTORY records the total number of CPUs applied so far to a given target. Querying this table is useful not only for the DBA to determine the CPU level applied against the database, but also for audit tasks to assess if a given database meets the company's patch level compliance requirements.

This query can be used to get the CPU information (the use of column formatters is suggested):

```
SELECT ACTION_TIME,
       ACTION     ,
       VERSION    ,
       COMMENTS   ,
       BUNDLE_SERIES,
FROM REGISTRY$HISTORY;
```

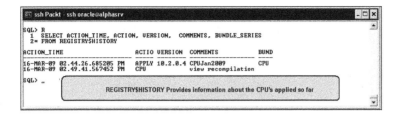

Critical Patch Advisory

If your environment has Enterprise Manager Grid Control you can use the Critical Patch Advisory, which is a valuable tool to diagnose the whole environment and diagnose among the targets which ones require a CPU to be applied. Grid Control can connect to Metalink and download the required patches. It also supports an offline operation mode for those targets that don't have a direct Internet connection available. Note that this requires both the Metalink account and the Configuration Management Pack option. The Critical Patch Advisory is also available in Oracle 11g.

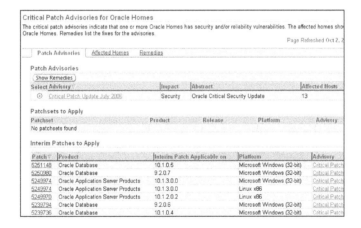

Hot patching (11g only)

Normally when a patch is applied the Oracle services must be shutdown. This means a downtime and a maintenance window must be open while the operation takes place. The DBA must ensure that the process will be successful on the first attempt otherwise there it must be a fall back procedure in place.

Among the high availability features provided by 11g, Oracle introduced the Hot patching concept. Hot patching allows the DBA to install, enable, and disable a patch online without disruption to Oracle services. Hot patches don't require instance shutdown, and they are installed with the traditional OPatch tool. This tool can detect conflicts between hot patches.

Not all patches in 11g can be installed in Hot patch mode. First you must find out if the patch supports the hot patch apply feature. You can use the following command to determine if this mode is allowed:

```
opatch query -is_online_patch <PatchLocation>
```

or

```
opatch query <PatchLocation> -all
```

The patches reported as Hot Patch enabled are shipped as dynamic or shared libraries which are mapped into memory by each Oracle process. When installing a patch in hot patch mode the oracle binary is actually not changed; even though the patch persists across instance restart operations.

Not all OS platforms currently support hot patching, you must refer to Oracle support to find out if your platform supports this mode.

Troubleshooting OPatch

There may be several circumstances that cause OPatch to fail in the patch apply task. The DBA must always read the instructions and make sure they are fully understood and the prerequisites are fully met. This reduces the number of possible failures during the patch apply process.

Let's assume a scenario; the DBA tries to apply a patch but it is only partially applied, OPatch works in an idempotent way, that is, the steps required by OPatch to apply a patch are executed only once. It doesn't matter how many times the user manually restarts the patch apply task. So if the user wants to rollback a partially applied patch the only way to start the rollback procedure is by first finishing the started patch apply task.

PATH environment variable

The PATH environment variable is critical. You must always make sure it is properly set and the OS commands required by OPatch are visible; otherwise, the patch process will fail.

OPatch log files

The OPatch log files are located under the ORACLE_HOME/patch_storage/ patchNumber directory. The log file is named <PatchNumber>_Apply_<date>.log. This file contains all the steps sequence applied by OPatch. If a patch fails, the DBA should refer to this file to start diagnosing what could have gone wrong during the apply phase.

Using Enterprise Manager for software maintenance

Enterprise Manager can be used to perform software maintenance tasks. EM can be configured to access Metalink, query the patches required by the database, download them, and store them in a reserved area known as the Patch Cache; the DBA can take them from this region and schedule them to be applied at a later time. You must remember that there are licensing concerns; you require the Configuration Management Pack.

Enterprise Manager Metalink configuration

There are a couple of requirements the DBA must meet to have Enterprise Manager connected to Metalink and perform the Patch download process.

Configure the Metalink Credentials: This can be done by clicking on the setup link.

1. There will be a link named **Patching Setup**.
2. Here we will find the form where the Metalink credentials are stored.
3. In this form, there is a section to configure the **Patch Cache**.
4. Make sure to reserve enough space to store the patches to be downloaded.

The URL, `http://updates.oracle.com` is valid at this time, Oracle may change it any time in the future, and you should contact Oracle Support Services to configure the updates URL properly.

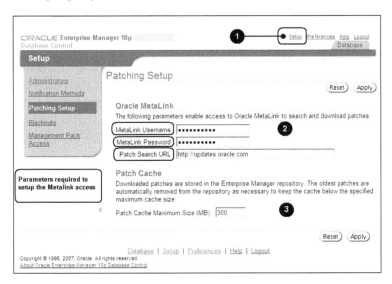

When the credentials are introduced, Enterprise Manager performs a test connection to Metalink. If this operation is successful then the user credentials can be considered valid.

In the case of Oracle 11g, the procedure to set up Metalink access information is the same, although the page has a different style from the one used in 10.2.0 version.

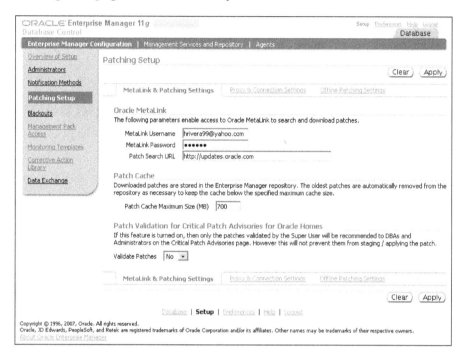

Refresh from Metalink Job

Configure a Job to perform a periodic refresh from Metalink. If you don't configure this Job then you will receive an error while trying to access the Patch Cache that will warn you about running a **RefreshFromMetalink** Job. Configure the Job that will be periodically accessing Metalink to refresh the Patch Cache. If you take a look at the bottom of the database page, you will see a **Jobs** link; by clicking on this link, you can access the section where you can schedule this Job.

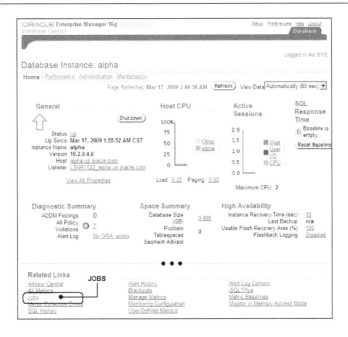

This link leads to the Enterprise Manager Job definition page, these jobs are different from the regular jobs managed by the DBMS_SCHEDULER. This is an Enterprise Manager Job that is stored in the repository tables. These jobs work the same way and with the same mechanism as the jobs manage with the DBMS_SCHEDULER package, but the EM programs cannot be redefined, although they can be rescheduled. In the **Job Activity** form page, you can create a new job of **RefreshFromMetalink** type. The next form will ask you to provide further details; the job **Name**, the schedule, and the access to the job.

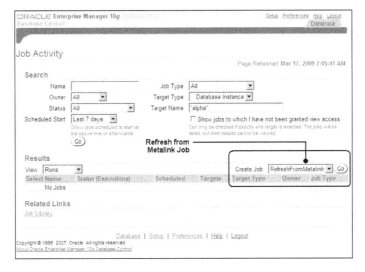

Once the job has been launched you can monitor its progress and verify the output log. You should make sure the job has ran smoothly, otherwise a troubleshooting session should be started. If the credentials, and if applicable, the updates URL and the proxy parameters are properly set, then some other issues that show up may have to do with connectivity to the site, updates site maintenance, or time out issues.

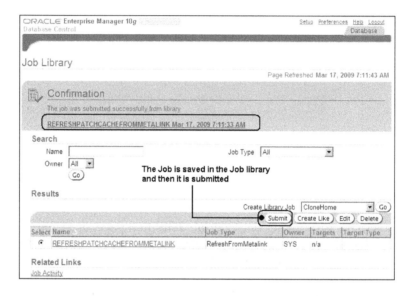

Once the process is finished, check the log for successful completion. If the process was not successful; then diagnose the cause of the error and, if required, raise a Service Request at Metalink.

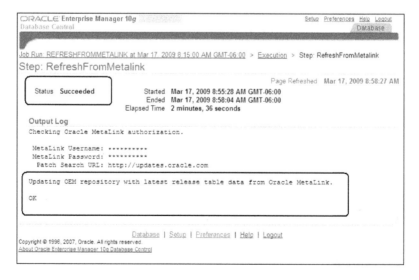

Currently, the name of the product and the platform names have increased in size, so you may face an issue with the column length of the SYSMAN.MGMT_ARU_PLATFORMS and SYSMAN.MGMT_ARU_PRODUCTS tables. If this is the case it is strongly suggested to raise a service request at Oracle Support Services. This is documented in the Metalink Note 459027.1.

Downloading and staging patches

Once the setup procedure is finished and you are able to synchronize with Metalink, you can query all the patches that apply to your platform. Selecting the maintenance tab from the main page, you can click on the **Apply Patch** link in the **Database Software Patching** section. This will show you the available patches for the target platform ordered by the patch release date in descending order.

You can see a process train at the top of the screen. This will lead you through the process of downloading and applying or staging the patch for later application. The following instructions will show you how to do it:

1. **Select Patch**: On the first page you have a **Search Criteria** form that allows you to look up patches on Metalink. You can enter the search criteria. By default it is related to the specific platform you are currently using. Once the query is executed a **Search Results** table is filled with the patch information that was found, there you can select a single patch to be either staged or applied at a later step.

2. **Select Destination**: This screen originally was designed for the Grid Control environment, so the target selection is based on multiple platforms where the patch can be applied which are filtered depending on the specific release and platform. The destination is filtered based on the patch destination type.

3. **Set Credentials**: The patch stage or apply operations require you to have access to the OS as a valid user. In this case Oracle, the owner of the installation, is the user selected to perform the tasks at the OS level. You must provide both, the user name and the password.

4. **Stage or Apply**: Once the patch has been downloaded to the target destination, you can optionally proceed to apply it or just stage it. On this page you select if you want to run the script to apply the patch or just leave it at the Patch Cache area. If you wish to apply the patch after it is downloaded you must make sure your system is at a maintenance window that allows you to perform the task and you must make sure the patch application process won't affect system availability afterwards.

5. **Schedule**: The process can be scheduled to run immediately after the user interrogation is finished or you can schedule it to be executed at a later time. This is the same scheduler form seen in the Job Manager. Here you define a meaningful Job name and a Job description that allows you to positively identify the task at a later time. This kind of task doesn't allow future repetitions. It is assumed the patching task will be run just once, so the only parameters you can specify have to do with the time your task will be scheduled.

6. **Summary**: This final stage is the point of no return where you validate the operation. If you feel comfortable with the parameters set then just proceed with the task execution. The job execution time depends mainly on the patch size to be downloaded and the Internet speed.

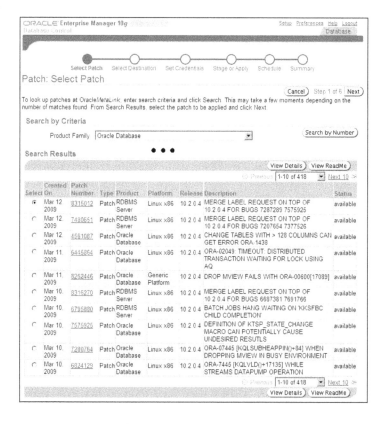

Enterprise Manager stages patches at `<Oracle Home>/EMStagedPatches`. Here you can find all downloaded ZIP files as well as the unzipped patch under a directory named the same as the patch number. If you want you can manually apply patches directly using OPatch from this stage area and use Enterprise Manager as a query and download tool.

The Patch Cache

Patches downloaded from Metalink are stored in the Patch Cache. This allows you to stage multiple patches. If a patch is not already in the stage area Enterprise Manager can automatically download it. You can manage the Patch Cache area by manually uploading patches to it.

The Patch Cache manager allows you to manually upload patches, apply patches currently stored in the Patch Cache and remove patches.

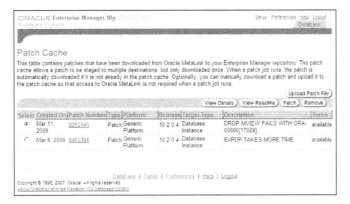

In this window you can select the patch and schedule when this will be applied by clicking the **Patch** button. This will proceed with an interrogation procedure to gather how and when this patch will be applied. At the end of the patching procedure you must read the patch-apply log files to make sure the patch was properly applied and all steps were successfully executed.

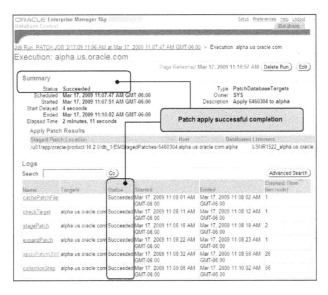

The tool used by the Patch Cache to proceed with the patch apply task is OPatch. Applying patches by means of Enterprise Manager frees the user from manually interacting with OPatch, providing the user with a friendlier, intuitive and more productive interface. However, as you have seen in other scenarios, such an action reduces the tool's manageability, restricting the options the user has to further customize the process.

Managing Patches in EM 11g

Enterprise Manager in 11g is slightly different from the 10g interface; it is oriented to provide the DBA with proactive advice on patch management and reduce the need for user intervention during the patching process. The Oracle Configuration Manger is the same as the one in 10g and it also requires the user to provide the connection information to the Metalink account as well as a valid CSI. This allows Enterprise Manager to connect to Metalink and download information about the available patches and products. At the setup link you must configure your user name and password to access your Metalink account. If the connection is successful then you will start to see information about the Critical Patch Advisor displayed on the main page, letting you know that there is a CPU available for your system.

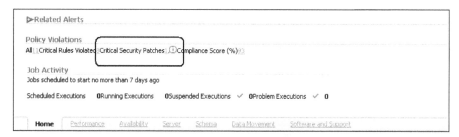

Oracle created a new tab named **Software and Support**, and among the many sections created there is one particular section named **Database Software Patching** which is the section where all patch management is performed.

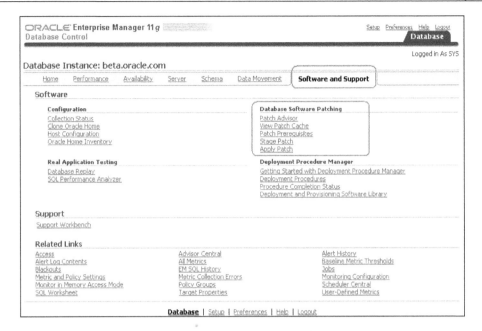

The goal of the Database Software Patching section is to manage Oracle software maintenance more efficiently by providing information about the latest patch releases found in Metalink. You can patch recommendations for your current installation, stage and apply patches, and display information about the patches and patchsets automatically downloaded from Metalink by Enterprise Manager along with those manually added by the users.

Database Software Patching comprises five sections:

1. Patch Advisor
2. View Patch Cache
3. Patch Prerequisites
4. Stage Patch
5. Apply Patch

Patch Advisor

Patch advisor collects information from Metalink about the most suitable patches for your system. It has two sections, one named **Critical Security Patches**, and a second one named **Patch Recommendations by Feature**. The first section displays information about the Oracle Critical Security Updates recommended for your current installation. Meanwhile the second section refers to the recommended patches according to the feature usage, this is also known as **Feature Based Patching**.

Critical Security Patches

When clicking on the recommended Critical Patch Update you can get the information related to this particular quarterly CPU release, which is a general purpose document that explains the CPU and displays the platform this particular release affects. By clicking on the **Show Remedies** button you can focus on the specific patch that relates to your platform. You can download, stage, and apply the suggested patch.

Patch Remedies is a combination of patches that may consist of Patch Sets and the interim patches most suitable for your platform chosen to resolve the selected Critical Patch Advisory. The Remedy Details gives you information about the patch or patches you are looking at. You can proceed to apply or stage the patch directly from this section.

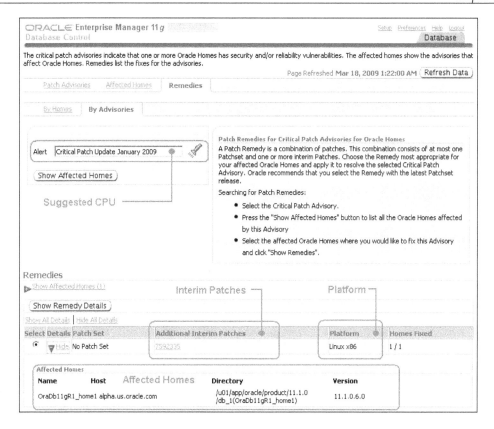

If you choose to stage the patch this will be visible from the Patch Cache section and you can schedule it to be applied later.

Feature based patching

Oracle classifies patches according to the feature they affect. This classification allows you to easily select the most suitable patches according to the features used in your target database. You can subscribe to a feature so you can direct Enterprise Manager to look for patches specifically for the feature you are using. This can be accessed from the **Patch Recommendation by Feature** section in the Patch Advisor page.

View Patch Cache

This section contains the patches that have been downloaded from Metalink or manually added by the users. The Patch Cache works the same way in 10g and 11g, and it is a convenient way to manage patch application in your system.

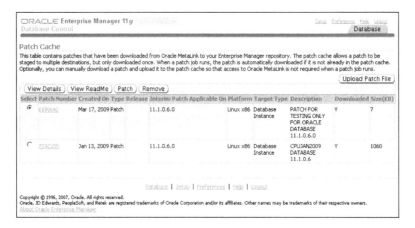

Patch prerequisites

When a patch is downloaded you must make sure your system meets the prerequisites for its installation. You can perform a manual checking or let Enterprise Manager to take care of this task.

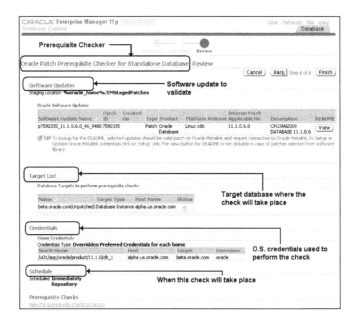

In order for Enterprise Manager to perform the prerequisite checking, you must provide the information related to the patch to be applied and the target database where this patch will be installed. Set the OS credentials to perform this task and also set when this job will be scheduled.

After a while the results are displayed in a three column table which shows the check performed, the status (failed or passed), the details specifying the tasks performed during the check, and in case of failure what should be done in order for the patch to meet the install prerequisites.

This is a proactive tool that frees the DBA from manually checking if the system meets the conditions to guarantee a successful patching session.

Stage patch

The Stage Patch section looks at Oracle Metalink for patches that meet the current platform OS and Oracle version to be downloaded. You can use a search form to look for a particular patch and have it downloaded and staged in the Patch Cache area.

Apply patch

Patches can be directly applied from this section. You can choose to look for a particular patch on Metalink and have it downloaded and staged or get a patch from the library. The forms presented interrogate the user about the specific patches to be applied, the target list where the patch will be installed, the OS credentials that will be used for this task, and when this job will be scheduled.

Summary

One of the most important tasks the DBA must periodically perform is apply patches. This ensures that the Oracle installation is kept updated and reduces the chances of encountering known bugs. Your company policy should define whether you should proactively patch your database or patch only when a symptom is noted. You should always thoroughly read and make sure you understand the instructions contained in the README file. There are two ways to patch the database; by means of interim patches, or by means of Patch Sets. The main difference between the first and the second option is that interim patches don't change the Oracle version and they are applied with the OPatch tool, while the Patch Sets are installed using Oracle Universal Installer and they change the fourth digit of the Oracle version number.

CPUs are quarterly patch bundles released by Oracle Support. It is important to keep the software protected up to the last available CPU. This ensures your database will be protected against any known security breaches.

You can manually manage patches by looking for patches and downloading them from Metalink, and manually checking the prerequisites on your target platform, or you can use the patch management tools provided by Enterprise Manager. This helps the DBA from performing most of the manual tasks and allows the DBA to download and stage patches, and schedule the time a patch will be applied. Oracle 11g is oriented to use a more proactive patch maintenance approach. It makes patch maintenance tasks less susceptible to human error.

Index

K

KILL_JOB command 23

L

LISTENER parameter 357
Loading Large Objects. *See* **LOBs**
load performance, enhancing
  tips 61, 62
LOBs
  about 52
  Binary Large Object (BLOB) 52
  Character Large Object (CLOB) 53
  CLOB(Character Large Object) load demon-
    stration table, preparing 53, 54
  external LOBs 53
  internal LOBs 53
  loading 53
  multimedia files, loading 54
  National Character Large Object (NCLOB)
    53
local parameter 319
lock enqueue mechanism 166, 168
log file, SQL*Loader demo user
  data file format 41
  file names, bad file 41
  file names, control file 41
  file names, data file 41
  file names, discard file 41
  header 40
  path used 41
  space allocated for bind array 42
  summary 42
  timing 42
LogLevel <level> parameter 318
lost inventory
  recovering 334

M

MAIL_SERVER parameter 357
Media Management Library (MML) 92
mkstore utility
  options 238
  using 251, 252
multimedia files, loading
  demonstration table, preparing 54, 55

FILLER file 54
multi-section backup
  about 113
  commands, issuing 113
  issues 114

N

Network Configuration Assistant (netca)
  267
network environment, changing
  DBSNMP password, changing 366
  host name, changing 364
  IP address, changing 364
  SYSMAN password, changing 364, 365
network mode, Data Pump import
  10.1.0.5.0, source database 30
  11.1.0.6.0, destination database 30
  about 29, 30, 31
  CREATE DATABASE LINK command 29
  db10gR1 link 30
newdbid utility (nid) 108
nobackground 320, 322
noclusterEnabled 320, 322
noconsole 320, 322
nologging option 159, 160
nowait 321, 322
nowarningonremovefiles 320, 322

O

OPatch tool
  about 369, 370
  command execution output 370
  failed session, rolling back 376
  in Oracle 11 g 378, 379
  latest version, downloading 370, 371
  log files 384
  PATH environment variable 384
  requirements 371
  syntax 372
  troubleshooting 384
  used, for applying single patch 374
  using, for Oracle maintenance 373
Oracle
  deadlock, handling 174, 175
  generic validation 312
  Hot Patches 383

R

record -destinationFile <Path> parameter
319
Recovery Manager. *See* RMAN
Recovery Manager Encryption, Oracle Wallet Manager
Advanced Encryption Standard (AES) 258
dual mode 256, 262
password mode 256
password mode, using 259, 261
supported encryption algorithms 258
transparent mode 256
transparent mode, using 256-259
redo log files' loss
current log group 151-155
inactive group loss 150
query used 149
scenarios 148, 149
relink parameter 320
remotecp <Path> parameter 321, 322
remoteshell <Path> parameter 321, 322
removeallfiles parameter 320
removeAllPatches parameter 320
Resource Manager
about 181
implementing, steps 183
OS level problems 181
Resource Allocation Method 182
Resource Consumer Group element 182
Resource Consumer Group Mapping element 182
Resource Plan Directive element 182
Resource Plan element 182
service assigned resources, configuring 184
user assigned resources, configuring 183
response file, DBCA
Add instance section 304
ASM configuration section 304
Configure database section 304
Create clone template section 304
Create Database Section 303
Create template from existing database section 304
Delete database section 304
Delete instance section 304
general section 303

Generate scripts section 304
locating 303
responseFile <Path> parameter 318
response file, silent installation mode
Automatic Storage Management Options (ASM) 323
Backup and recovery options 323
Configuration options 323
creating, from actual installation 325
customizing 324
Database configuration 323
General Section 323
Privileged operating system groups 323
Read only section 323
uninstall task, performing 329, 330
Upgrade an existing database section 323
variables 323
RMAN
about 91, 92
advantages 91
Archivelog mode 93
BACKUP DATABASE command 108
block media recovery 114, 115
critical datafiles loss 109
DUPLICATE command 121
encryption modes 256
format masks 100
multiplexed backup, configuring 104, 105, 106
non-critical datafiles loss 109
recovery catalog, configuring 106, 107
recovery catalog database, using 92
repository, creating 106
simple backup, creating 108, 109
TARGET database 92
User Managed Backup (UMB) 101, 102
rman command 154

S

schedules
about 225
creating 226
using 225
Scheduling tasks 199
service
about 179

T

three tier application
row lock contention, monitoring 172
throttling 118
time expression syntax
about 211
combined schedule 216
examples 221
regular schedule 211
regular schedule, frequency definition 212
regular schedule, interval 213
regular schedule, timing specification 213, 214, 215
repeat interval 211
Transparent Application Failover (TAF) 277
Transparent Data Encryption (TDE) feature 33 258

U

updateNodeList parameter 320, 322
User Managed Backup (UMB), RMAN
limitations 91
offline backup 101
online backup 101
online backup, myths 103, 104
util command 378

V

VERSION clause
COMPATIBLE value 76
LATEST value 76
VERSION NUMBER value 76

W

waitforcompletion 320, 322
Windows Scheduler
about 199
cron utility 199

X

XML files
mapping, as external table 87

Z

ZLIB algorithm used, backup compression
BZIP2 algorithm 112
No Compress option 111

Thank you for buying
Oracle 10g/11g Data and Database Management Utilities

About Packt Publishing

Packt, pronounced 'packed', published its first book "*Mastering phpMyAdmin for Effective MySQL Management*" in April 2004 and subsequently continued to specialize in publishing highly focused books on specific technologies and solutions.

Our books and publications share the experiences of your fellow IT professionals in adapting and customizing today's systems, applications, and frameworks. Our solution based books give you the knowledge and power to customize the software and technologies you're using to get the job done. Packt books are more specific and less general than the IT books you have seen in the past. Our unique business model allows us to bring you more focused information, giving you more of what you need to know, and less of what you don't.

Packt is a modern, yet unique publishing company, which focuses on producing quality, cutting-edge books for communities of developers, administrators, and newbies alike. For more information, please visit our website: www.packtpub.com.

Writing for Packt

We welcome all inquiries from people who are interested in authoring. Book proposals should be sent to author@packtpub.com. If your book idea is still at an early stage and you would like to discuss it first before writing a formal book proposal, contact us; one of our commissioning editors will get in touch with you.

We're not just looking for published authors; if you have strong technical skills but no writing experience, our experienced editors can help you develop a writing career, or simply get some additional reward for your expertise.

Mastering Oracle Scheduler in Oracle 11g Databases

ISBN: 978-1-847195-98-2   Paperback: 240 pages

Schedule, manage, and execute jobs that automate your business processes

1. Automate jobs from within the Oracle database with the built-in Scheduler

2. Boost database performance by managing, monitoring, and controlling jobs more effectively

3. Contains easy-to-understand explanations, simple examples, debugging tips, and real-life scenarios

Oracle SOA Suite Developer's Guide

ISBN: 978-1-847193-55-1   Paperback: 652 pages

Design and build Service-Oriented Architecture Solutions with the Oracle SOA Suite 10gR3

1. A hands-on guide to using and applying the Oracle SOA Suite in the delivery of real-world SOA applications.

2. Detailed coverage of the Oracle Service Bus, BPEL Process Manager, Web Service Manager, Rules, Human Workflow, and Business Activity Monitoring.

3. Master the best way to combine / use each of these different components in the implementation of a SOA solution.

Please check **www.PacktPub.com** for information on our titles

www.ingramcontent.com/pod-product-compliance
Lightning Source LLC
Chambersburg PA
CBHW081501050326
40690CB00015B/2876

* 9 7 8 1 8 4 7 1 9 6 2 8 6 *